The Dirty Dozen

John Kenny has broadcast on Radio 1, 2FM, Lyric FM, RTÉ television, SKY TV, TG4 and the BBC on a wide range of sport including GAA, soccer, cricket, swimming and motor sport. His radio programmes include *Saturday Sport*, *The Olympic Years*, *Ireland's Motorsport Legends* and *The High Atlas Challenge*. He has covered the Olympic Games and the Cricket World Cup for both RTÉ Radio and Television as well as the prestigious *Test Match Special* for BBC Radio in the Caribbean in 2007.

John Kenny's first visit to Mondello Park was in September 1987 for the Leinster Trophy races where he witnessed a future Formula 1 World Champion, Mika Häkkinen win the Formula Opel Euro Series, and since then he has presented various television motor-sport programmes, including the *Racing Green* series for TG4 in 1999, as well as commentary from Mondello and the Phoenix Park Races plus the Killarney Historic Stages Rally for RTÉ and SKY TV and the A1GP and MotoGP series for RTÉ Television. John has been the motor-sport columnist with the *Irish Daily Star* since 1989.

He is married to Catherine and has three daughters, Danielle, Nicola and Jane. This is his first book.

The Dirty Dozen

Ireland's Motor-Sport Legends

John Kenny

THE O'BRIEN PRESS
DUBLIN

PUBLISHED IN ASSOCIATION WITH RTÉ

First published 2007 by The O'Brien Press Ltd,
12 Terenure Road East, Rathgar, Dublin 6, Ireland.
Tel: +353 1 4923333; Fax: +353 1 4922777
E-mail: books@obrien.ie
Website: www.obrien.ie

ISBN: 978-1-84717-050-7

British Library Cataloguing-in-Publication Data
Kenny, John
The dirty dozen : Ireland's motorsport legends
1. Automobile racing drivers - Ireland - Biography
2. Motorcyclists - Ireland - Biography
I. Title
796.7'0922'415

1 2 3 4 5
07 08 09 10

Typesetting, editing, layout and design: The O'Brien Press Ltd
Printing: Creative Print and Design, Wales.

Contents

Foreword

Ireland has produced more than its fair share of top-class motor racers in all disciplines from car-racing and bike-racing to rallying, and many have become household names on the international scene.

At Jordan, we would like to think that we had a hand in spreading that message across the motor-racing world, and it's a privilege to be part of John Kenny's book about Ireland's motor-sport legends.

To be included in first the radio series on RTÉ and now the follow-up book is indeed an honour. When you consider that I'm named with the likes of Derek Daly, Billy Coleman, John Watson, Eddie Irvine, the Dunlops and Paddy Hopkirk, it shows just how much this small island of ours has contributed to the world of international motor sport.

John Kenny was a regular visitor to the Jordan Grand Prix motor home during our halcyon days when our team was at the forefront of Formula 1. Indeed, I received a very excited call from him when we won the French Grand Prix in 1999, as he was at Magny Cours sitting in the stands with his daughter Danielle, cheering on what was only our second victory. John became part of our family at Jordan, and it was a pleasure to host him and his fellow journalists during their regular trips to our grand-prix races.

It is important that somebody gives an insight and documents the history of Irish motor-sport competitors, whether it's John Watson's and Eddie Irvine's grand-prix victories, Billy Coleman's double of Irish and British Rally championships, Jeremy McWilliams' success in grand-prix motorbikes or Rosemary Smith's World Rally win.

There are moments of heartbreak combined with moments of glory, and *The Dirty Dozen: Ireland's Motor-Sport Legends* encapsulates many of those.

John Kenny has a genuine passion for sport, and motor sport is just one of the many strings to his bow. I wish him every success with this, his first book.

Eddie Jordan

Preface

Who is the greatest living Irish motor-sporting hero? I won't attempt
to answer that question here because much depends on whether you
follow cars or bikes, two or four wheels, rallying or racing. However,
when you read this special book, you can surely decide for yourself.

John Kenny's concept was brilliant: to interview a dozen of the
greats within the Irish sport, to suss out their thoughts and ideas,
their likes and dislikes, their highs and lows, and then to make twelve
separate radio programmes. A good idea and great for the sport!

The programmes made riveting listening on RTÉ, and now John, in
conjunction with the O'Brien Press, has extended his idea to the book
stage. Another bright scheme! We need such books by the bedside to
lull us into dreamland. All his subjects dreamt of being successful, and
do you know what? They all made it in their own way.

I have my own favourites within the 'Dirty Dozen' and my own
preferred stories. I admire and applaud the courage of the veteran
motor-cycle road-racer Jeremy McWilliams who has retained sheer
raw speed together with a delightful pleasantness into his forties.
Nice man, Jeremy!

Eddie Jordan's story has been told in several ways, and, just like
old wine, it improves as the years pass by. Eddie did what he wanted
with his life, he struggled and suffered, but in the end, when he sold

Jordan Grand Prix, he was a very rich, if unemployed, team manager.

The John Watson yarn was also worth telling and makes good reading, while both Austin MacHale and Billy Coleman epitomise what is good and great about Irish motor sport, and rallying in particular. They were bitter rivals at the height of their exceptional careers, but in their golden years they have mellowed and now have a high if not glowing regard for each other. Great men both! Great sportsmen are like that!

Billy Coleman's accomplishment in the British Rally Championship in 1974 was an exceptional success story. He then added the Irish Championship and became a legend. Joey Dunlop was a legend both on and off the bike, and one of the nicest blokes one would meet in any sport. So is his brother Robert; both are the subject of one of John Kenny's interesting interviews.

Derek Daly was the Dubliner that made it deep into Formula 1 – a driver who was prepared to starve and toil so that he could drive a racing car. And Michael Roe . . . here was a young fellow who had extraordinary success despite his laid-back attitude. Was he the best racer?

I'll accept that Eddie Irvine was brilliantly successful and became a Formula 1 giant. Strangely, Irv the Swerve (nowadays property owner, publican and boatman) got more notice for his beddings and avoidance of weddings than for his for four great Grand Prix victories.

The last three that I remember from John Kenny's Irish motor-sport legends book are, indeed, special people – Rosemary Smith, Martin Donnelly and Paddy Hopkirk – three titans who carried the Irish flag to extraordinary heights and whom, I am glad to say, I knew very well during their competitive years.

'Hoppy' was world-championship material when there was no World Rally Championship. Martin Donnelly had his career cut unfairly short by a horrendous accident, and Rosemary Smith was the best female driver ever produced in this small country.

It's John Kenny's book. A labour of love for the radio-head and a delightful read from start to finish. I still can't make up my mind as to who was the greatest of them all. Read on, my friend, and you can give me the answer when you have scanned every chapter of JK's writings!

Michael O'Carroll
Editor, *Irish Motorsport Annual*

Introduction

I began this project back in early 2005 when Declan Quigley, the motor-sport journalist and broadcaster, sat with me in Todd's Bar in Naas one Friday afternoon, compiling a list of twenty Irish motor-sport legends, be they in circuit-racing, rallying or motorbike riders. The idea was to present the list to RTÉ Radio with the view of making a documentary series on those involved in all three disciplines who had distinguished themselves both nationally and internationally.

I took the list to Eithne Hand, who was the Head of RTÉ Radio 1 at that stage and Paddy Glackin, overall manager in charge of RTÉ Radio sports output.

'A list of twenty!' they cried. 'Far too many! Cut it and make it six.'

'Only six?' I replied. 'Far too few.'

We settled on a list of twelve, and, thus, *The Dirty Dozen: Ireland's Motor-Sport Legends in Conversation with John Kenny* was born. (Quigley still asks me why they are Dirty.)

I cut the original twenty down to twelve, leaving out from the original list: (sorry, guys) David Kennedy, Gary Anderson, Kenny Acheson, Tommy Byrne, Eddie Laycock, Kenny McKinstry, Jonny Kane, Tommy Reid and Richard Lyons.

Although I didn't do interviews with the nine I left out, they were all mentioned by many of the twelve in the original RTÉ Radio 1 series, which was sponsored by Volvo and which eventually went out at 8pm on Friday nights from January to March 2006. All nine drivers I omitted have, in their own way, contributed to Irish motor-sport successes both here and abroad and, like the radio series, are all included, one way or another, in this book. Some will argue that I left out perhaps some more deserving names from the past, but I hope I struck a balance between Irish rallying, circuit-racing and motorbike riders.

Actually, the radio series is still on the RTÉ website at <http://www.rte.ie/radio1/dirtydozen> if you fancy a listen.

When the programme ended, I thought that was it, move on. However, Adrian Moynes, the Head of RTÉ Radio, stopped me in the corridor of the Radio Centre one day. He mentioned that because the programmes were only half an hour in length, I must have left a lot of material out, naturally enough. It was Adrian who put the idea for the book in my mind, and he encouraged me to pursue it.

I had a word with Paddy Glackin, and he suggested I get someone to transcribe the original interviews. Brian Tuite, one-time manager of Thin Lizzy and Mondello Park (how about that for a CV?), found for me one Siobhan O'Connell to do the transcription work. Thanks for your patience and diligence, Siobhan.

To all those, especially the Naas Racing Mafia, who regaled me with stories to add to my own, a heartfelt thanks, especially Paddy 'Glass' Byrne, Leo Nulty and Mr Quigley. Thanks as well to Felix Muelas from the excellent Formula 1 website www.forix.com for allowing me to use his memories of Martin Donnelly's terrible crash in Jerez in 1991, and to my RTÉ colleague Michael O'Carroll for writing the foreword and for giving me my first break in television motor-sport commentary. Thanks to Peter Collins for helping me continue with RTÉ Television motor sport and also to Brian Carthy for all his help and advice and to Seán McAongusa of RTÉ Television sports library for his help with the clips for the radio series.

Thanks to the twelve superstars in the book for giving of their valuable time. The original series had twelve racers and, indeed, there are a dozen chapters in this book. But, as you can probably guess, the great Joey Dunlop had passed away before the interview process had begun, so one chapter is the Dunlops' story, told by his brother Robert.

Thanks finally to my family, Catherine and my daughters Danielle, Nicola and Jane, plus my brothers Noel, Colin and Evan and sister Miriam and my best friend Michael Phelan, for help and support and for just being there.

1

Derek Daly

Finishes to a Formula 1 race didn't come as dramatic as the 1982 Monaco Grand Prix, where three drivers, including Derek Daly, led on the last lap, before Ricardo Patrese, who had spun at the Mirabeau hairpin, incredibly took the win when mishaps befell the three drivers in front of him.

For Daly, it was heartbreak. His Williams, with its rear wing ripped off in an earlier accident, was on the way to victory, with the chequered flag in sight. But victory was cruelly snatched away from the Irishman when his gearbox seized on the exit from the tunnel, and with it went his only chance of recording a Formula 1 grand-prix victory.

Daly remains one of only a handful of Irish drivers to take part in Formula 1. Others include Eddie Irvine, John Watson and Louth man Tommy Byrne. His good friend David Kennedy (now a Formula 1 commentator) also tried – but still holds the unenviable record of the most 'did not qualifys' (DNQs) in Formula 1 history. Daly and Kennedy were amongst a crop of young and ambitious Irish racing drivers who were around at the time, which also included Eddie Jordan and Byrne, who won the British Formula 3 championship in 1982 and who tested a McLaren Formula 1 car before having a very short career in the world's top formula. Michael Roe (see Chapter 3) from Naas in County Kildare and Dubliner Bernard Devaney were also part of what was a very talented bunch of drivers from the Republic of Ireland who raced on the world stage in the 1970s and 1980s.

Although recognised as not as naturally talented as Roe and Byrne, Daly was one of the more successful ones. After working his way up the motor-sport ladder in Formula Ford and Formula 3, he began his Formula 1 career racing for Hesketh and Ensign, scoring his first Formula 1 points when sixth in Canada for Ensign in 1978.

In 1979, he continued with Ensign before being taken on by Ken Tyrrell in 1980, where he produced some encouraging results, including fourth and in the points twice in Argentina and the British Grand Prix at Brands Hatch. In 1981, he switched to the RAM team, which had the new March 811 chassis, with sponsorship from Guinness and Rizla (strange combination). It was a poor campaign, and at the start of 1982, Daly moved to Theodore and looked set to race at the back of the field in an underfunded car. But he soon got his big chance when the great Carlos Reutemann prematurely retired and Daly took over the second Williams, racing alongside teammate Keke Rosberg. The Finn went on to win the World Championship that year.

Daly was dumped by Williams at the end of the 1982 season after the Las Vegas Grand Prix, and there his Formula 1 career ended. In all, he raced in sixty-four Formula 1 races, picking up a total of fifteen championship points before he went to America and began racing with the Wysard team in their CART (Championship Auto Racing Teams) IndyCar series (the US equivalent of Formula 1). In all, he raced in sixty-six CART races, including six Indianapolis 500s.

In 1984, while driving for the Provimi Veal March team, he had a massive accident at the Michigan International Speedway. The front of the car was torn off in the impact, and Daly suffered serious leg injuries. It nearly cost him his life. He did, however, make a return to IndyCars with the Raynor Garage Doors team. In all, Daly had twenty-one Top 10 finishes in the IndyCar series but only once stood on the podium – when he was third in the Milwaukee Indy race in 1987.

After his CART career, he moved on to sports cars with Nissan and Jaguar, claiming two victories in the Sebring 12 Hours with Nissan. He retired from motor-racing in 1992, taking up commentating for US television and opening a motor-racing school in Las Vegas, which he sold in 2006.

Daly had worked his way up through stock-car racing and Formula Ford, in which he won the Irish Championship and Formula Ford Festival at Brands Hatch. He was also a British Formula 3 champion before graduating to Formula 1 and actually led his first race, the International Trophy at Silverstone for Hesketh Racing before spinning off, a race won by his team-mate James Hunt.

Not a bad career overall. Daly is, in fact, the most successful Formula 1 driver from the Republic of Ireland and, outside Watson and Irvine, is the only Irish driver to score World Championship points. Pretty good for a driver with no family background in the sport and who hailed from Dundrum, a suburb of Dublin on the southside of the capital city.

'Growing up in Dundrum, ah, it was very basic,' says Daly. 'My dad sold meat for a company called Shines Sausages in a place over in Crumlin in south Dublin. We had no motor-racing background, and we lived at Wyckham Park in Dundrum.

'I don't know what year it was, but one of my dad's customers . . . her brother was coming from England and was going to race at Dunboyne. Her brother's name was Sid Taylor, and I'd never heard of Sid Taylor, never heard of Dunboyne. Anyway, I'm walking home from school one day, and I walk by her house, and here's this big van which had just come from England, and inside it was a racing car. I would have been twelve and it had enough of an effect on me.'

Daly professed that he had a happy childhood in his working-class family, living in a much different Dublin to the Celtic Tiger that was unleashed in the 1990s.

'Your entertainment revolved around what you did yourself with your family. We had hens and chickens in the back garden of the house. It wouldn't be unusual to go and chop the head off the chickens for the Sunday dinner, and your entertainment might be walking along the railway track, which was two fields over from our house, and that was what we knew.

'But there was plenty of love in our house. There was obviously nowhere near the wealth that there is now, nowhere near the opportunities. Life was simple. My parents, like most families in our area, looked after the kids, and sometimes the neighbours' kids as well. It was very different, but it was very simple, I suppose, in a way, very enjoyable because we didn't really need much or miss much.'

Daly had one brother, Vivion, who was also a racing driver and who, sadly, succumbed to cancer in 2002. He also had three sisters, and they all pretty much lived around the same area, even when they got married and lived within a 5-mile radius of the family home in Dundrum.

'I probably would have been the black sheep of the family. I was allergic to school. Went to Terenure College and struggled to get my Leaving Cert. I was a visual learner. I had to be active – out doing rather than sitting listening. So I started racing when I was sixteen, but I was anxious to move on as much as possible. I couldn't say that I had an ambition to get to Formula 1. From our background, it was almost impossible. They were almost at a different level, like superstars. A bit untouchable. But when I went to England, it all happened really fast for me, going through Formula Ford, Formula 3, Formula 2 and then Formula 1.

'But when I was twelve, and I saw that racing car of Sid Taylor's for the first time, it seemed like a different world. There was no Formula 1 on television. I can remember calling reporters in the *Evening Press*, hoping they might have the results of the races because it wasn't widely reported here. I pressurised my dad into going to see the racing in Dunboyne, and he drove me out on a Saturday. We sat on the banks in the grass right beside the road watching these cars going by. So much freedom just to roam around and be involved. I can still remember the drivers, the cars, the noises and smells that weekend.'

And that visit to Dunboyne in County Meath was the catalyst for Daly's interest in motor sport that would take him to the very top. Dunboyne once hosted the now-famous Leinster Trophy meeting, which was first awarded in 1934 to Fay Taylor and has been an integral part of the Irish racing calendar ever since.

Outside of Dunboyne, it was also raced for at Skerries, Tallaght, Wicklow and Bishopscourt before finally taking up permanent residence at Mondello Park in 1968, where it was raced for and won by two future World Champions in Ayrton Senna and Mika Häkkinen, along with John Watson and Eddie Jordan, who also put their names on the famous old trophy.

'After that weekend in Dunboyne, I was going to be a racing driver. Getting a normal nine-to-five job . . . it wasn't an option for me. It never was something I considered because work would have taken so much time out of my day. How could I become a racing driver if I had to have a job? I was so naive that it didn't compute; you know, racing/money – you need one to do the other. But I was going to do it, and that was that.

'I can remember coming home from school and, almost on a daily basis, the first thing I would do was get the keys of my dad's car and go out and sit in it and mock the driver, practise driving, when I was thirteen or fourteen. I would practise emergency stops and pulling the handbrake and going into reverse at the same time because that'd be the best way to stop. I had it all planned and worked out in my head.

'Dad was great though. I would say he was very open to me. When I think back on it, I didn't understand it at the time, but I was never really told you need to do this or that. I was never told you should be a doctor and you should be whatever. It was pretty much left up to me to decide what I wanted to do, and I didn't understand at that time that that was a great freedom that I was allowed to chase my dream. Remember, we knew nothing about racing, but I had nothing but support.'

So, at the tender age of sixteen, Derek Daly went motor-racing, and a very humble beginning it was too.

'Stock-car racing was the start, an E93A Ford Anglia I raced on the stock-car track in Santry. I went down to Smithfield in Dublin and paid a guy called Jack Murphy £7 for it and towed it back up to Wyckham Park, and the neighbours laughed at us as we towed it down to where we lived and put it in the back of the garage. That was my first racing car.

'I'd also an Austin Cambridge I modified in Dundrum at a place called Larry Byrne's where I took an afternoon and weekend job at times. And I can remember that car, turning it upside down and getting smashed to pieces, destroyed. It got hit while it was on its side, and I crawled out through this broken glass that was still lying on the bottom of the doors, crawled out on my hands and knees, and I can still see my dad running across the track between the cars just to pick me up and say, "Let's tow it home and see can we fix it and get you going again." There was never, *ever* a case of him saying, "Why don't you get a bit of sense and do something else" – never. Total support.'

Stock-car racing was the beginning, but when did Daly get the idea of getting into competitive single-seater racing?

'I was about two or three years into stock-car racing, winning a lot of races, and I thought I'd like to have a go at something new. David Kennedy was a step ahead because he had set his sights on a Formula Ford earlier than me, so had Eddie Jordan. I had a 1966 Ford Anglia and £400. I went over to Eddie's house, and on the side of the road he had a trailer with a Lotus 61 on top. I gave him my pride and joy, the Ford Anglia, and my £400 and got Kennedy to tow the trailer away for me. And that was my introduction to single-seater racing.

'Nowadays, there's a school for everything, including racing schools. I should know. We had to learn by trial and error. You had to get yourself to the race track, and you learned by your mistakes, and I made many of them.'

It also required a certain degree of finance to go racing, as well. Daly's parents may have been supportive, but there wasn't enough money to raise the children and financially support his burgeoning motor-sport career.

'No, because they weren't really in a position to do it. I was able to buy the Lotus from Jordan with the £400 I had earned and the Anglia. To run it for a year, I needed money. I went down to the local bank in Dundrum, signed on for a loan of £1,000; my dad co-signed it. I told the bank manager I was going to use it for a used-car business. He didn't need to know that it was a racing car I was in the process of buying. I decided I'd have a lifetime to pay it back if I didn't make it. But I had to. I just felt a compulsion to give myself an opportunity. I got the £1,000 and began to use that for entry fees, doing hill climbs and racing in Mondello. In fact, the trailer that we took the car home on was Eddie's, so we didn't even buy the trailer. We towed the Formula Ford on the road at the end of a rope to Mondello for the first race back in 1973.'

Formula Ford, then, was a single-seater open-wheel class with a 1600-cc Kent engine. There were many chassis manufacturers, the top two chassis being the Van Diemen and the French-built Mygale, while the Crosslé was also a feature of the Irish championship.

Many drivers, including Senna and Michael Schumacher, raced in Formula Ford as they worked their way up the ladder, and the likes of Daly, Kennedy, Eddie Irvine and Roe did likewise, as it remains, to this day, an entry-level series to the world of single-seater motor-racing.

When the series, which, in time, became the top junior worldwide formula, came into being, the intention was to offer an affordable form of single-seater racing. John Webb of the Brands Hatch circuit in the UK, Geoff Clarke of Motor Racing Stables (Brands' race-driving school) and Jim Russell, who is credited with founding the racing-school industry, were largely thought to be responsible for its creation, and the first Formula Ford race took place in July 1967 at Brands.

'I was sponsored by another friend of mine in my early Formula Ford days, Kellogg's Poultry Farm. He sold eggs, and I think he gave me about £300 or £400. We painted the car blue and went down to scrutineering for a race at Mondello Park in County Kildare. I was on Avon tyres because they lasted longer; everyone else was on a Firestone tyre. I remember that well. I qualified last or second last; I think Kennedy might have been last or second last along with me at the back of the grid, and I was nowhere.

'But in the fourth race of my career, I landed at Mondello, and it's raining. I win it but my engine was illegal. However, I was the first southern guy to win an Irish Formula Ford Championship race for a long time, because the northern guys like Jim Sherry and those in the Crosslés would dominate in those days. Ken Fildes had built the engine for me. So Ken walks over and proudly says, "I'll tell you, everybody, now, that was a perfectly legal engine."

'My first year was 1973, and at the end of that season, the bank needed the £1,000 back – I didn't pay it – and I needed a new car to go into the 1974 season. My girlfriend at the time . . . her brother had just come back from the mines in Australia, and he said, "If you go down there you can pay back the bank and get enough money to go racing."'

Daly and Kennedy took off for the Australian tin mines in the winter of 1973, both determined to raise the necessary cash to keep their careers alive.

'Well, the bank note needed to be paid back, and I had no real means of income, so I'm with my girlfriend, whose brother tells me if you go and spend the winter in the iron ore and tin mines in Australia and do the heavy labour, you can make £4,000 in about a six-month period. About a week or ten days later, myself and David were standing in the middle of Perth, Australia, signing on to fly up to the single men's quarters in a place called Cliffs River Robe right through the middle of the bush in Australia. We stayed for just under six months, just for the winter, to raise the cash and go back racing in the Irish summer.

'When you are young, doing something like that is a real adventure. The place was just a small single-men's quarters, so one room to a man, and you all ate in the mess hall. Every two weeks you got paid. And you got paid straight time for your first eight hours, you got double time for your second eight hours, and if you did twenty-four hours straight you got triple time for your last eight. There were some people there to buy a yacht, some people there to buy a house – we were there to buy two racing cars.

'I came back with £5,000, which is more money than I'd ever seen. Went to a fella called Gary Gibson, bought his Crosslé Formula Ford, put it on the track down at Mondello and was *almost* fast enough. Actually, the funny thing is, on our way back from Australia we stopped in London, and the International Trophy was on at Silverstone. Myself and David were standing outside the fence looking over at these Formula 1 cars going by. Little did I know that in four years' time I'd be leading that same race in a Hesketh.'

In the intervening years, Daly began to learn his trade. He won the 1975 Irish Formula Ford Championship before decamping to England to take part in their Formula Ford series driving a Hawke, and, at the end of the 1976 season, Daly became one of a number of Irish drivers to take part in and win the Formula Ford Festival and World Cup at the Brands Hatch circuit in Kent. The track was, at that stage, home to the British Formula 1 Grand Prix and was considered to be the best circuit in these isles.

The Formula Ford Festival, which began at Snetterton in 1972, ran for four years at that track and, in fact, Daly was the first winner of the prestigious end-of-season shoot-out when it switched to its new and permanent home at Brands Hatch in 1976. The festival, which introduced a world-cup element for all the competing nations in 1981, is still one of the top end-of-season festivals for the 'young lions' of world motor sport, although it has been diluted somewhat as Ford changed the specification of their engines down the years, introducing the Zetec 1800 cc in the early 1990s and the Duratec version in 2005. Thus, there are now festival races for all three versions, and, to a certain extent, it has lost its lustre.

Nevertheless, winning the festival is seen as a huge stepping stone for a young driver who has to overcome over 150 fellow competitors through heats, quarter-finals, semi-finals and final. A lot of Irish drivers, including Daly, passed through the Formula Ford Festival and have gone on to bigger and better things.

'My Crosslé was almost, but not quite, fast enough. In the Irish Formula Ford Festival (in late 1974), there was a big dust-up between myself and Bernard Devaney. He was in the Hawke from

England, I was in the Crosslé. On the last lap at Mondello, I made a big lunge, and I tried to go past him. He saw me; I actually saw his eyeballs in the mirror. I saw his eyeballs watch me coming down the inside. He turned inside to block me because I was coming too fast, and I went over the top of him, rolled this thing upside down, destroyed it. And again, as the marshals are pulling me out from under the car because I landed upside down, there was my dad running down the track again. He drags me out, puts his arm around me and walking back says, "I'm glad you had a go – doesn't matter about the car." Can you imagine that type of support?

'So we take the Crosslé back, put it on the trailer, and we're all looking at it, just standing around and looking at this wreck because my season was over. At this stage now, the racing car was gone, the loan was not paid back from the year before, it was over.

'But a fella called John Crosslé walked up. I didn't know him from Adam. He said, "If you're interested, we'll take that wreck and give you a brand new Crosslé 30F if you can get enough money to buy an engine." I went to David Kennedy, as I knew he hadn't spent all his money from Australia. I says, "You need to loan me the money for an engine." He obliged. We got a Minister engine and sent it up to Crosslé. There were nine races left in the Irish season. I had nine poles, eight wins, one second, four lap records and won the championship.'

At that time, Daly came across Derek McMahon in a bar at the Kirkistown racetrack in Northern Ireland. McMahon was involved with a number of Irish drivers down the years, including Eddie Jordan who raced for his team in the 1970s. Daly needed sponsorship to go racing in the UK, and he approached McMahon, but, according to Daly, got short shrift.

'I met him in the bar at Kirkistown and I walked up to him. "I'm Derek Daly. I want to go to England. I need a bit of help. Would you be interested in helping a young Irish fella to get on his way?" He was, let's say, "happy" at the time, but he says, "I'll tell you what, I need you like I need a six-inch hole in me head."'

Daly didn't know it then, but McMahon eventually came on board to back the Irish driver when he made the Irish motor-racing fraternity sit up and take notice after his win in the 1976 Formula Ford Festival Meeting at Brands Hatch.

'The Crosslé I won the Irish championship with was a valuable car. So I went to England in an old bus. I took all the seats out of it and cut the back door, put two wooden ramps in. My mother made the curtains; my dad made the sponge mattresses that I slept on. Rolled the car in, put in a toolbox, said goodbye to everybody. When I got to England, I sold the Crosslé, and Hawke gave me a car, and I drove it around England for the year, which is when I won the Formula Ford Festival at the end of the 1976 season.

'You went to measure yourself at Brands Hatch. There were huge entries on a regular basis. Vivion went there many times and ran well. But I go and I win the festival. The reason wasn't that I was naturally brilliant or anything like that. It just happened to rain – I was very gifted in the rain. I didn't like it necessarily, but I was very good in the rain, and I won the heat, quarter-final, semi-final and final. James Hunt was the World Champion at that time and *Autosport* had a picture the following week saying, "World Champions Present and Future? James Hunt Presents Derek Daly with the Trophy." The reason that's significant is Derek McMahon was in Donegal, read this, rang me up. He says, "Meet me at the Dorchester Hotel for the British Racing Drivers Club Dinner Dance." Walked in, completely out of place, everybody's dressed in monkey suits, he sits me down, he says, "I'll back you for British Formula 3."'

Recognised as perhaps being the unofficial Junior World Championship, Formula 3 was spilt into two series in 1977.

'Yeah, and in those days, too, everybody that won the British Formula 3 Championship went to Formula 1 at some time or other. All the Europeans went to England, the Brazilians – Nelson Piquet was there. We were a very small team. Derek bought a Comer walk-through van, two concrete blocks, two wooden ramps into the back. We had a tent and towed a caravan on the back and drove round the place. It was right before the era of team managers and engineers. We just caught that last time when it was a sort of free-spirit era – look after yourself, make some half-decent decisions and you could still be successful.'

And it was a great year for the McMahon-backed racing team in 1977, which ran a Chevron for Daly. By season's end, Daly had won the BP series, while Britain's Stephen South took the Vandervell Championship. South went as far as trying to qualify for the 1980 Long Beach Formula 1 Grand Prix in a McLaren but failed to do so. His career ended after crashing in a Can-Am race later in the year. The accident destroyed his leg so badly that it had to be amputated.

'Myself and Stephen were the two fellas going head to head all the time. I remember leading the Formula 3 support race to the British Grand Prix in the Chevron. The car was not quite fast enough. South was very fast on the high-speed corners, but I'd block him just enough. He tried to pass me one time, and he tried to chop me off going into the left-hander that leads onto the Hangar Straight. So I had to back off. We touched wheels; he turned upside down immediately. I remember seeing the underside of his car as he flew off through the grass. I spun, got back on and finished seventh or eighth. But South said afterwards that "Daly tried to kill me – if that's what it takes to win a champion-ship, I don't want to have anything to do with it." The fact was, I didn't. I just didn't want to have to back off. I was telling Derek McMa-hon, I said, "I'm so close to winning," I actually started to cry trying to explain, because I felt this was the big one I was going to win. And he says, "Well, if you really think that way, why don't we go to the Aus-trian Grand Prix, that's another Formula 3 support race."

'In Austria, I put the car on pole position and won with Nelson Piquet behind me. And on the grid was Sid Taylor, the same Sid Tay-lor whose car I saw when I was twelve years of age back outside his sister's house. He was now running Teddy Yip's Theodore Formula 1 team. He walks up to me, he says, "If you win this race, I'll put you in a Formula 1 car."'

Daly won the race in Austria and was now on his way to Formula 1 – not initially with Theodore, as he first thought, but with the Hesketh team. Before his move to Formula 1, Daly also drove for Ron Dennis's Project Four racing team in Formula 2, driving an ICI-sponsored March-BMW in 1979, and, in between, the Irishman got his Formula 1 chance with Hesketh.

'I'd gone from Formula Ford, winning the Formula Ford Festival and the Formula 3 Championship, and Guy Edwards called me up to go to Estoril to drive a Formula 2 car that Ray Mallock couldn't make go fast. I jumped into that at Estoril, set a new lap record five laps from the end, finished fifth and was in a Formula 1 car – all within thirteen months. If I read that rise with anybody else . . . '

Hesketh Racing was owned by the somewhat eccentric Conservative MP, formally titled Alexander Fermor-Hesketh, the 3rd Baron Hesketh. He was directly responsible for bringing James Hunt into Formula 3. Hunt and team-mate Anthony 'Bubbles' Horsley wrote off car after car in the 1972 season. Hunt, though, stayed with Hesketh until he reached Formula 1, and he scored the team's first championship point at the 1973 Monaco Grand Prix, fitting for a team owner and driver who revelled in the champagne lifestyle.

'Hesketh had Rolls Royces, champagne and lived the good life. A very wealthy English lord who owned most of Silverstone and all the land around it. They won the Dutch Grand Prix with James Hunt, and he went on to McLaren. They had Olympus sponsorship. I think, in fact, it was James Hunt's brother Peter Hunt, an accountant, that arranged that sponsorship.

'For myself, in Formula 3, I was big news. In Formula 2, I did well at Estoril, so Hesketh called me up and said, "Do you want to drive this car?" So I tested it. It was designed by Frank Dernie, who went on to work with Williams.'

Daly's first official Formula 1 grand-prix drive for the Hesketh team was ignominious, as he failed to even pre-qualify the Hesketh-Ford for the US West Grand Prix at Long Beach in California and was classed last of the twenty-nine drivers in a race won by the Ferrari of Argentine Carlos Reutemann. Daly also failed to make it to the starting grid for the next two races in Monaco and Belgium and then left the team to go to Ensign. He did, however, get on the grid for one non-championship race with Hesketh, the International Trophy, also in 1978.

'The first race was the International Trophy at Silverstone. Since the World Championship came into being in the 1950s, it was no longer part of the series, but it was still a prestigious race, held under Formula 1 rules. In my first race, the car was 150 pounds over the weight limit, but we elected to drive it anyway as I'd nothing to lose because I didn't have any money and had to jump into anything I could.'

It was a good start for Daly who qualified the car in seventh.

'I remember it was raining going into the first corner. I'd passed two or three cars, and Hunt was outside me. He chopped across and I let him go. He was leading and I was second into the Old Becketts. Braking for the first time, I went down the inside of James, and I actually led halfway round the very first lap. But I spun off going through Club Corner and got her back on again. Ten laps further on, I went into the lead again and was actually ahead and looking good when the visor on my old Bell helmet broke on the Hangar Straight, and it's raining cats and dogs . . . So I'm sort of blinking as best I can. Led for another three or four laps but went off the road for good, braking onto Woodcote. That was my baptism in Formula 1.'

Finland's Keke Rosberg, who was to become Daly's team-mate at Williams four years later, won that day in his Theodore-Cosworth in what turned out to be the last Formula 1 International Trophy race at Silverstone.

'After that, I went with Hesketh to Long Beach and didn't qualify. That was the era of pre-qualifying. Two cars out of six went into official practice, and those two cars were always the worst at that point. After trying to pre-qualify the Hesketh three times, I stopped.

'I was also doing Formula 2 at the time with Chevron and got a phone call from a chap called Mo Nunn. I'd seen Mo Nunn racing at Dunboyne when I was twelve years old, that very first weekend. He was now running the Ensign team.'

Ensign began racing in Formula 1 in 1973 with one car and one driver, Rikky Von Opel, who was born in Lichtenstein. The team were mostly at the back of the Formula 1 grid and had to pre-qualify for many years. The likes of Clay Regazzoni, Jacky Ickx and BBC motorsport reporter Tiff Needell all drove for the team until it folded in 1982.

Daly's first race for Ensign in 1978 was at the French Grand Prix, where he again failed to qualify in the Ford-powered machine, but he did manage to put the car tenth on the grid for the following round, the British Grand Prix at Brands Hatch in July of that year alongside Hunt, who was now at McLaren.

Neither finished the race.

'I qualified tenth. Ran seventh in the race and the rear wheel upright broke going through Paddock Bend. Out.'

But it got worse before it got better for Daly and Ensign. He missed the next race in Germany and was disqualified for a push start in Austria before he retired with transmission problems on Lap 10 of the Dutch Grand Prix in the sand dunes of Zandvoort. He managed tenth in the Italian race at Monza and eighth in the second US Grand Prix of the year at Watkins Glen before picking up his first World Championship points with a sixth-placed finish at the Canadian race at Montreal – a race, incidentally, won by Gilles Villeneuve, Jacques's father, for Ferrari.

'Myself and Didier Pironi in the Tyrrell just had a *huge* dust-up the whole race long. He was right behind me, the whole race, inches apart, but I brought it home in sixth place, my first World Championship point, which was the only reason Ensign then got free travel from FOCA (the Formula 1 Constructors Association) for the following year so they could continue on in the sport.'

Daly drove eight more times for Ensign in the following 1979 season. His best-placed finish was eighth in Austria, before being taken on by the legendary Ken Tyrrell for races in the USA and Canada. Daly retired on both occasions, but he had done enough to get a contract for the 1980 season. He was a stunning fourth in the opening round in Argentina, just seconds behind Rosberg in the race for a place on the podium, and he matched that result with fourth at the British Grand Prix at Brands.

His relationship with Tyrrell ended after fifteen of sixteen races, at the end of the 1980 season, after five consecutive retirements, and 1981 saw a move to the RAM team who were racing in a March chassis with one of the sponsors being Guinness, an Irish company backing a team with an Irish driver. It was another up-and-down season. Daly only finished four races out of fifteen, his best a seventh place in Britain, before another move, this time eventually to Theodore in 1982. However, he only raced three times for the team from Hong Kong before he got a massive break.

Carlos Reutemann had suddenly announced his retirement. The brilliant Reutemann had won twelve grands prix during his career and opened the 1982 season with a second-placed finish in South Africa. However, he had a falling out with Frank Williams the next race in Brazil over team orders and, sensationally, quit.

Daly joined Frank Williams as Rosberg's team-mate for the remainder of the 1982 season, which included that now infamous non-finish in Monte Carlo.

'Carlos Reutemann was one of the most gifted drivers I'd ever seen. He had the ability to run a car on the ragged edge, but he did it with such grace and with such ease. He just had that feel and that gift, and I was a huge fan of his, even though I'd hardly ever spoken to him. He was very quiet, very moody, and if he was not in the right frame of mind, he would not be able to produce those magical performances.

'When Rosberg went to Williams, he was a very much larger than life and didn't live to anybody's protocol in particular. He smoked, drank and was out late every night, and when he jumped into the car, he was quicker than Reutemann immediately. Reutemann detected for some reason that this was not going to be an easy season for him. So, if it wasn't going to be easy, he didn't want to have to get into a mental fight to get himself in the right state he needed to be in to produce the goods. He just said, "I'm done. I'm not going to do this. I don't want to fight this out for the whole season."'

And what was it like driving for Frank Williams?

'Frank is emotionally cold. He is driven by the results and the numbers and is old school in that he has an intimidation style – the complete opposite to a team like Eddie Jordan. Eddie understood people. Understood that to get the best from a person he had to put them in an environment in which they would flourish. Frank didn't care. He'd say, "If you don't like it, leave." I think that's to his detriment. I believe if Williams understood their drivers, they probably could have got more from them. Having said that, from my point of view, it was a golden opportunity. A great team to be in.'

Mario Andretti ran in the second race of the season for Williams alongside Rosberg in Long Beach. The team, like many others in Formula 1, didn't take part in the next race in Imola due to an ongoing dispute between FISA, the world governing body, and FOCA.

By the fourth race of the 1982 season, Daly was on the grid for Williams at the Belgian Grand Prix in Zolder. He didn't finish, as he spun off on Lap 60, and the weekend was overshadowed by the death of Gilles Villeneuve, who died in qualifying when his Ferrari crashed.

Daly's next race, Monaco, made international headlines and is still spoken about today as the day that he so very nearly became the first driver from the Republic of Ireland to win a Formula 1 grand prix.

'I remember what happened as if it was yesterday. We brought four cars to the race. On the first practice session, something broke in my first car. The spare car was sitting there, but I wasn't allowed use it. That one was for Keke. They went to get the other one, but I was never as comfortable in that car. Anyway, qualified twelfth and got stuck behind Nigel Mansell going around the first corner. Followed him for I don't know how long, lap after lap, a typical Monaco. By the time I got by Mansell, I'd begun to absolutely fly. Caught Keke. He hit the kerb going onto the seafront. I saw him break his front suspension, and I was catching fellows hand over fist.'

Alain Prost was leading the race in his turbo-charged Renault and looked well set for victory with less than ten laps remaining, but it started to rain, and the cars on slick tyres found conditions now much more slippery than when the race started. Ricardo Patrese, who was driving for Brabham, and Didier Pironi in a Ferrari, began to close in on the leader, while Daly move from sixth to fifth, when Michele Alboreto's Tyrrell went out with a broken suspension after whacking the barriers. Daly himself got caught out in the wet conditions and slammed into the Armco, losing his rear wing, and, unknown to him, the gearbox oil began to spill. Surprisingly, after such a heavy impact, the car was still drivable, even without the rear wing, and he set off again, still in fourth.

The rain was now heavy, and it caught out the leader, Prost. His Renault tore off a wheel in another impact that handed the lead to Patrese, who crossed the line in the lead with one lap to go. But, through Mirabeau, the Italian lost it at the hairpin and stalled. Pironi got by, as did Andrea de Cesaris in the Alfa Romeo, and the wingless Daly, incredibly, was still circulating and now passed the stranded Patrese, elevating himself to third.

Pironi's Ferrari then suddenly ground to a halt in the tunnel. He had run out of fuel, and, just behind him, de Cesaris's Alfa Romeo did the same thing as he coasted to a halt behind the stricken Ferrari. Daly now led on the last lap and only had a few corners to negotiate to take his maiden grand-prix win. But the craziness continued.

'I was about to start the last lap when the gearbox broke. I had crashed at Tabac, the fast left-hander after that chicane, right before the swimming pool. I came in there so fast I got it sideways and hit the rear wing off the Armco barrier, which straightened the car up perfectly. I left the rear wing on the road, and the car was still going, never missed a beat. The oil cooler for the gearbox was on the rear wing, so as I drove round, it was only a matter of time until it spat all the oil out and the gearbox overheated – which it did, starting the last lap.'

Daly's race was over, and he parked it by the barriers, just seconds away from winning.

In a further dramatic twist, Patrese got a push from the marshals, and his engine restarted. He passed the stranded Pironi, de Cesaris and Daly, under the chequered flag, in first place and was declared the most unlikely winner, while Daly had to be content with being classified sixth for Williams.

'I've seen the video of the car stopping. I stepped out, stepped onto the side pod, stepped onto the wall, walked away and never even glanced back. I don't know why. It was just something that happens in motor-racing. I knew the outcome of the gearbox breaking was as a result of me driving too hard anyway, so there was a logic in what was going on. But they were pretty heady times – I mean, I was only two races into the season.'

Daly was looking for a long association with the team but played a distant second fiddle to Rosberg for the rest of the season. The Finn won the World Championship in a year that no driver won more than two races. Daly scored points in five of the remaining races, but his Formula 1 career ended with a sixth-placed finish in Las Vegas, the final race of the 1982 season, where fifth was enough to give Rosberg the title.

At the end of the year, Daly, who had also competed in his first IndyCar race in the USA, was replaced by Frenchman Jacques Laffite. A Formula 1 career that spanned five years and included sixty-four grands prix was over. He finished with the world's top racing formula, having accumulated fifteen championship points from 1978 to 1982 and wrote himself into the annals of Irish motorsport history with that dramatic non-finish in Monaco.

'The reason I left Formula 1 was that my contract wasn't renewed. For the second half of the year, I didn't drive well.'

But it was not the end of his motor-sport career. America beckoned.

'I got married at the end of 1980; it was probably a mistake. It wasn't right for me at that time to get married because I was living out of a suitcase. I was selfish and focused, which you had to be at those times. Being married and having the baggage of my environment . . . There was nothing wrong with the person I married – it was the environment I created.

'I knew I wasn't able to drive right, so I ended up getting divorced at the end of 1982, and I needed a complete break. I just needed something different, and I began to believe I'd reached my limit as a driver in Formula 1, which is why I went to America. I went to Phoenix to do an IndyCar race. The cars had 250 horsepower more than a Formula 1 car. It was 200-mile-an-hour racing between concrete walls.'

In 1983, Daly began driving in the CART IndyCar series after that one-off event in Phoenix and continued through until 1989. In all, he competed in sixty-six CART races, finishing in the Top Ten twenty-one times. His one and only podium finish was a third place in Milwaukee in 1987. Daly also raced in six Indianapolis 500s from 1983 to 1989, missing the 1986 event. He also survived a massive accident in Michigan in 1984.

'Yeah, big crash: 217 miles an hour initial impact, straight into the wall. I actually survived the highest impact a driver had ever survived at that particular time. Intensive care, skin graft, bone graft, wheelchairs, crutches. It was six months before I actually could put weight on my rebuilt left leg, and that changed the direction my life went. I was never the same driver afterwards – now racing at 95 per cent instead of 100 per cent, because I was aware of the consequences. I really didn't want to go there again. So I just stopped myself going out on that ragged edge; I knew I couldn't do it. While I enjoyed racing at that level, when I stopped, I never missed it for a day. I walked away in 1992 after three years with some of the best sports-car teams in the business, including Jaguar and Nissan.

'But, back in the mid-1980s, I'm on crutches after Michigan. It's about a year after I got hurt, and I'm still on a walking stick in orthopaedic shoes. Then somebody says, "Will you come and do an interview on live television?" "Sure." I did a little piece. I'm about to leave, and the director says, "Would you stay for another little bit?"

'And about a week after that, ESPN, which is the largest sports broadcaster in America, calls me up and says, "Would you like to become a colour analyst?" I said, "Yeah." I never heard the term, I didn't know what I was saying yes to, but I was doing nothing else: I wasn't racing, I was injured. So I began to do television work on Formula Ford races, and I liked it. And they thought I did a good job, and it got bigger and bigger, and I ended up contracted to ESPN for ten years.

'So, I'm racing and doing television at the same time. It was sort of a natural fit: when racing stopped, I just fell right into doing television. It was easy for me, and I just fell into it. I was so lucky.'

One of Daly's final races was the 1988 Le Mans twenty-four-hour race where he and Kevin Cogan of the USA and Larry Perkins of Australia finished a stunning fourth place in the Jaguar XJR-9 LM for the Silk Cut Jaguar team, all the while cultivating his television work, where he progressed from doing commentaries on Formula Ford to Formula 1 and IndyCar racing – the whole spectrum.

'Live television for me is a bit like the feeling I had in a racing car. I get that same adrenalin, you're on your toes, you're alert, and you're wide eyed.'

Having driven before and won races through all the different formulas, Daly's views as a colour analyst became respected.

'That was my biggest advantage. When a driver made a mistake, I could feel it, because I've been there, I've made that mistake – so it was easy for me. I got criticised by drivers for telling the truth quite often. My answer always was, "Did I say something wrong or something you didn't like?" It's professional criticism rather than a personal one.'

While his broadcasting career continued with ESPN, he also opened the Derek Daly Performance Driving Academy in Las Vegas.

'I was in a position potentially to win the British Formula 3 Championship in 1977, and I went to Brands Hatch for a practice day. The chief instructor of the school, who for some reason took a shine to me, liked the Irish in general, and he said, "I'll walk you round the circuit here, and I believe I can show you three or four key areas that'll make you faster." He walked me around the "so-called" racing line. Next race, I went out, put the car on the pole, won the next five in a row and won the championship. And that day, where he actually took me and influenced me to be a better driver, stuck with me all those years, which is why I ended up opening the school in Las Vegas.'

Many drivers passed through Daly's doors before he sold the school in 2006 to the American Racing Academy, owned and operated by Robert Prevost. A.J. Allmendinger, who is now in IndyCar, and actor Sylvester Stallone were two. Stallone came to Daly when he was practising for a movie called *Driven* in which he starred with Burt Reynolds.

'We had nothing to do with the movie, but a friend of his, Emerson Fittipaldi, recommended him to us, and I spent six days with him. He was OK, but it was a rubbish movie.'

While Daly was cultivating his career in the USA, there was an immense amount of sadness for him when, in 2002, he lost Vivion, his brother, who died of cancer. Vivion was a veteran of Irish motor sport. He raced occasionally in the UK and Europe but spent most of his career in Ireland and was an Irish Champion in Formula Ford and Formula Opel. It was only after his death that Irish single-seater circuit-racing began to disintegrate. He was a master of Mondello Park and Kirkistown, the Northern Irish circuit, and also won numerous races in the Phoenix Park.

The yardstick for a young driver coming through the ranks in the 1980s and 1990s was to beat Vivion Daly. If they couldn't, it was pointed out time and time again that there was little point in pursuing a career abroad.

'It was claimed that if you couldn't beat Vivion, it was time to call it quits. He used to come and help me in my Formula Ford days when we'd go across on the ferry, towing the car on the end of the rope. We'd push it on because we couldn't afford the space to bring a van. He raced go-carts, which I never did, and raced with the likes of Ayrton Senna. He stuck it out so much longer than me. He had sponsorship when people never had it. He had long-term relationships with sponsors to keep his career going, but he never had the ambition to necessarily be a professional. He knew what he enjoyed. And you know, if people could measure themselves against him, that was great. If you beat him, you were ready to go and take an international step, and if that's part of the legacy he left behind, great, because he enjoyed what he did.

'I miss him. When I left to go to the UK, I would send helmets and overalls which I was finished with back to him. He had a large collection of photographs with me, of me. I'm just glad he enjoyed what he did, even though he wasn't around to enjoy it for as long as we all were.'

With the sale of his driving academy in 2006, Daly, now in his fifties, remains involved with motor sport and still commentates for US television. He has three boys with his second wife Rhonda, and Conor, the eldest, is now racing go-carts in the USA. He flew to

Ireland to take part in a go-cart weekend at Mondello in 2006, the circuit where it all began for his father.

Daly Snr. is naturally proud of his son's abilities.

'Conor has a remarkable feel. What he does in a go-cart is just natural; you can't coach what I see him do. He tells me he wants to do it seriously, so my joy from here on in will be just to see where he'll develop. I'll try to give him opportunities and the type of support that I had from my mother and father. I'd love to be in a position to transfer my information to young kids of the future. Every driver has their strengths and weaknesses. Racing drivers, above anybody else, are scared that anyone would notice they have weaknesses. Believe it or not, it's what they should expose and work on and turn into a strength as soon as possible, because if you can recognise your weaknesses and turn them into a strength, you can be pretty much unbeatable.'

There have been many tributes to the only driver from the Republic of Ireland to race a modern grand-prix car, and Derek Daly was the first driver inducted into the Motorsport Ireland Hall of Fame in 2000.

2

Rosemary Smith

osemary Smith remains, to this day, the first lady of Irish motor sport and a Continental rally winner to boot. In 1965, her Hillman Imp, powered by a tiny 998cc engine, won the Tulip Rally in Holland. It was a successful event all round for the little car, as Smith led home an Imp one-two, with 'Tiny' Lewis finishing second for the Rootes Works Team in another Imp.

Smith fashioned a successful career for herself in a male-dominated sport, which included not only the win in the Tulip Rally but also numerous outright ladies and class titles on the Circuit of Ireland and drives on the London-to-Sydney Rally, in which, at one point, she had to reverse over the Khyber Pass due to mechanical problems. She also raced on the track in the British and Irish Saloon Car Championships and at one stage held the Irish land-speed record for a car, which was set on the Carrigrohane Straight in Cork in 1978.

More recently, Smith has been one of the leading lights in the road-safety campaign with her Think Awareness programme designed for transition-year students, which was started in 2001.

Although Smith remains an Irish racing icon, she doesn't have much visible evidence of those years, as many of her trophies and a lifetime of photos taken during her career were stolen from her house a number of years ago and never returned.

One of three children, with elder siblings Pamela and Roger, Smith was born on 7 August 1939 into what was considered a middle-class family in South Dublin. She spent her childhood in the suburb of Rathfarnham. Smith remembers it as a time of contentment and harmony.

'Well, looking back on it, it was a very happy childhood – innocent,' said Smith. 'We were never bored, because we didn't even know what the word meant. My dad had this idea that if you had nothing to do he'd find something for you do, so it was just happy-go-lucky, going away for summer holidays down to a little cottage in Bettystown.

'I had one sister, Pamela, who was the eldest, then my brother Roger, he was the middle, and I was the so-called baby. But I was totally different to the other two because Pamela was small and dainty and very pretty, Roger was brainy, clever – one of these people that everybody liked automatically – then I was the afterthought. And I was very tall from a very early age and blonde, blue-eyed and skinny, and I remember my mother saying one day, "Ah well, I'm not really going to worry about Rosemary. After all, she'll grow up and get married and live happily ever after," and that was the sort of attitude.'

(Rosemary Smith did eventually marry and subsequently divorce a bullying husband who was to refer to her many rallying events abroad as 'ego trips.')

A life-changing experience for the young Dublin girl was at the tender age of eleven, when she was allowed to drive one of her dad's old bangers around a field near their house on the southside of Dublin.

'I was quite small, and I'd have to have cushions on the seat, and then my feet wouldn't get down as far as the pedals, but I loved it. I really loved it. It was a way of getting out and about and doing things, something different than just playing with dolls and making mud pies. Roger and myself spent hours and hours driving around this field that we had up near Tallaght, and I remember it was such a big old car, I think it was a Vauxhall, and the steering wheel was so large, I had to look between the top of the steering wheel and the top of the dashboard so I was sort of crouched down, but it was still something I enjoyed. It came quite naturally to me, but I was always fine with my hands and my feet. It was the bit between the two ears that rather was my problem.

'I went to school in Loreto, in Beaufort, but school and I never really got on too much. I enjoyed the things I could do with my hands and my feet but, unfortunately, the old brain power wasn't the best, and I just really didn't get on too well with the nuns. And the day that the Head Nun, the Principal, told my father that his beloved daughter was stupid was the day I left school, and I was only fifteen.

'That was a bad mistake on my dad's part. Looking back on it, I should have been taken away from that school and sent to another one, but I wasn't. I just left school at fifteen, which was far too young. So they sent me to the Grafton Academy, which I thought was great fun because, again, that was using my hands and my art – I was quite artistic.'

Rosemary graduated from the Grafton Academy after only nine months with the accolade of Designer of the Year, and then she hit the outside world and got into full-time fashion design. It was on a small scale but, amazingly enough, it was to offer her a way into the world of motor sport. She wasn't to know it yet, but cutting cloth and working in the fashion and clothes-design business was to be the start of the career of Ireland most successful woman's motor-sport driver.

'I was designing outfits for some quite well-known people around Dublin. I worked for a few companies – Irene Gilbert being one of them. I did a bit with Sybil Connolly, and then I went into a factory to learn the ins and outs of cutting cloth, and we got some colossal orders on my designs.'

Gilbert recognised that Rosemary had a little more to offer than just dress design and began to use the teenager's face and figure to model her creations, and the designing began to fade into the background. Her mother, alarmed at what she saw, put her foot down and insisted the modelling stopped and made her return to the design business.

'My mum and the man who eventually became my step-dad set me up in business in South Anne Street, just in two rooms. I got a few machinists, and I started doing specialised stuff. But having worked for somebody like Irene Gilbert and also having won the overall award at the Grafton Academy helped. I specialised in wedding dresses, ball gowns and all the lovely things that were around in the 1960s, and that's where it all started.'

One of her customers gave Rosemary Smith her first introduction into the world of motor sport.

'A woman called Delphine Bigger came into me a number of times; she used to own the Coffee Inn in South Anne Street. Her husband was Frank Bigger. My dad raced, and so did my brother, but I hadn't thought about doing it myself. This woman kept coming in and out of the shop for things that weren't really worn back then by women – trousers and the like. I used to make all these things for her, lovely silk shirts, scarves made into blouses – very expensive stuff, lovely stuff.

'I kept thinking to myself, why do you need all these trousers and tops? And eventually she said to me, "Oh, I'm going rallying this weekend." Now, I knew about racing, but I didn't know about rallying, and I said, "Oh great, do you know where you are going?" She said, "Kilkenny," and I said, "Is this why you've been getting all these outfits made?" "Oh yes," she said, "I go all over Ireland, and I rally here and I rally there." So that's what caught my imagination, and I thought, all over Ireland – that sounds interesting. She pointed a long manicured fingernail at me, and she said, "You will come to Kilkenny this weekend," and I said, "For what?" and she said, "You may navigate me, we're doing the such-and-such rally." I don't even remember the name of it, just this little event. I was afraid of her because she was terribly sophisticated and smart, or so I thought. She was older than I was, well groomed, and her husband was this big rally driver who drove for Jaguar. She intimidated me completely, which she succeeded in doing practically up to the day she died. Actually, I discovered after going on a few events with her that she was only going rallying because even though she was married to one man, she was having an affair with another, and she went on these events to meet the other man.'

In that event in Kilkenny, Delphine Bigger, navigated by Rosemary Smith, got lost three miles into the rally. Smith, reading a map on her lap, turned it as the car turned and got the pair stuck up on a mountaintop. It was a quick end to her co-driver days.

'We ended literally up a boreen at a farm gate which was firmly locked, and Delphine started using words that I had never even heard before, so I was totally flummoxed. I knew she was annoyed because she was purple in the face, and she said, "You drive and I'll navigate." So we did, and we happened to come in third in our class in that very first event.

'But before we got a mile from the finish, we stopped. She hopped into the driving seat again, and I was meant to do navigating into the finish. So we did that for about, oh, a year and a half, I suppose. I just enjoyed it so much, even with the fact that she was getting all this kudos because we were winning everything we went in for, even in the ladies class in the Circuit of Ireland the very first year we did it. There were something like twelve women's teams, which was incredible, including people like Pat Moss and Ann Hall – all the big names.'

Smith took over the driving responsibilities, with Delphine Bigger on the maps. But one major incident nearly cost her co-driver her life on the 1959 Circuit of Leinster Rally.

'I was down as the named driver, though Delphine was down as the owner of the car and the entrant, and we went to do the Circuit of Leinster. We had a Mini, and it was an all-night event, which I never liked particularly, and September was a bad month because of the fog and mist and so on. We were coming down this road at three in the morning, and it was very hard to see, extremely hard to see. Delphine said, "We're coming up to a crossroads, straight through the crossroads."

'So, 3 o'clock in the morning, not really seeing where I was going, I dropped down a gear and continued. But unfortunately, we were on the wrong road, and it turned out to be a T-bend with a very hard stone wall at the end of it, and I literally drove straight into it . . .'

Smith discovered later that the Mini had slammed into the wall at the appropriately named Goresbridge in County Kilkenny.

'There was this *awful* silence. I mean, *awful* silence. The engine had stopped; the windscreen had come in on us. There was just nothing. There wasn't a sound outside, and I turned around to say, "Oh gosh, sorry Delphine." I got the flash lamp, which was in the pocket of the door, and I put it up to look at her to discover that the top of her head was virtually gone. She'd been scalped, basically, on the windscreen; the visor had just taken the top of her head off. And the flap of head was rolled over backwards. As I looked at her, the blood just started, and it just gushed down her face, and I thought, I've got to do something to help this woman. I've caused this, and the only thing I could think of was to take the flap of skin and slap it back down on top of her head again. There was a box of tissues, so I got those, planted them on her head; then I found a scarf, and I tied that tightly around her head and right round the back of her neck. She was unconscious.

'What had happened was that when we'd hit the wall, her seat belt (she was a very heavy woman) had broken, she'd shot forward, and she'd been caught with the sun visor. So what could I do then except get out and go looking for help?'

In the middle of the night, she struck out to look for help, leaving her unconscious navigator inside the car. She says she remembers the incident as if it were yesterday.

'I couldn't initially get out of the car because the doors were smashed in against the side. So I had to open the window, and they didn't wind down as they do today, they slid backwards and forwards. It was freezing cold. The fog was right down, and I started to run down this road, and I remember I had no shoes on. Somehow, I lost them in the car. I started to run down the road, and I fell over something, which turned out to be a calf sitting on the side of the road. Absolutely silent, not a noise around, and because we were on the wrong road, no other rally cars came along.

'So I just kept going, and eventually I saw a pinprick of a light at an old farmhouse. Bang bang bang on the doors, and the dogs came rushing out, barking. The next thing, this upstairs light went on, and I looked up, and all I could see was the nozzle of a shotgun down through the window, and the old farmer said, "Who's there? Stand back!" I said, "Don't shoot, please," and realised then that I was covered in blood at this stage. Of course, it never dawned on me. He took one horrified look and said, "Oh, I'll help, I'll help."

'The only thing he had was a cattle truck, and he'd been to the cattle mart that day, so you can imagine the state of it. We drove back up the road, got Delphine (who remarkably was still alive), got the door open, got her into the truck and drove to the county hospital.'

That wasn't the end of their troubles. When the trio got there, with Delphine in the back of the filthy truck, they were met by the matron who said there was nothing they could do as all the doctors had gone to a party. The cattle truck had to turn around and drive back into Carlow.

'They were waiting for us in Carlow because she'd rung through to say that this was serious. When we got there, there were two doctors waiting for us and a nurse, and they took one look at Delphine and just sort of shook their heads. I had a gash on the side of my face, and they insisted on sewing that first before they even looked at Delphine, which I was really upset about. They didn't even give me an injection. They got a big curved needle and started sewing it all up, and then they turned their attention to Delphine. She had forty-nine stitches around the top of her head.'

Incredibly, Delphine Bigger survived and lived into her eighties. She passed away in 2004.

Amazingly, after such a horrific injury to her co-driver and her amazing brush with death, the pair stayed together and even went so far as to compete in the RAC Rally of Great Britain in 1962.

'She was a big woman, and she was strong, so it stood her in good stead. When she came back out, out of the hospital, she decided that it was all getting too expensive, so we discussed it and decided we'd go to the end of that particular year [1962].

'But the RAC was such a gruelling event. I mean, it's not like it is today. We drove day and night. It was awful, and it was one of the first years that we went in the forests. The Mini was running at number 173, way back, and was so low to the ground. So you can imagine going through the forest stage! All we had were these wheel tracks and the grass, and the centre was up in a big heap. It was the most difficult event I think I ever did. But we got to the end, and I think we were third in the ladies section again, and then we more or less said "Well, that's it."'

Bigger retired and took her cars and money with her, leaving Smith without a drive and looking like she was at the end of a very short career. Luckily for Smith, not long after the RAC Rally, a telegram arrived from a lady by the name of Sally Anne Cooper of the Cooper Fly Spray family, who wanted a partner for the Monte Carlo Rally in 1963. Copper was well backed, and there was no financial input required from Rosemary. Cooper asked her would she come and do the Monte with her because she was getting married the following May, and she wanted to do something exciting before she got married.

'It sounded very odd, but I agreed to take part, and I really enjoyed it. We started in Glasgow. I drove most of the way. Sally Anne sat in the back with her picnic basket and her fur coat and waved to the crowds along the way, and another girl navigated me. And we got to Monte Carlo; I think we were third or fourth in the class. As I left the car, this man came over, and he said, not "Will you?", "Would you like to?", or anything else. He just said, "You are now going to be a member of our Works Rally Team," and that was Norman Garrard from the Rootes Group.'

Garrard was offering Smith a place in his team, looking for her to replace Mary Handley-Page who drove the Works Sunbeam Rapier Series II for the team in the late 1950s and early 1960s. Initially, Smith did not accept, but Norman wasn't taking no for an answer.

'I said, "I'm sorry, I didn't like the snow and ice. It was too long and too hazardous, and I'm going home now." And, of course, when I got home . . . it's the first time I ever saw my father really,

really annoyed with me, and he said, "How could you be so stupid?" And I think either he or my mum actually wrote to Norman and said, "Look, she was tired, but I think she would really like to do it."'

'So I got the letter back saying you're a member of the Rootes Works Rally Team. They were going to pay me, I think, £2,000 a year plus expenses, and I mean that was just phenomenal – to be paid for something I really enjoyed was unbelievable.'

According to Rosemary, Norman Garrard also had an ulterior motive in signing her.

'It was only years later I discovered it was just that Norman fancied the look of me and thought a nice "dolly bird" on the team would be good for publicity. Which was quite right, because one of the first things he did when I joined was to enter me for the Le Mans twenty-four-hour race.'

A golden era for Smith had begun, and there was hardly any rally in the subsequent years that did not have the young Dublin woman on its results sheets. In the 1963 Tour de France, Rosemary, along with navigator Margaret Mackenzie, finished tenth overall and third in class in a Sunbeam Alpine. But the Le Mans twenty-four-hour race of 1964 was a different kettle of fish. Garrard was a man who liked to raise the profile of his team. Having a stunning-looking woman in his outfit was good for business, and sex sells. Unbeknownst to Smith, women drivers were banned from racing at Le Mans. Garrard knew the rules but still went ahead with processing her entry that year, and Smith headed to France.

'Well, I went out, and I thought this was wonderful, meeting all these big racing drivers. Then you had to go in and have a medical. I went into this room and there was this very good-looking young doctor, who had his back to me at this stage. It was reminiscent of Benny Hill. "Drop your trousers," he said, without looking around. And I thought, "Oy, oy, I've heard of the French, but this is ridiculous," and I said "What?" and he turned around. He was so upset! "What are you doing here? You're a woman! Non, non, non, you cannot be here. You cannot drive here because you're a woman," and so on and so on.

'Of course, I went out, and I told Norman what had happened, and Norman beamed from ear to ear. He had about half a dozen journalists around. That's the publicity he wanted. He knew his cars couldn't do well at all, and I think I was in every newspaper, every television show, every radio interview, everything all around the world; even the American channels got in touch with me.

'So from there on, I'd made my name. But he was lucky in as much as I could drive. The next event I went in for, I won my class plus the ladies class, and then, bit by bit, I gradually moved up, and I was in the Top 10, and then I started getting in the Top 5.'

Garrard also knew that Smith could help sell cars – ladies cars – and to this end the Rootes Group persuaded her to drive the Hillman Imp, starting in 1964. It had a 998-cc engine, with Stromberg carburettors producing around 65 brake horse power. Performance was a very modest 0–60 mph in fifteen seconds, with a 92 mph top speed. With the Imp, Smith finished fourteenth overall in the 1964 RAC Rally and second in the Coupe des Dames, or Ladies Cup.

In April 1965, Smith competed in the Imp in the Tulip Rally in Holland. There was no organised WRC at that stage, but it was considered to be one of the top European rallies of its time. She was also changing navigators like light bulbs, and for that event, teamed up with Valerie Domleo, driving car registration number EDU 710C running with the number 35.

The Tulip that year was run in very bad weather, and of the 157 starters, only forty-seven finished. The event was also on a very complicated handicap-scoring system to make cars of different performance levels more comparable; thus Smith's Imp could compete on a level playing field with her more powerful competitors. Overall performance was judged by a driver's advantage or disadvantage compared to those in their class and classes above and below them.

'The Imps had only just come into being at that stage, and from the time they'd come out, people really laughed at them. They called them tin boxes; the engine was the wrong end. But I loved them, and I still love them.'

In the unusually snowy conditions, the Imps of Rosemary Smith and 'Tiny' Lewis revelled and claimed a one-two victory for the Rootes Group Team.

'What nobody had banked on was that it was going to snow the entire way. It started in a place called Nordvik in Holland and went across some of the very high cols into France. I think we went into Germany as well, and we came the whole way back around and back into Holland again. One of the particular cols we went up, it was so steep that the little car wouldn't go any further, so my unfortunate co-driver Valerie Domleo had to get out and sit in the boot, put the weight on the rear end, even though the engine was the rear as well. But I didn't care: "Sit on it," I said.

'And this girl, she got out and sat and clung onto the boot lid and bounced the whole way up, and we passed everything from Porsches to Fords, to you name it, until we got to the top of that col. Once we got it going down the far side, I stopped, and she got off the boot. Well, she tried to get off the boot, but her hands were frozen solid around the edge of the boot lid. We got her back in the car, and even with the fact that she was crying from the pain of her hands, she was still navigating. She gradually thawed out, and we eventually got back into Nordvik.'

At that stage, it was still not known who had won the rally, and it would be some hours before the handicappers worked out the overall result.

'When we finished, we had a great party and went to bed. About 11 o'clock that night, the phone rang, and this voice said, "Ah, Miss Smith, you have won the rally," and my answer was, I'd learnt a few swear words at that stage, "Would you go away and stop f***ing annoying me." Put down the phone, and it rang again. Put it down, it rang again. Then there was banging on the door, and Norman was there, along with quite a few of the team with the press, and they said, "You've won, you've won!" It took a while to sink in. It was brilliant, there's no two ways about it, the feeling of beating all the men.'

Accolades poured on Rosemary Smith and Valerie Domleo. Back in Ireland, she was presented with the 1965 Texaco Sportstar of the

Year Award for motor sport. Since they were first presented in 1958, the annual Texaco Sportstar Awards have stood as a celebration of Irish sporting achievement in national and international competitions and are a coveted prize. Corgi later made a die-cast model of the winning car, and Rosemary bought and restored the original Imp in 2003.

Smith also had success with the Imp at other events in 1965. She won her class and the Coupe des Dames in the Alpine Rally, the Coupe des Alpes with navigator Sheila Taylor in the blue Imp, Reg. No. EDU 710C with competition number 105, as well as First in Class and eighth overall in the Canadian Rally that year.

Illegal headlights, though, robbed her of the Monte Carlo Ladies Cup in 1966, the same set of rules which were to cost Hopkirk and the Mini Cooper S a one-two-three in the same event. (See Chapter 6.)

There was also the Classic Marathon Rally, which covers a gruelling 4,500 kilometres from Paris to Marrakech. Rosemary was partnered by English co-driver Elizabeth Jordan driving a 4.8 litre 1964 Sunbeam Tiger. The pair finished in tenth position overall and first in the ladies and their class.

Smith drove for the Lombard and Ulster team and Dealer Opel Team Ireland when she rallied at home. Her best result came on the 1968 Circuit of Ireland when she not only lifted the Ladies Cup but was also third on the overall standings behind the late Roger Clark and Adrian Boyd.

She also contested the 1968 London–Sydney Marathon, driving a Cortina for Henry Ford of Ireland. Her co-driver was a Belgian woman Lucette Pointet, who didn't speak much English, while Rosemary's French was negligible.

'I don't like driving with someone who natters at me. Anyway, we had sufficient vocabulary to get along.'

The pair won the Ladies Cup and were forty-eighth overall, the year Paddy Hopkirk, Tony Nash and Alex Poole were runners up.

They were heady days for the Dublin woman, mixing it with some of the top names of her sport at that time. Pauli Toivonen, Hopkirk and Timo Mäkinen, plus Pat Moss, with whom she had great battles in the ladies sections of various rallies. Moss was the younger sister of Stirling Moss, who also won the Tulip Rally (1962) and who was third overall in the 1965 Monte Carlo driving for Saab.

'It was a great life, there's no two ways about it. But my private life has never been hectic, and driving professionally . . . well, I was always away, and it's very hard for a marriage to survive if one is away eight months of every year, and you come back and you're talking about all these different people, who in those days were household names, but the person you're married to doesn't really know anything about it. Not the ideal situation from that point of view. But, in general, "Yes, I have enjoyed every moment of it".'

Smith also combined her rallying with circuit-racing, which she took right up into the 1990s when she raced in the Irish Saloon Car Championship in a Tulip Computers-backed Peugeot (smart bit of advertising on the company's behalf). She also raced in the British Saloon Car Series, where she won her class for three successive years and almost won the famous Sexton Trophy, narrowly losing out to Derek Shortall in 1975. Shortall, in fact, was a close friend of Rosemary and her husband Tom, but they fell out, and Shortall tried everything to win the Sexton that year just to deny Rosemary.

'I went to America, and I raced in America for about two or three years and had a wonderful time over there and then went down to Australia, New Zealand and South Africa. You name it, like, I've been there, and I've rallied or raced in all these countries.'

So, if Rosemary Smith had the choice, which was the best, rallying or circuit-racing?

'Oh rallying, rallying every time. circuit-racing to me was monotonous because once you got to know circuits you just went round and round. I didn't enjoy it very much really. I enjoyed when I won, obviously, getting out and getting the little wreath around my neck, but no, I began to find it very monotonous.

'I did the twenty-four hour in Daytona, and that was exciting. The first year I went to Daytona, we were driving in an all-girls team. There was a girl called Donna Mae Mims, she was known as

"Think Pink" because she had pink overalls, pink helmet, pink hair, pink nails, pink everything, you name it. She wasn't really a very good driver, but because she was good for publicity they used her. There was another girl called Janet Guthrie [the first woman to qualify for the Indianapolis 500] who raced with us as well.'

Ever mindful of publicity, Rosemary Smith also hatched a plan to break the Irish land-speed record in 1978 on the Carrigrohane Straight on the outskirts of Cork city, attempting the record in a Formula 5000 car while motorcycle importer Danny Keany came along for good measure and attempted to set the motorbike equivalent on his Yamaha.

Danfay Limited, a company set up by Keany and Fay McHenry, celebrated its fortieth year in business in 2005. It was established back in 1965 to import Yamaha motorbikes into Ireland. Keany raced on Yamahas in Irish motorcycle championship races and was a regular on the Isle of Man TT in the 1970s.

The city of Cork and the Carrigrohane Straight in particular became synonymous with the Irish land-speed record attempts. Indeed, in October 1930, Joseph Wright set a then world motorbike record of 150.65 mph on a 994-cc OEC Temple JAP on the same piece of road. The basic idea was to run through a quarter-mile section of the road twice in opposite directions, and the aggregate of the two runs counted towards the overall speed record attempt.

This is an extract of an article written by Rory Egan of the *Sunday Independent* about just how Keany came to be involved in that weekend in Cork back in 1978.

SOME dinner party invitations should come with a health warning. At least, that's what Danny Keany thinks. In 1978, he was invited to Rosemary Smith's house in Donnybrook to break bread with the legendary rally driver. Rosemary was the pin-up girl of the European motor-racing scene. With her Hillman Imp, blonde hair and perfect figure, her girl-next-door smile belied the aggressive driving that had made her so successful. Danny was no slouch himself; not only was he king of the motorcycle circuits at one stage, but he was the sole importer of Yamaha in Ireland.

After dinner, the port was passed, and Danny remembers little else until he received a phone call from Rosemary the next day asking was he still on for it. Being the gentleman he was, he said, 'Of course,' but then had to ask, 'On for what?'

Apparently, the Irish land-speed record was open for the taking, and Rosemary wanted a crack at it. She thought it would be fun if they turned it into a contest, with Rosemary in a car and Danny on a motorbike.

He decided to give it a go, but he was worried about letting the side down: a 750-cc motorbike was no match for a 2-litre Hillman Imp in racing gear. He rang up his good friend, World Champion Kenny Roberts from the USA, who came over to the shop in Aungier Street to soup it up.

Their biggest problem was keeping the tyres on the rim at over 160 mph. The centrifugal force at that speed could make the tyre expand, as had happened Barry Sheene at Daytona, in a crash which had very nearly killed him. However, Danny had his own solution. He literally screwed the tyres to the rim and headed off for Cork.

The 1-kilometre, perfectly flat stretch of road was the only place acceptable to the recorders. Rosemary arrived, not in a Hillman Imp but in a Jaguar, with a massive American V8 engine bolted into it. Rosemary took off 'like a bat out of Hell' and recorded an aggregate speed of 178 mph. Danny decided to go for it and ended up reaching 204 mph over the finish line and aggregating 185 mph to hold the Irish land-speed record, on 21 June 1978, on his 750-cc TZ Yamaha four-cylinder, two-stroke motorcycle. The bike now resides in a museum owned by Gerry Stephens, the distributor of Kawasaki, in Ballymore.

It was a day that lived long in the memory for Ireland's fastest lady. 'We had to rent a car, something that would be fast enough. So we got a car from an English guy called Mick Hill. He was a very big racer in England. And this car – oh, an enormous thing – it had a Jaguar body, a fibre-glass Jaguar body, which covered in the whole of the Formula 1 chassis, engine, everything else. The engine was at the back, and until I started the car on the straight down in Cork that morning, I'd never sat in, never mind driven, that car.

'A huge crowd turned up first thing, and on the left-hand side of that straight there used to be an old dump, and, of course, in the morning all the seagulls came down. Some of the marshals went up and down the road firing shotguns in the air to get rid of these enormous seagulls before we started, because, obviously, Danny on his motorbike, if he'd been hit by a seagull he was a goner, and even if it had hit my car I wouldn't be here.

'It turned out to be the most beautiful day, and we were there at 5am on that June morning. What we hadn't counted on was the numbers of people that were going to come out to watch this thing. They were everywhere.

'The other thing I hadn't counted on was that the surface on part of the road was ridged concrete. Now, when you're doing 40/50 miles per hour in an ordinary car you don't feel it. When you're doing nearly 200 miles an hour in a car with racing tyres on it, you certainly do. Another extraordinary thing was that we were doing another run, both of us, before the roads were reopened at 7.00am, and somebody got down on the ground and said, "Stop, don't go one inch further." What had happened was that the car had been set up for the English circuits, which were clockwise, and nobody had thought to straighten the wheels into a dead straight line. So the inside of the front left-hand tyre had got a bulge on it, literally sticking out about 6 inches. One more start and it would have blown.

Smith, by now into her forties, didn't let up. She raced in an Escort with an FVC engine, which she bought off Tony Brennan and raced across the length and breadth of Britain, winning her class three years on the trot in the British Saloon Car Championship (now the British Touring Car Championship, BTCC). The Cosworth-built FVC was designed for endurance racing.

'I loved that. My brother was still alive at the time, and he used to come down and help in the pits. After that, I got drives with Porsche and Lancia. I did the Safari a number of times, late '70s/early '80s. I really only gave it up sometime around the mid-'80s up to the early '90s, and then I got bitten by the bug again, and I had the little 205 Peugeot, and I used to take it to Mondello. The Tulip Computer-sponsored car raced for a number of years in Mondello and Kirkistown. Then all the classic and historic rallying started again, and I was asked all over the Continent to take part in events or to be a guest.'

After her retirement from racing, Smith got involved with a programme set up a couple of years ago for Irish transition-year students called Think Awareness.

'That is something that I saw in America first of all. I thought, the carnage on our roads is so bad for such a small country. It really is appalling. Initially, I found it difficult to get it going because people weren't used to the idea of training young drivers before they got their licences.

'Ford of Ireland, though, realised what I was trying to do, and they came in and backed me. I've a lot of instructors, and the youngsters get the feel of starting and stopping in perfect safety. It's an educational programme. It's not just a fun day out for the kids.'

'I'm delighted with its success, but it's taken over a decade for people to wake up to the fact that the youngsters must be trained to drive. If you look at what's happening on the roads, it's the seventeen- to twenty-five-year-olds who are the most vulnerable. You see, I'm not entirely convinced about this thing of speed. Obviously, speed in the wrong place, on the wrong roads, the wrong conditions, it's all going to contribute. But if they were educated to read the roads, read the road markings, take into consideration whether it is day or night, what the conditions are . . .

'The other train of thought is, "Oh, the roads aren't that great," but that's not true. Our roads are improving all the time. The driving is not improving, and, quite honestly, I think our drivers here are dreadful. They say, "I've been driving for twenty years, and I've never had an accident." That's not the attitude. I often take out people who've been driving for twenty years just to try and see what they're like. They go through Stop signs; they go through red lights; they've done it for twenty years so they're going to continue doing it. Now this all comes back to education. And the young people, they're like sponges. They're brilliant. I just love teaching them because they absorb everything. They are so into learning and staying alive, basically. But if you can't get to them early, and if you can't train them, you're still going to go on having just as much carnage as we have been having.'

Rosemary Smith was inducted into the Motorsport Ireland Hall of Fame in 2001 and was honoured along with the likes of other recipients Michael Roe, Billy Coleman and Alex Poole. It's an award she cherishes.

'I was absolutely thrilled, because I always reckoned that they didn't really give me an awful lot of credit in Ireland. Not the general public now – the general public were great to me, always were – but I felt that the drivers themselves, they sort of slightly resented me, so to get an award and an honour like that, I was absolutely knocked out. I thought it was wonderful. I was thrilled.'

3

Michael Roe

hile this book deals with the motor-sport careers of Irish legends like Derek Daly, Paddy Hopkirk and the Dunlop brothers, all are well known, not just in Irish motor-racing circles, but on the international stage as well. However, there remains a clutch of Irish drivers who had successfully worked their way up the motor-sport ladder but, for some reason or another, just failed to get to the pinnacle of their chosen profession, despite having the obvious talent to do so.

County Louth's Tommy Byrne, Dubliner David Kennedy and Kildare's Michael Roe are amongst the crop of Irish drivers who rose to the cusp of Formula 1. While they still had half-decent careers in other forms of motor sport, they never managed to crack the ultimate prize, Formula 1. So near and yet so far. Roe, for example, won the British Formula Ford Festival and the Can-Am series in the USA and was on his way to a Formula 1 drive with the legendary Ken Tyrrell before others intervened, and one of Ireland's most talented drivers ever was lost to the world's top formula.

There are not many outside of the small circle that is Irish circuit-racing who knew of him, but ask any who do, and they will tell you that Michael Roe was one of the greatest and most skilful drivers this country ever produced. Roe was one of a very special breed of Irish drivers who raced in the 1970s and 1980s. Many are still talked about today by dewy-eyed nostalgic motor-sport supporters who still reckon that the era had, in the likes of Roe, Byrne, Derek Daly, Kennedy and Bernard Devaney, some of the finest drivers this country has known. Daly was the most successful, driving for five seasons in Formula 1 for the likes of Tyrrell and Williams, but Roe was also considered amongst the best, and it's with much regret that we didn't get to see the Naas man drive in the world's top formula.

Roe won the Irish Formula Ford Championship in 1976, following that up by winning the 1978 Formula Ford Festival at Brands Hatch before moving onto British Formula 3. A career in the USA followed, where in 1984 he won the Can-Am series, a championship which was also won in the past by the likes of Australian Alan Jones, who became the 1980 Formula 1 World Champion and by Al Unser Jnr., two-time Indianapolis 500 winner.

Roe was in exalted company with his 1984 Can-Am win, a series for Formula 5000-cc cars with a sports-car shell. However, with Formula 1 beckoning, Don Walker, the millionaire businessman who backed the Irishman to the championship win, persuaded Roe against moving to Formula 1. Walker, in effect, blocked Roe's upward progression, waving a chequebook in his face in order to keep him with his Can-Am team. It was a decision that Roe was to regret.

It all began for Roe back on 8 August 1955 when he was born in Naas, County Kildare, then a village on the north side of the county about half an hour's drive from Dublin city. It was an unremarkable town then, with its major claim to fame its being part of the Dublin-to-Cork route, with drivers welcomed by a sign on the Dublin road, 'Naas, a nice place to shop.' The property boom of the 1990s saw the town grow, swollen from its original size to encapsulate a population of over 25,000, becoming, in effect, a satellite town to the capital city of Dublin. The 'nice place to shop' sign is now long gone.

'I was born on the Sallins Road in Naas. It was a very small town then, with a population of about 3,000, and, obviously, you knew everyone in it,' said Roe.

In secondary school at Newbridge College, Roe wasn't too in-volved in motor sport, instead preferring to play in the front row as hooker for the school rugby team – a sport which was, according to Roe, 'nearly compulsory at that stage.' Roe is still involved with rugby as one of the coaches at Naas Rugby Club.

'I've always been keen on sport as a spectator as well as playing and coaching. My son Shane was Captain in Newbridge College Snr. Cup team, and he's now playing with Naas. If fact, we have a back-ground in field sports as my Dad also played a little bit. I read in an obituary of his that he was one of only a few people who played in Croke Park, Dalymount Park and Lansdowne Road in the same year. I think it was when he was in veterinary college. He played rugby and soccer, and he played junior football with Dublin.'

And it was Michael Snr., a veterinary surgeon from Naas, who introduced Michael Jnr. to the world of motor sport when he pushed him towards running in an auto-cross special.

'In fact, his first interest was motorcycles. He was a frequent visi-tor to the Isle of Man, and he recounted great stories from there. But he always had an interest in cars, and in the early '70s, he decided to take up auto-crossing. I remember the little Special he bought for £100, and we knocked serious sport out of it. Initially, it had a Volks-wagen engine, but we went over to England and bought a Porsche engine for it, and it was very successful.'

When Roe was a teenager, his father would allow him to drive the car at the end of meetings, and, by the time he was fifteen, he was competing himself, one of a crop of underage Irish drivers who kept their dates of birth to themselves in order to fool the scrutineers of the meeting, who more or less turned a blind eye anyway.

'Dad then put me in that car, and I did a year in auto-cross. I learned so much from it in terms of car control and traction. I think it's underestimated. It's probably one of the best forms of motor sport that you can learn to drive in.'

By the time he had left school, young Roe had now forgotten about playing rugby and started to concentrate on motor-racing. In 1975, he decided to buy a Formula Ford car, an ex-Bernard Devaney

Crosslé 25 F, financed by various jobs, including buying and selling second-hand cars, driving cattle trucks and, at one stage, working as a movie stuntman.

'I remember the car was brought to Naas cinema, and we had to do various laps around Naas and Mondello in it in 1975. I can't remember the name of the movie, but previous to that I had been driving a 1912 Humber in *The Blue Max*. Kennedy and Daly went off working in the Australian mines to try and earn money around that time. I worked on the films, driving that Humber, and that raised enough for the 1975 season.'

It was a wild start to the Formula Ford career of the Naas driver, and he was off the track more than on it. But he soon settled into it, and his biggest chance that year was at the Phoenix Park races when he led both Daly and Kennedy. But his inexperience showed when he went off while leading on the last lap.

In 1976, Roe knuckled down to racing with a little more serious intent. Those involved at Mondello Park, a circuit just a couple of miles from his family home, saw his potential. Their racing school, run by John Murphy, supplied a Royale RP21 to Roe. He won nine races that year from eleven starts and took the Irish Formula Ford Championship. World Champion James Hunt presented him with the Irish Racing Drivers Association trophy for Driver of the Year.

'I was lucky in that at the end of 1975, John Murphy arrived in Ireland, and he had an agency for the Royale cars. Aldon supplied the engines, and we maintained it ourselves with John Murphy's great help. One of the big races that year was when the works team came over to Mondello with Derek Daly in the Hawke. Jim Walsh was driving a Royale for the factory team, and one of my great memories is of Rory Byrne, who went on to become the Ferrari Formula 1 designer, in the garage at home on Sallins Road helping me set up the car and get it ready for the Sunday race, which we duly won. I think we won everything in Ireland that year.'

With an Irish championship win under his belt, Roe joined the exodus to the UK to try his hand at the British Formula Ford Championship in 1977. Under-funded and on shoestring budget, he struggled in his first season but still managed to race against the likes of Nigel Mansell, who was to become Formula 1 World Champion.

By now, Roe had hooked up with the legendary Formula Ford team owner Ralph Firman Snr., a former mechanic of three-time World Champion Emerson Fittipaldi, who ran the works Van Diemen team. (His son Ralph Jnr. raced for one season in Formula 1 with Jordan and also with the Team Ireland A1 Grand Prix outfit.)

The Van Diemen team was founded in 1973 by Firman Snr. and Ross Ambrose, whose son Marcos won the Australian V8 Supercar Championship in 2003 and 2004. Their company's name came from the island of Tasmania, which was formerly known as Van Diemen's Land, where Ross Ambrose was born.

Roe drove a Van Diemen in the 1977 season, which proved to be a steep learning curve. He did manage to take third place in the British Fusegear Championship and set Formula Ford lap records at European circuits like the Österreichring in Austria. Clearly, the Van Diemen was the car to be in, and, by 1978, Roe and Firman began an assault on the two British Formula Ford Championships: the Townsend Thoresen and the RAC Series.

'Actually in the late 1970s in England, the Irish took over everything in Formula Ford. Derek Daly won the Festival in 1976. I won it in 1978. Tommy Byrne also won it. We were unbeatable in Formula Ford, and a lot of it was due to the connection we made with Ralph Firman. Ralph was married to Angela from Kilcullen, and he was very favourable to the Irish. He was a tremendous help to me and Tommy Byrne, and Derek also drove a Van Diemen for him. Right through, he's been a great help to Irish drivers.

'In 1977, I went with Ralph. He supplied the car, and a company called Scholar supplied the engines. I basically lived that year in a house with Ralph and Angie.'

The following 1978 season, again in the UK, proved to be a fine one for Roe. He was second in the Townsend Thoresen Formula Ford Championship, a series he should have won had he not lost fifteen points for a disqualification for passing another Irish driver, Kenny

Acheson, under a yellow flag. Acheson won that series by three points as a result and went on to race in Formula 1 for the RAM team, where he managed to qualify for three races – his best finish twelfth in the 1983 South African Grand Prix.

Roe also finished second in the RAC Formula Ford Championship in 1978, but he rounded off the year in fine style when he beat a world field of nearly 200 drivers to take Formula Ford Festival honours at Brands Hatch.

'Kenny was a fierce competitor. It was all Kenny and myself throughout the season that year, and we had some great battles. One of the biggest things I learned that year was that we had to develop the car. At certain circuits on long corners, we were slowing a lot to Kenny, and we couldn't figure it out. One night, we just happened to be passing the car in the garage, and I turned the crank shaft, and it spun freely. So immediately that night I called Dave Baldwin the designer. I said, I think we've found the problem here. He came down to the workshop – it was possibly 11 o'clock at night – checked it out and decided to make a new engine-mounting system. I think for the last six races we literally tore away with every race.'

Roe had over twenty race wins that year in the two championships, but it failed to bring him either series titles. He did have a major success in the end-of-season Formula Ford Festival shootout at Brands Hatch, the Mecca of Formula Ford racing.

'The biggest thing in the Festival was getting through the heats; you had to be careful not to get knocked out. In those days, there were so many entrants that we had to do heats, quarter-final, semi-final, final. So, in the early stages, you had to be very careful to try and finish in the top four without damage, and that was the key to winning the Festival – being careful and measured early on in the races.

'I think it was in the semi-final that I had a massive battle with Bernard Devaney, who was driving for the PRS team at the time. Something happened to the carburettor, the top came off or something. I had a bit of a misfire, and he overtook me. The second-last lap, I went around the outside of him at Paddock, and Ralph wasn't very happy about that because I was taking a chance to win the race. But in those circumstances you just say, 'I have a good chance of winning this one,' so I took it, but Ralph was annoyed because I did it, not in the final, but in the semi-final.

'I started on pole for the final and went on to win. In fact, Van Diemen had a one-two that day with another one of their drivers coming second, James Weaver. Actually, I knew I was going to win it, strangely enough. I bought a suit in Coughlin's in Naas for the presentation. I remember I gave £18 for it.

'We had everything right. The car was right, the engine was right. I worked a lot down in Scholars, the engine builders, getting it ready. Everything was right, and I felt right, so I was very confident I was going to win it.'

Roe had become good friends with Dubliner Bernard Devaney, who himself had almost won the 1977 Festival at Brands but who was knocked off while leading the final. Devaney went on to Formula 2, where he took part in European Formula 2 and American IndyCar championships in the 1970s and 1980s. Roe was now a man who liked to socialise, and alcohol started to play a role in his life. He and Devaney liked to socialise more than most drivers of their day.

'That is true. There are various stories about that. One of the funniest I can remember is in 1978 after we'd won the Donington Festival. There was a big prize for it – around £500 at the time – and Ralph was there. There was a meeting at Thruxton the next day, and Ralph said we were not to go to it. However, another driver, Trevor Templeton, and Bernard and I all went for a few jars in the Donington clubhouse. The following day, we forgot that we were told not to go to Thruxton, so we duly loaded up in the transit and headed for Thruxton in convoy. I won the race and set a new lap record, and I rang Ralph from a pay phone to tell him. He roared at me, "I told you not to go to Thruxton!"

"But Ralph," I said, "Royale with Kenny Acheson just introduced their new car, and we beat them, won the race and set a lap record."

'Let's just say he was speechless.'

Roe is a quiet, shy man. Indeed, some who were there to witness his early days racing would have called him a little lazy. Roe has admitted that he turned to alcohol to combat his shyness, and while the stories of his antics in his motor-racing career are legendary (he claims that he and Al Unser Jnr. tried to qualify for the Indy 500 after a feed of pints), it was also his undoing; his social life clearly interfered with his racing and was to cost him in terms of family relationships as well.

By 1979, and four years behind them in the same racing class, Formula Ford was over for Roe, and he continued his career by moving to the British Formula 3 Championship, following Devaney, Acheson and, indeed, Eddie Jordan into the series which was the real first port of call for drivers moving from the likes of the rather unsophisticated Formula Ford into real racing cars complete with slick tyres and wings. Roe's first attempt at the series was in a B47 Chevron which went well in the wet but was a real dog in the dry, and it was ultimately a frustrating year.

'I had an offer from a guy called David Clarke, car dealer in London, who previously ran Bruce Allison, and he was teamed up with John McDonald from the RAM Formula 1 Team. It looked a very impressive outfit. I started off very well; there was no apparent problem with money, but we only realised about three races into it that they didn't actually have any cash. The car was on loan from Chevron, the engine was a used one; but it was very well presented, it looked the business. But Derek Bennett, who was the owner of Chevron, died the previous year, and they were in financial problems.

'I started well at Silverstone. I think I was second on the grid, and, if I remember, I led the first couple of laps, but Chico Serra, who was racing in a March, overtook me, and I finished second. It all looked very hopeful, but I was used to a very intensive testing programme and professional set-up with Ralph and Van Diemen, and that was lacking in the Formula 3 in the Chevron set-up. Bernard Devaney had a Chevron that year, and so did Eddie Jordan, but Eddie changed to March about four races into the season. Bernard stuck with the Chevron, also to no avail, so we just slid further down the field due to lack of funding and the wrong choice in chassis.'

Roe spent just one season in British Formula 3.

'There were some bright moments. I had a race win, and I was third in a European round at Donington. I won the Gunner Nielson Challenge race at Donington, where Mike Thackwell was second in a March. So there were a few. I think I only did about nine races in Formula 3, and it just petered out.'

After his year with Chevron, the money had dried up, and, by the beginning of the 1980s, America was calling.

'After Formula 3, I did nothing really in 1980. I had various chances to go back with Ralph in Formula Ford 2000, but nothing came of it, and there was nothing in Formula 3 because we didn't have any budget. By then, Ralph was starting to market quite heavily in the States, and he suggested I go over there and give him a hand setting up cars and racing Formula Ford again. He set up a deal where I had a chassis and engine, and in 1981 we pretty well won everything over there. There was a good bunch of guys in Formula Ford over there – the likes of Michael Andretti and Al Unser Jnr., so we had a good time in that.'

'Really though, my career had stalled, and, again thanks to Ralph, he resurrected it. There were various things I could have done in the UK, like Formula Ford again, but having won the Festival, I didn't want to stay at that.'

Despite his race wins at the start of 1980 in the USA, offers began to dry up over the next two seasons, and by the end of 1982, Roe's career looked to be over, but he and his new bride Gaye, daughter of Dr Karl Mullen, who played international rugby for Ireland, arrived in Texas in 1983 and met Don Walker. Walker, who had made his money in real estate, wanted Roe to head up his Can-Am team for the 1983 season.

The Can-Am Championship, originally the Canadian-American Challenge Cup, was established in 1966, and there are two distinct periods in its history. The first, from 1966 to 1974, was for Group 7 sports cars, which were totally unrestricted – something that made them quicker then Formula 1 machines at the time. The first title went to Britain's John Surtees in a Lola. Surtees was the only driver to win world championships at both motorbike and Formula 1 levels.

The initial Can-Am series petered out and came to an end in 1974. It was resurrected in 1977 and lasted until 1986. Sports cars with engines of up to 5 litres became the norm in its second coming.

'They were single-seater, closed wheel, open-top sports cars with a 302-cubic-inch engine, which is 5000 cc, and they had to be Chevrolets. Chevrolet produced about 400 of them with 560 brake horsepower. They had loads of down force and were very very fast.

'Some of the top racers in Can-Am when I started were Jacques Villeneuve (uncle of the 1997 Formula 1 World Champion) and Scotland's Jim Crawford (who also raced in Formula 1 with the likes of Lotus). They would have been the leading two that year. We came into the series late, with an old ex-Patrick Tambay Lola, but we got a couple of results, and then VDS, who were running Geoff Brabham, put their cars up for sale, and Don Walker decided to buy them.

'It was by pure chance I met him. I did a few Formula Super Vee races between Formula Ford and Can-Am in 1982. I was down at a local meeting, and we used to sell things like brake fluid and duct tape just to get a little bit of extra income. This particular crew kept buying litres and litres of brake fluid, so I said, "What are you doing with it? What's the problem?" They said, "We can't bleed the brakes." Walker was running the team, and they asked me would I come down and have a look. I went down and had a look at their car, and they had one of the rear callipers on upside down so the brakes wouldn't bleed. I got talking to the owner, Walker, and he asked would I come along to his workshop in Dallas, and that's where it started.'

Walker took a shine to Roe and invested in the Irishman. He bought the best of the VDS Can-Am Team, and in 1983, Michael Roe finished sixth in the championship with a second and two third places his best showing.

'I asked him to hire some people towards the end of 1983, which he did. Basically, he gave me whatever I wanted in terms of personnel and back-up equipment, and we set out on a development programme between the end of 1983 and the start of the 1984 season to improve the car, and it worked really really well.'

So well, in fact, that Roe won the 1984 Can-Am Championship title with seven wins, ten pole positions and nine lap records in the ten-round championship which began in Mosport in Ontario and worked its way through tracks such as Lime Rock and Road Atlanta. At the Dallas race, which was a support to the Formula 1 Grand Prix in July 1984, Roe actually broke the outright lap record in his Can-Am Chevrolet and was the fastest car on the track that weekend, faster even than the Formula 1 cars.

'We were sharing the pits at the Dallas Grand Prix. It's not like grands prix now, where their cars were housed and then brought down to race. We were sharing the pits with Tyrrell in between practice sessions, and we got friendly with them. I broke the lap record. Niki Lauda was the fastest Formula 1 car, but we were about half a second quicker than him in the Can-Am car.'

And that was achieved despite a badly sprained right ankle. It made the Formula 1 team sit up and take notice, and Roe was suddenly in demand. Braham and Toleman made enquiries, but it was Tyrrell who asked Roe to race in Formula 1. It never happened.

'Martin Brundell broke his ankle in the race, and Ken Tyrrell asked me would I go to Australia for the next round. I can't remember how many rounds were left at that stage. So I rang home, and through the good office of Wilf Fitzsimons at the RIAC, he organised a grand-prix licence, which that was done pretty well overnight.

'I was all set to go with Tyrrell, and Don Walker, the guy I was driving for, wouldn't release me. He said he had big plans for Indy-Cars the following season, and he waved a carrot in front of me. Partly out of loyalty, partly out of stupidity, I decided to stay with him, and unfortunately he ended up in jail the next year.

'Roberto Moreno went instead to drive the Tyrrell. There wouldn't have been a big change in the way grand-prix cars ran at that time because there was probably a bit less horsepower. In fact, they were lighter to drive than Can-Am cars, and I'm sure I would have fitted in quite well. So, it was a missed opportunity.

'That's one regret, that I just wasn't headstrong enough to go and do it, or ruthless enough to go and do it. But, in reality, there were lots of other reasons why I didn't go to Australia. I probably wasn't the pushiest guy. I might like the social end of things a bit more than other people, and I probably wasn't as professional as a lot of the boring drivers that are around now.'

And did his social life come in the way of his driving?

'I'd say it did, yeah. Yeah, no doubt about it. If I was to go back again, I would do it differently.'

Roe still had to see out the Can-Am season. He had eight more races to go as the Formula 1 circus moved on, leaving the Irish driver behind. Jim Crawford's March was his only serious rival, but by the time the last round came about, at the Green Valley circuit in Texas, the championship had been all but decided in Roe's favour. But there was still one more title to be won: the Triple Crown and, with it, a prize of $100,000.

'At the start of the year, the promoter of the series decided to have what they call a Triple Crown, and they picked out three races during the year. The first one was at Mosport, which I won. So, now I'm the only one who could win it. I won the second leg of the Triple Crown at the Dallas Grand Prix. We knew that the bonus was $100,000, and it was a lot of money at the time, because the dollar had reached parity, so it was, in effect, £100,000. The deal was that the promoter was to have taken out a bet with Lloyds against anyone winning, but he hadn't paid his premium, and I was nobbled in the last race.

'One of their accountants was part of our team, working as crew chief. He decided he'd work out the fuel windows for the last race, and two laps before I was due to come in, it stuttered to a halt out on the track. I had run out of fuel.

'How did I find out about it? Well, I called a meeting for 8 o'clock the following morning with the crew, and when we got to the workshop, our crew chief, tools, bag and baggage – everything – was gone. I did a bit of investigating. We rang Lloyds of London, and the premium had never been paid, so the $100,000 was gone as well.

'Actually, I was very disappointed, not so much in the bonus, but I could have lost the championship if a couple of other permutations had gone against me, and that's what annoyed me most.'

That was it for Roe and the Can-Am Championship. Walker had promised to take Roe further up the motor-sport ladder, but he failed to do so and ended up in jail for commingling funds from one of his many companies to prop up another.

By this stage, the CART IndyCar racing series had emerged as the new king of circuit-racing in the USA. The better Can-Am teams moved over, and there followed a major decline in the series. In fact, if truth be known, the year that Roe won the championship, he and Crawford were the only real serious contenders lapping many of the other drivers throughout the year.

With Walker now out of the picture, and the chance to go to Formula 1 now, seemingly, gone, Roe looked at the IndyCar series himself and competed in four races in a Lola Cosworth in 1985, racing at Long Beach, Portland, Meadowlands and Cleveland, where he picked up eleven championship points, his best placed finishes being a seventh in Portland and an eighth at Meadowlands.

'I went and did a few IndyCar races with Ron Hemelgarn Racing at the start of the year. Again, that was another uncompetitive team, and they put different drivers into it all season. That team petered out as well, and, for me, it was into sports cars. In fact, my first sports-car race was in 1984 in Japan in the World Sportscar Championship, driving the Skoal Bandit Porsche 956 for John Fitzpatrick's team. That was our first foray into sports cars.'

In 1986, Roe went full-time sports-car racing with the Toyota Team Tom's, driving the 85C car in the Japanese Sportscar Series or the All-Japan Endurance Championship, as it was officially known, with the Team Ikuzawa outfit, ironically partnering Kenny Acheson with whom he had some great battles in their Formula Ford days.

'I did a season for Toyota, got on very well with the owners but had a few rows with Kenny. But Japan and, indeed, racing in the States paid very well.'

Roe and Acheson finished third in their first race for the Ikuzawa team, the Suzuka 500 Kilometre, their best result of the year, and followed up with a number of Top 10 finishes. Roe had the opportunity, or so he thought, to race for Lola in the Japanese Formula 3000 championship, but, like many opportunities that presented themselves during Roe's career, that too fell through.

'I went over to Lola for seat-fitting to drive for their Formula 3000 Team in Japan for 1987, and they were to be sponsored by John Player Special, JPS. I had the seat-fitting; they had everything organised; and about the middle of February Tetsu Ikuzawa, who was a Formula 1 driver at one time, the owner of the team, called up to say that JPS had pulled out, so we were in limbo again.

'But I did Le Mans with Aston Martin, and, starting out in 1989, it was going to be a massive set-up. They had budgets of $30 million and they had great people. Ray Mallock was the engineering director there, and he was fantastic. We started with that car qualifying twentieth, twenty-second, and at the end of the year we were qualifying fourth and fifth behind Jaguar and Porsche. Ray put in a huge amount of work, and it would have evolved into a very nice car the following year, but the regulations changed. They brought in a new 3-litre formula, and at the time, Aston Martin was bought over by Ford. Ford was also involved with Jaguar, so the money went to Tom Walker and the Jaguar outfit rather than to Proteus Technology, which Ray Mallock was running. We had a very very good team organised for that year – good drivers, and Gary Andersen was going to join us as designer for the new 3-litre formula and, again, at the last minute, it just fell apart.

'Sports-car racing could take you anywhere. It was very enjoyable with Aston Martin because we did a lot of testing, and there were very good, really good, people involved. Ray was tremendous, and I'd look on Ray Mallock and Ralph Firman Snr. in the same light. They were totally dedicated to what they were doing. They understood the nuts and bolts of it. There was no bullshit with them. If you found something wrong, you fixed it. A lot of other high-profile teams were more image-conscious. Their image quality was much better than their engineering quality. And the one thing I've noticed throughout the years in motor sport is the amount of money that's being wasted by people really not knowing how to get it right.'

Roe took part in the 1989 Le Mans twenty-four-hour race for Aston Martin, partnering Britain's Brian Redman and Costas Los of Greece. The trio finished eleventh in a race which is now famous for the fact that six Irish drivers were part of different teams that raced over that weekend, with Acheson in second place in the Sauber Mercedes team, while David Kennedy, who was part of the Mazdaspeed outfit classed in seventh. Derek Daly, who was driving for Jaguar, failed to finish, going out after eighty-five laps. John Watson's Toyota Team Tom's car lasted fifty-eight laps, while Martin Donnelly, with Nissan Motorsport, only managed five.

'I also competed in some races for Nissan in the States, and I drove for Nissan in Le Mans with Geoff Brabham. We also had a problem in the twenty-four hours of Daytona with Derek Daly who was driving with Jaguar. What happened? A twenty-four-hour race, and we collided on the second corner, which put him out.'

Roe claims that both cars went out on the first lap, but, in fact, the records show that Daly actually went out on lap one, but Roe continued for fifty-one laps before the brakes gave way in the Electromotive Engineering Nissan.

'My last race was Le Mans 1990 (partnering New Zealander Steve Millen and American Bob Earl, helping to take their Nissan to seventeenth place). Then I got involved in a development programme with Aston Martin. Yamaha took over the Aston Martin factory, and they were building this super-car to compete with the McLaren Formula 1. It was going to cost £600,000 or £700,000, so we spent a year working on that – that brought us all around the world – both on the road and on the track. That was very enjoyable because you could see progress each week, and their plan was to run this new car in a new sports-car series, but – it seems to be the story of my racing – Yamaha pulled the plug on that as well.'

It was the end of Roe's motor-racing career, and he headed back to Naas to the house he had bought and paid for from the winnings of his Can-Am career. It was a career punctuated with race wins, championships and what-might-have-beens. Had he taken the Formula 1 drive at Tyrrell in 1984, he might well have eclipsed Daly as the top driver from the Republic of Ireland in Formula 1, such was his talent. But we shall never know.

'I regret racing for some teams I've driven for. I should have been more patient with Formula 3, and I should have been more patient after winning the Can-Am Championship. But, you know, you make these decisions, and you must remember, in those days, we never had anybody like the drivers have nowadays: managers and management groups behind them. We were just dealing from coin boxes, really.'

How does he respond to the suggestion that he was the best Irish driver to ever race on the international stage?

'Well, in my opinion, Tommy Byrne was the talent. He was an exceptionally quick driver. I remember at a McLaren Formula 1 test at Silverstone, and I went to him, I think it was after he won the British Formula 3 Championship. Tommy was unbelievably quick, and he made a comment about the handling of the car to Ron Dennis, which Dennis disliked, but Tommy was right. A lot of people that knew Tommy well could see that he really had it every way on the track. Gary Anderson thought the world of Tommy and was there the day of the test of that Formula 1 car. He could tell you stories about Tommy that would make the hair stand up on the back of your neck.

'I was very friendly with Tommy. He stayed with us quite a bit in the States, and we drove together for Budweiser in the Daytona twenty-four hours in a March. I helped him anyway I could to get drives, but I don't see him much now because he's down in Florida somewhere, and I haven't seen him in a couple of years.

'At a professional level in motor sport, you don't tend to make friends. That's one of the reasons why I enjoy team sport such as rugby or GAA. The camaraderie is very different to professional motor sport. I would certainly have more friends who are mechanics or crew people than drivers because, basically, we're trying to knock each other to bits all the time.

'I've often looked at jockeys; they always seem to be great pals afterwards, but then they're riding different horses each day for different owners and for different trainers, whereas in motor sport, it's your own car, and you're trying to beat up on your team-mate all the time. You're also trying to beat up on your competitors, so it doesn't lend itself to friendships that you might see in other sports in later life. When I say "in motor sport," I really mean at that professional level. I still have loads of friends from Mondello from the early days who are purely doing it as a hobby. They're all great friends, but from professional racing there are very, very few. I love team sports. I love watching Eadestown playing GAA, Naas playing rugby, any form of GAA or rugby I love. I'm a big advocate of team sports for kids, more so than individual sports like motor-racing. I would certainly go to a lot more matches now than watch motor sport.

'Overall, I've had some amazing times, and I loved it while I was at it. I had downs, but the great times were great. I possibly should have stayed on in the States, but I felt at the time that I had to think about the family. Gaye was pregnant with our first son Shane at the time when I was in Japan, and I was commuting to Japan from Dallas. I didn't like it; I just felt it was time to come home to see the kids grow up and enjoy themselves around Naas. I'm glad I made the decision from that point of view. From a racing point of view, I would have been much better staying in the States, but I've no regrets. Naas really has always been home, even when I was in the States. As they say, a savage loves his native shore. Hopefully I'll never have to leave here.'

Does he ever sneak down to Mondello Park to have a look for old time's sake?

'Oh very much so. I go there whenever we're not involved in a rugby game or on days with big meetings. I still love Mondello, but I don't have an involvement in it anymore. My son Shane was keen about doing something down there, but it's so expensive now for what you get. It was relatively much much cheaper when I started, and yet there was something to achieve because you had works Formula Ford teams in the UK who were looking for drivers with no money. You don't have that now. You have to have a bundle of money no matter where you go, but in those days you could try everything, and if you won something you'd be offered another thing in the UK.

'To give you a comparison to today's paying driver, the car we bought off Bernard Devaney back in 1975 was the first and last money we ever spent in motor sport.'

For Michael Roe, has motor sport lost its romance?

'I think it has, in a way, because there are so many more classes both in the UK and Ireland now. In Ireland, you basically have Saloons, Formula Ford, Formula Atlantic, and Formula Vee was just starting to come in. You had three premier classes, and of those three classes in Ireland, you could take your outfit to the UK and compete with the best over there. I don't think there is any car you can race in Mondello now that you can take over and compete in a major championship in the UK.

'That was the great thing about Formula Ford. We had the same engines, the same access to the equipment as the top guys. Obviously, the works cars were that little bit better. I know that myself, that when I had a works car, I had a better one than customer cars. When I had a works engine, I had a better one than a customer engine.

'That's because I was down in Scholars, and if I saw a customer engine that was better, I'd say, "I want that." But our finger was on the pulse then. We didn't have managers; we had no motor homes, no mobile phones, it was just purely focused on the fact that I wanted the best engine and the best chassis, and the only way to get that is by sitting down with the engine builders or sitting in the factory building the car. We were admired greatly by English team owners for that.

'I remember the Brazilians, in particular, would come over, and they'd turn up for their testing or they'd turn up for their race, and they'd be done afterwards. We'd go straight back to the factory working on the cars, straight down the engine builders working on the engines. We were very focused. The only reason we were focused was because we had no money; we couldn't do anything else. It's as simple as that.'

4

Joey and Robert Dunlop

William Joseph 'Joey' Dunlop and his brother Steven Robert Dunlop are considered among the greatest motorcycle riders of all time. Joey's achievements are staggering and include five consecutive Motorcycling Formula 1 titles from 1982 to 1986. But it was on the Isle of Man at the famous TT races where he excelled. The 'King of the Road' won twenty-six TT races, including three hat-tricks in 1985, 1988 and 2000. His career also included countless wins at the North West 200 and numerous victories at the Ulster Grand Prix.

Robert, born 25 November 1960, lived somewhat in Joey's shadow, but while his elder brother, born eight years earlier on 25 February 1952, was winning all around him, Robert was also making his mark. He is a winner of a record fifteen North West 200 races, British 125-cc Champion and a winner of five TT races.

Nicknamed 'Yer Maun' by some on the Isle of Man (but not so much in Ireland), Joey was also awarded an OBE (Order of the British Empire) by Queen Elizabeth II of England for his humanitarian work for children in dilapidated Romanian orphanages. Unbeknownst to many outside his family, Joey would load up his race transporter and head off on his own, sleeping in the truck on a plank of wood in order to deliver clothing and food to underprivileged kids in Bosnia, Hungary and Romania. He was also awarded the MBE (Member of the British Empire) for services to motorcycle-racing.

Joey was shy, more introverted, preferring to do his talking on his bike right throughout his career, while Robert was much more talkative – two completely different characters. Coming into bike-racing eight years after Joey had started, Robert felt more than a bit overshadowed at times.

'In fact, I was embarrassed,' said Robert, 'because Joey and I would be in the same race together at times. We used to go into the pubs, and they would say, "Well, how'd you get on?" I think they were just basically being polite because Joey had maybe won three races, and I had finished eighteenth or twentieth. But I never lost sight of what I could achieve, and, in fairness, I wasn't on as good a machine. I took a long time to learn the trade, but, you know, any-thing I learned, I never forgot.'

Both courted death throughout their careers. Robert very nearly lost his life on the Isle of Man in 1994 when he had a major accident in the Formula 1 TT as the back wheel of his Honda RC45 750-cc ma-chine collapsed at Ballaugh Bridge. Although he received multiple injuries, Robert survived, and, after two years of recuperation, he was back racing again, despite the fact that the crash left one leg 2 inches shorter than the other. Joey also had accidents – big ones too, at the likes of Brands Hatch and Tandragee in Armagh, County Down. He didn't survive his last crash in 2000 in Tallinn, the capital of Estonia.

Joey had been to Tallinn before and was part of a remarkable BBC Northern Ireland Television documentary that showed a previ-ous trip to Estonia alone with his bikes and a crash that broke his collarbone and severed a finger. He clearly liked the track there. Rather like himself, it was a no-airs-and-graces circuit with none of the hype that surrounds the likes of MotoGP. Many wondered just why he had taken himself off to Tallinn that weekend. When his long-time sponsor and friend Andy McMenemy took his own life in

2000, Joey was stunned. Perhaps as a way of dealing with Andy's death, he loaded up his van and headed to the former Soviet enclave. After taking victories in the 600 and 750-cc races in the European Road Race Championships, Joey was leading the 125 race when he appeared to lose control in the damp conditions. He was killed instantly when he hit a tree.

A massive crowd from all over the world and from the length and breadth of Ireland descended on Ballymoney for Joey's funeral on 7 July 2000, including Robert, who was one of the pall-bearers. It was an ignominious end to a fantastic career.

Joey and Robert were two of seven children born to Willie and May Dunlop. In fact, Robert is a twin to his sister Margaret, and the family squeezed in together in a semi-detached stone cottage about a mile or so from the County Antrim village of Dunloy. The family moved three times and eventually to a council estate in Killyrammer near Ballymoney.

'We come from a very humble background. My father, sadly not with us any more, was a mechanic all his life, and my mum came from a farming background. Dad had an old Norton to go to his work on, but racing didn't really come into the scene until my sister Helen, who's the oldest girl in the family, met Mervyn Robinson, the late Mervyn Robinson. He and Joey used to work in Ballymoney. They had bikes to get in and out of town, and they used to race in and out from work. I remember coming home from school and going down to see them. There was a great S-bend just over a wee railway line down the road from us, and we used to go down there about 5 o'clock and wait for them. It was a great spectacle to watch the two of them coming out round, and that's what got Joey involved in the racing, and then, obviously, I started because of Joey.'

Joey and Robert attended Ballymoney secondary school, and the elder Dunlop struck up a friendship with Mervyn Robinson and Frank Kennedy. Together with Joey's and Robert's brother, Jim Dunlop, they formed what was known as the Armoy Armada. Robert came later, but too late to really be considered a full Armada racer.

'Actually, when I was a young boy growing up, I wanted to be Tarzan – that was my hope, you know, but it didn't work out that way. Joey and Jim, Mervyn and Frank made up the Armoy Armada, and they used to race at circuit meetings in Northern Ireland. Our biggest rivals were the Dromara Destroyers (Ray McCullough, Ian McGregor, Trevor Steele and Brian Reid) who came from County Down. We were from North Antrim, which, in financial terms, is quite a lot further down the scale. It was always a great achievement to beat fellas with plenty of money, and that was the drive that we had.'

Joey left school with very few qualifications and worked at various jobs including driving for one of his uncle's haulage firms. He even contemplated joining the British Army before his passion for bikes began in earnest.

He met Linda Patterson when he was sixteen and she fifteen in the Killyrammer estate, and at the very tender age of twenty they were married. Being eight years older than Robert, Joey's motorcycling career began ahead of his younger brother with his first race in 1969 at Maghaberry, riding on a Triumph Tiger Cub. Before the race, Joey took an ivy leaf and traced around it on his helmet, and Robert coloured it in. The symbol was a mark of respect to the late Bill Ivy, one of Joey's heroes.

By 1973, a man called Danny McCook became Joey's first major sponsor, buying him a 350-cc Harley Ameracchi on which he entered his first North West 200. Joey didn't get far after breaking his chain on the start line.

Joey joined the Rea Racing Team in 1974, and in 1975 won his first road race in the 500-cc class on a Yamaha at the Temple 100. He and the rest of the Armada had some terrific battles with the Dromara Destroyers, and Ray McCullough in particular, who was one of the dominant riders of the early 1970s on his QUB Yamaha.

Joey raced for the first time in England in 1976, and the following year, Johnny Rea, his team owner, persuaded him to race on the Isle of Man at the TT races, with him and his crew heading over to the island with the bikes in tow on a fishing trawler.

On his first visit, Joey's love affair of the island began with two second places and a third in the qualifying races. He won the first of his twenty-six TT titles in the Jubilee Classic in 1978.

Ballymoney businessman Sam Taggert then parted with some of his cash to buy a Joey a brand-new 250-cc Yamaha for the 1979 season, and with it he had his first win on an English circuit, winning a 250-cc race at Brands Hatch.

By this stage, Joey, Jim and Robert were now all racing motorcycles. Robert's career began in 1978.

'I wasn't really interested in bike racing, but when I turned seventeen, I got a bike just to go in and out to my work on, an old 250 Suzuki. I fell off it a few times on the road, just riding too hard I suppose, trying to be somebody I wasn't. I was breaking my mum's heart every time I went out on it. She was really worried by the time I got back. So Joe said to me one day, "Robert, you'd be better out on the track," and I said, "Well, I don't have a bike." He says, "I've got an old one lying in the garage. You can have that," and I said, "Right, I'll do that so."

'I went and I got a racing licence. I was seventeen years of age at that time, and I forged my age to get the licence because you weren't allowed to race until you were eighteen. The very last meeting of the season was up at Aghadowey in County Derry. Joey landed up with the bike about 7 o'clock in the morning before the race, and I remember pushing it up and down the avenue where we used to live, trying to get it started. I went to Aghadowey, and I pushed it the full length of the straight, but I eventually got it started and got on it. I just got the bug. The sensation of the G forces when you open the throttle, it really gives a buzz, and I sold my road bike then to finance my racing, and I never had a road bike since. Funny that.

'I'm a determined fella anyway, and once I set my mind on something, I usually succeed. But not in my wildest dreams did I ever think I'd have won fifteen North West 200s – I mean, I never thought I'd even win one of them.'

The following year, 1979, tragedy struck the Armoy Armada. Frank Kennedy was injured at the North West 200. He never recovered and died six months later. Joey's good friend and fellow competitor Tom Herron was also killed at the same meeting. In 1980, again at the North West 200, Mervyn Robinson hit a pole after his bike seized and was killed outright. Jim Dunlop decided he had had enough and retired.

With death all around him, Joey also considered retirement but, in the end, he decided to continue. In fact, he won the Classic 1000 race in 1980 at the TT when his Yamaha beat the Honda team of Mick Grant and Ron Haslam.

Suzuki signed up Joey to race in the Formula 1's motor-cycling championship in 1981, assisting team-mate New Zealander Graham Crosby to the title. In 1982, Joey was picked up by the Castrol Honda UK Racing team run by Bob McMillan, and it started the greatest partnership ever in road and circuit-racing in these isles. Joey helped to develop the Honda, and he was to dominate the Formula 1 scene with five championship wins in a row from 1982 to 1986.

Joey and Robert both almost lost their lives in 1985 when the trawler *Tornammona*, in which they were travelling, sank just outside Portaferry on the way to that year's TT races.

The brothers Dunlop, together with friends and crew, headed out to sea in May 1985 for the Isle of Man on the converted fishing boat. The trawler headed out without Brian Reid's bikes, which were due to be loaded but turned up after the boat has sailed. They got word that they were on the quayside, and they were forced to turn back. By the time the bikes were loaded and they headed out to sea again, the tide had turned on Strangford Lough.

'Yeah, the tide had turned, sure,' says Robert, 'as we headed out of the Lough. I was up top on deck talking to the captain, and I said to him, "What speed are we doing?" and he says, "We're actually going back," because the tide was coming in so fast, and it was a treacherous bit of water anyway. By this time, it's about 12 o'clock at night, we went down below, and Joey, he's put the pan on. He was going to cook some pork chops or something like that. Of course, we were having a beer or two as well, but I was feeling a bit sick because it was a bit choppy, and I says, "Joey, I'm going to lie down," and he says, "Aye, lie near the middle of the boat and you'll not feel the same."

'So I lay down, but I wasn't down that long until there was a big thud. It sounded a bit heavier than most, but I was half asleep. Joey obviously realised that it was a bit more than just a heavy wave, and he nipped upstairs, and the next thing, he comes down through the wee hatch and says, "Right boys, everybody up," and I knew by his face and the tone of his voice that there's something wrong.

'There were no life jackets on the boat, and that particular year there was a fuel strike, and we were carrying aeroplane fuel over with us in drums, and Joey said, "Empty the drums out lads, it'll be something to float with." Joey was very calm about it, very calculated and great to have there that particular time. But, luckily enough, the lifeboat came out for us. A lot of people ask me, "Do you ever get scared on a bike?" but I never have been. I got frights, sure, but it's just over in a split second, but that particular night now, I was afraid – I really was.'

A lot of expensive bikes ended up at the bottom of Strangford Lough, but they were eventually brought back to land and raced again after the crew steeped them in diesel to clean off the salt water.

'Funny enough, Joey didn't have any racing bikes on the boat. He only had an old trials bike that he was going to ride in the Isle of Man from his digs down to the garage. But I had my two racing bikes on it, leathers and helmet – everything I had, wee boxes that I had inherited from Joey and Jim, with jets and wee things that you take for granted – all gone. We got the bikes back, and I rode one of them on the Isle of Man, a 250, and I borrowed a 350, but I didn't do very well, broke down on the 250 actually.'

While Joey was blitzing all before him in the Formula 1 World Championship during the 1980s, Robert started to carve out a career of his own.

'I raced pretty much every race I could get. I'd an old 250 Yamaha that a few business people from Ballymoney had all clubbed together and bought off Joey for £600. Joey had originally lent it to me before the boys came in to buy it. I still have that bike. I got it re-stored, so it's a nice bit of nostalgia.'

Robert followed Joey to the Isle of Man, where, in 1983, on his first visit to the island, he too had his first TT win in the Manx New-comers Race.

'At that particular time, I was still riding old Seeley bikes, while Jim and Joey were all on Cantilever bikes, which were the new suspension-type Yamahas. Jim had fallen off at Faugheen in south-ern Ireland, broke his pelvis, and he was out for most of the season. It came near September time, and I says to Jim, "You know, could I ride your bike instead of my old one?" and he says, "Well, yeah, phone up John Rea," who owned the bike. I phoned John, and he said, "Yeah, I didn't buy it to sit in the garage"; he says, "You can have it, but you gotta look after it yourself."

'My father and I went over, obviously on a shoestring budget, and I can remember going out on Michelin tyres. They weren't that good, but they were cheaper than the Dunlop variety. They were al-most falling off at Greeba Castle, which is a fast section of the circuit. I just lost the back end of the bike. I didn't know that much about tyres at that time, but I really struggled. I couldn't get over 100 miles an hour in practice, and that was my goal. Dad said, "Take your time, it'll come, it'll come," and I never got it in practice. I was really disappointed that I didn't do it. The clutch was a bit dodgy on it, and Martin, John's brother, said, "I'll put a clutch in it for you." I thanked him very much and went out in the race and did 105 mph with a set of Dunlops we managed to get.'

Robert says that right throughout their careers, their late father Willie was a major influence.

'Obviously, my dad knew that the circuit was very dangerous al-though I would think he was fairly confident in my ability and my awareness of the bike and the circuit. I think he was just trying to nurture me to get round safe, but obviously he wanted me to go fast as well you know, so, yeah, a big influence.'

While Joey was infatuated by the Isle of Man (his twenty-six TT wins prove that), Robert was a little less thrilled to be hurtling around the mountain course with speeds of over 150 mph. It's a unique event where bikers race against the clock, setting out individually at regular intervals, whereas races at the likes of the North West 200s and Skerries in North Dublin are one on one, rider against rider, a race from the start. The Isle of Man is a different kind of bike race, and it's a different kind of mindset. The circuit is 37.73 miles long and runs from the start in Douglas in a westerly direction before the riders swing south and head up the daunting mountain climb rising from sea level in Ramsey to some 1,400 feet at the highest point at Brandywell, before descending down the mountain and back to Douglas. Those who've never ridden it can probably never know and not quite understand just how difficult a circuit the Isle of Man is.

'The Isle of Man TT was really my least favourite race of all time. I didn't like it at all. But it was part of the calendar, and there was, obviously, a lot of media coverage and money to be won. I did it for a living, so I suppose I had to go there, but I really never liked it. I think that Joey was good there because he didn't really like mixing it with other riders. If he got off to a good start and got out in the front, nobody caught him, but I don't think he really liked the pushing and shoving, the cutting across each other's wheels, you know? Joey didn't like that.

'I didn't mind it actually, because it only made me more aggressive. When somebody did something on me that I didn't really think was fair, it just made me more determined to beat them, so they were making a stick for their own back basically.'

Falling off a motorbike is an occupational hazard for bike riders, and both Joey and Robert had big offs in their careers. Sadly, the last one that Joey was involved in took his life, but the brothers had more than their share of broken bones throughout their careers. In 1989, Joey crashed heavily, breaking his legs at Brands Hatch. Resilient and tough as he was, it was still a number of months before he was back on the bike competitively, and, to further complicate matters, those who had attended to him made a mess of his rehabilitation as the bones hadn't been set properly and the pins that they inserted into his leg were the wrong size. It was only when he was brought back home to Northern Ireland that the pins in Joey's leg were correctly installed.

Around that time, Robert was really starting to come into his own, and, between 1985 and 1993, he ran up eight wins at the Cookstown 100. He also won the Macau Grand Prix in 1989 on a Honda 500, beating Phillip McCallen and Steve Hislop, who were both riding Honda 750s that weekend. He added to his Newcomers win of 1983 on the Isle of Man when he notched his first TT win in the 125-cc class in 1989. In 1990, there was a change to a Norton factory bike, which brought him more into public focus, the bike being sleek black, matching his black overalls. Robert took a superbike double that year in the North West 200, beating the likes of Carl Fogarty and Hislop.

'I never raced for myself. I always raced for somebody or something. I think the mental thing is more than 50 per cent of success; there's no doubt about it. You can get a great strength from the mind, and I always was mentally motivated anyway. I had a great mentor as well in Liam Beckett who helped me to win the British Championship. The Norton bike was a very fast machine, so I was confident before I even got on it, but it did raise my profile, and I think that it's because it's a superbike. You wouldn't get the same recognition riding a 125, and that's one of the reasons I didn't go 125 racing in grands prix. I come from North Antrim, and I didn't know enough people like Jeremy [McWilliams] knew who helped to get him into grand-prix racing. I'm not very well educated in that field anyway, so I really would have struggled to get finances together to go to the grands prix.

'But in 1990, I rode successfully for the Norton team, and in 1991 I asked them would they give me a British superbike ride. Barry Simmons, who was the team manager, and who, in fact, was Joey's team manager all though his early Honda days, said, "Well, you're a road racer. You can't ride short circuits, so we can't give you a ride at the British Championships." That's one of the reasons I went in 1991 with my 125 and won the British

Championship. I won every round and broke the lap record. I went back to him again in 1992 and said, "Will you give me a ride in the British Championships in 1992?", knowing full well that they couldn't say no.'

By 1993, Joey had notched up his fifteenth win at the TT, beating the record previously set by the legendary Mike Hailwood. Ballymoney Borough Council presented him with the Freedom of the Borough in recognition – this at a stage of his career when there were new up-and-coming riders just rushing to take Joey's place and many in the sport were just waiting to write him off.

Not only was he winning on the Isle of Man throughout the 1990s, he also produced the goods in Ireland, winning at Cookstown, Skerries and at the Ulster Grand Prix in Dundrod on what a mere mortal would have reckoned to be relatively uncompetitive bikes – until Joey got hold of them.

Robert's career was also progressing nicely, and it was aboard the 125s that he produced his best results.

'It wasn't a matter of liking them, it was just that my stature suited the smaller bikes better than the big ones. I struggled whenever I rode the Norton, basically just because I wasn't heavy enough to hold the bike down to get enough grip on the back tyre. On the smaller bikes, my weight and size were an advantage. I enjoyed all the bikes I rode.'

Bob McMillan, the boss of Honda's racing team in the UK and the man who backed Joey to the hilt, said at one stage, 'If Joey hadn't been around, Robert would have been our number one.'

'Well, it's very flattering now, but I did speak to Bob McMillan at Honda at the time, and Louise, my wife, also spoke to him about getting me a ride on their bikes. But he said, "We already have one Dunlop, we don't need another one."'

Joey's love affair with the Isle of Man TT races continued into the 1990s. He hadn't won on the island since 1988 when he landed his second hat-trick by winning the Formula 1, Junior and Senior TTs, but he rectified a four-year winless streak by winning the 125 races in 1992 and 1993.

After winning the Newcomers Class in 1983, Robert took his first TT win in 1989, winning the 125 class with a new lap record. In 1990, he repeated the previous year's 125 win with another lap record and was victorious in both the 125s (a class lap record of 106.71 mph) and Junior TTs in 1991. He didn't win in 1992 or 1993 but had podium finishes in the 125s and junior and senior races.

In 1994, Joey won the 125s and the junior races on the island, but Robert almost lost his life when the back wheel of his 750-cc Honda RC45 collapsed on the jump over Ballaugh Bridge in the Formula 1 race. The crash flung Robert off the bike and into a stone wall.

'It's ironic that Bob McMillan once told my wife to get me off the Nortons as "he's going to get killed on them," but it was a Honda that I was riding when it prematurely finished my career on big bikes. I remember that day. I was in third place in the race, but I wasn't going to get any further up. I was just riding round because it's quite physical. I was small in stature, and it was quite hard work for me (the Isle of Man TT) in comparison to any of the rest of them because of the mileage and the nature of the circuit as well.

'But I remember going over Ballaugh Bridge and going round the left turn when I was opening up the throttle as well. I changed into about third gear, and I just remember the back end going round and me going over the top of the tank of the bike. I thought the suspension had collapsed, but I don't remember hitting the wall. There was no pain or anything, even though I was conscious, but your body seems to take over like a . . . like a painkilling thing, because I didn't feel anything. I remember before I went into surgery saying to my mechanic Liam, "Liam, check the back suspension, there's something wrong with it. Something happened the back end of the bike, check the suspension." But then it emerged that it was the back wheel that just collapsed.'

Robert suffered massive injuries, breaking both his legs, badly breaking a wrist, and such was the impact that one leg ended up two inches shorter than the other. He had corrective surgery on the shorter leg in 2005 and was back racing the following year when he won his fifteenth North West 200 in 2006.

The crash in 1994 nearly killed him. As it was, he recovered but missed the rest of the 1994 season and the whole of the 1995 campaign as well while he recuperated.

'Even though I was damaged badly by motor-bike racing, it was motorcycle racing that made me determined to get my leg and arm fixed and get better again. There was a great girl from Monaghan, my physio Fiona Gilliland. She was motivated as well, and we had a rapport together. She came to the TT with me in 1998 when I was fairly fit but not as fit as some of the lads. I had a bad hand which I still have, but she really worked wonders, and I could see the effort that she was putting in; it made me more determined too.'

After the crash in 1994, it looked as if Robert Dunlop's career was over, but, aided by his family and his physio, he got back on the track. In 1996, he raced at Bishopscourt and the Cookstown 100, but his injuries were causing him problems, and it was painful at times to race.

Joey, meanwhile, continued on his winning way at the TTs, winning the lightweight and senior races in 1995, the 125s and the 250s in 1996, followed by wins in the 125s and 250s races in 1997 and 1998 – making it, at that stage, a record twenty-three wins.

Robert didn't race again at the TTs until 1997, when he was third in the 125s, but, amazingly, he showed all his determination to become a champion again on his least favourite circuit when he won the ultra-lightweight race in 1998.

'It wasn't a psychological barrier that I had to get over to win on the Isle of Man again, but obviously I welcomed it, there's no doubt about that. It's funny, Joey said to one of the lads, "I think Robert's going to win," and they said, "Well, why?" "I just know by the way he's . . . the way he even walks about the paddock," said Joey. He must have seen the confidence brimming out of me, and I *was* confident, you know. I knew I was going to be hard to beat.'

Joey was in the wars himself in 1998. Now forty-six and not as fit as the new up-and-coming racers, he went back to Honda, who promised to give him a new RC45 for the 1998 season.

Joey was the kind of man who would go away if things got too much. He would have spent many weeks in Donegal during his career, getting away from it all, and he actually headed to Australia in early 1998 to get fit for the season. He may have won the 250 race on the Isle of Man that year, but he wasn't fit enough to ride in the Formula 1 race as a result of an crash in a 125 race at Tandragee, where he broke many bones and lost part of a finger from his left hand.

The year 1999 came around, and the subject of retirement for Joey Dunlop raised its head. Although he still had contact with Honda, McMillan broached the subject with him. Joey wasn't happy with the bikes he was getting, and he didn't win on the Isle of Man that year. At forty-seven, he wasn't getting any younger. McMillan passed word of Joey's unhappiness on to the Japanese Honda outfit, who offered to help the 'King of the Road' to race in the 2000 season on a bike which was practically a full works machine. They also supplied technicians, engineers and Aaron Slight's mechanic Simon Greer to aid Dunlop's campaign.

It worked wonders, and the Honda-backed bikes gave Joey Dunlop his third hat-trick at the TT races, winning not only the Formula 1 TT but the 250 and 125 races as well. Joey also set his fastest-ever lap of the mountain course when he was third in the senior race behind the late David Jefferies and Michael Rutter, lapping at a speed of 123.87 mph. It was truly a remarkable achievement, which meant that his TT wins now stood at twenty-six.

It's a record unlikely to be broken.

After his three wins at the TT in 2000, McMillan again spoke about Joey's possible retirement, this time publicly. It would have been a fantastic way to bow out, and Ballymoney threw a party, affording Joey a civic reception and a tour of the town on an open-top bus to celebrate his record-breaking week.

'When Joey started racing, it was long hair, dirty fingernails, greasy – you know, that type of look. Jim was sort of the same mould as Joey, but things had started to change to a more professional approach. When I started off, the professional thing was starting off as well. So, Jim was caught in between the two. It worked for Joey because that's the way he was, and everybody loved Joey for that. Jim was caught in the middle, and he couldn't step up to where I was. But he couldn't go back to where Joey was, and I think that's why he struggled, as he couldn't work with his sponsorship, whereas I was able to do that because that era had come in by the time I'd started.

Sadly, the races in the year 2000 were to prove Joey Dunlop's last TT outing. After his hero's welcome in his home town, Joey had entered for the Dundrod 150 when news came through of the death of Andy McMenemy. He pulled out of the Dundrod event and decided to go Estonia instead. Once again, he left his family behind, packed up his bikes – a 125, a 600 and an RC45 Honda, which had been on display in 'Joey's Bar', formerly the Railway Bar, which he had purchased in Ballymoney, and headed off on his own, driving across Europe to Tallinn, to the little-known Pirita-Kose-Kloostrimetsa circuit on the outskirts of the Estonian capital.

He wasn't unfamiliar with the track. He seemed to enjoy racing there, and, after the euphoria of the three TT wins, the races in Estonia were perhaps what he was looking for to get over McMenemy's death. The organisers and races fans there adored him, and it was a no-mess, no-fuss kind of event, right up his alley.

Joey won the 600 race on the Saturday and followed that up with a victory in the wet in the superbike race on the RC45 on the Sunday. There was only a quarter of an hour or so between the end of the superbike race and the 125s, but Joey was ready, opting for a full wet on the front and an intermediate on the rear to race on the now drying track.

Joey was lying in second place on the second lap of the 125s when it began to rain again. He came into the last corner just before the start/finish straight. His rear wheel lost its grip coming out of the corner and headed for the trees.

Such was the impact that the bike split in two on one tree while Joey smashed into another. He was killed instantly.

'I wasn't surprised he went to Estonia,' says Robert. 'Joey raced for the love of racing, it wasn't for the money. He just did it because he loved it, and he loved being out there amongst ordinary people as opposed to the glamour and glitz that's involved now. He just loved the bit of craic.

'It really was a big shock because of all the miles that Joey had raced at high speed. To lose his life on the smallest bike, the slowest bike – really, it's very hard to fathom. And the fact that Joey was so experienced . . . I suppose we all thought it would never happen to Joey. You can accept when it happens to somebody else but not to Joey, you know? I find that hard to come to terms with now, I must say. But it's happened. In a way, I can get comfort from the fact that Joey was killed off a bike.

'When I fell off in the Isle of Man, even though the video footage shows me conscious, I don't remember anything about it. I could have been killed; I wouldn't have felt a thing, so I know that Joey didn't suffer at all, which *is* comforting.'

On 7 July 2000, around 50,000 mourners from all walks of life descended on the Garryduff Presbyterian Church in County Antrim for Joey Dunlop's funeral. Joey Dunlop's faith was Protestant, although his religion didn't matter to his legions of fans. People from every corner of the globe and from all parts of Ireland were amongst the mourners that day.

Robert says he was not surprised by the outpouring of grief and sympathy that his family received. He says they felt humbled. Joey's daughter Donna read out a poem in honour of her dad at the funeral. There wasn't a dry eye in the house.

> To people you were a number 1, to me you were a daddy,
> To people you were a quiet person, to me you liked to party,
> The smile of yours was real, nothing there was false,
> The knight in shining armour was always in a rush.
> The yellow helmet stood out bright,
> The number 3 there too.
> The Honda always shone out light
> but you always remained so true
> Now you know why John called you the gurk,
> on that face you have that smirk
> Up the paddock you'd go for a walk
> But then the folk would start to gawp
> You hated the publicity, you liked to go your own pace
> The only thing I have to say, I know you loved to race.

The racing was your life, you just couldn't stop,
But then again, why should you have done
Because you were the top of the plot.
The light is on, our hearts are pumping,
On the grandstand we are jumping
The only thing you ever wanted was another Formula 1,
You sure showed them you could do it by giving them your
twenty-fourth win,
At the Ulster last year there was an awesome fight
But you sure showed David Jefferies on the RC45
Our lives will never be the same, in our hearts you will remain
Deep in thought and in our laughter
Because we know you were the master.
We never thought this day would come
when we had to say good-bye
But the memories I have of you, God I wonder why
You were simply the best
We know you were better than all the rest
The only thing I'd like to say is
That you, Sir Joey, all the way.

Joey left a record of twenty-six Isle of Man TT wins, five Formula 1 World Championships, thirteen North West 200 wins and twenty-four victories at the Ulster Grand Prix, as well as countless other triumphs at other races in Ireland, Britain and across the world.

Robert, and, indeed, the rest of the family, had to decide how best to move on with the rest of *their* lives now that Joey was gone. Robert decided to keep on racing, but he had many moments of doubt about his decision.

'I never thought about stopping racing, but I was a bit conscious of would it be the right thing to do. I was afraid that I was going to be disrespectful, but my father was very supportive so he says, "If you don't want to stop, don't stop".'

After Joey's death, the big wins eluded Robert Dunlop. His 1994 crash on the Isle of Man was still causing him problems, and he delayed getting corrective surgery on the shorter leg. On 16 December 2003, Robert announced that he would quit motorbike racing after the 2004 season, hoping to add one more TT and North West 200 win that following season.

His sons William and Michael were now involved in the sport, racing on 125s, and he hoped that they would take up the mantle. So, while his sons began their motorcycling career, Robert went into hospital in Belfast in 2005 to have his injured leg broken and lengthened. He was on crutches when his two boys were in the support races at the British Superbike rounds at Mondello Park in 2005 and, at that stage, was contemplating life off the bikes.

The operation was a success, and, at the age of forty-four, Robert came back out of retirement during the 2005 road-racing season and, incredibly, took his record-breaking wins at the North West 200 to fifteen with a win in the 125 race in 2006.

Robert was back. He not only ran his two sons' team but he raced against them as well. At the Monaghan Road Races in 2006, William won the 250 junior race, with Michael second, while Robert claimed the 125 victory. Michael finished runner-up.

'I don't really fear for them when they go motorcycle racing. I know it doesn't look like it at times, but the sport has been good to me, you know, and I had a good living at it. I'll never be a millionaire, but I live comfortably. I get paid for doing something I would have done for nothing anyway.

'I think it's good for the young boys, because it gives them a focus in life and keeps them off the streets. It gives them something to focus on, and, if they're dedicated, they will make it alright. I think it's good that youngsters should have something. A lot of people say to me, "How can you let your boys race? Remember and look what's happened to you and look what happened to Joe." But I've got no qualms about it at all; I think it's good for them.'

On 8 February 2005, Robert Dunlop was the first person to be elected into the Irish Motorcycle Hall of Fame, while in February 2006, Robert and Joey were bestowed with honorary degrees from the University of Ulster to award their achievements in motorbike racing. Later the same year, the brothers were awarded with honorary doctorates from the University of Ulster.

The Dirty Dozen

Joey is survived by his wife Linda and their five children Julie, Donna, Garry, Richard and Joanne.

5

Eddie Jordan

'Winning in any capacity is always great. I believed that I wasn't good enough to be a driver. I chose the management role, and winning a Grand Prix is a very special moment.'

When Edmund 'Eddie' Jordan (or E.J.) was in Formula 1, it was a throwback to a different era in the multimillion-pound industry. While the big teams like Ferrari had a bottomless pit of money, Jordan scraped by, trying to get his cars on the track in the early years. As he said himself, he was on speaking terms with almost every bailiff in the Northamptonshire region when his Formula 1 team was based at Silverstone.

He was a real wheeler-dealer, who, while he was shaking your hand was at the same time looking over your shoulder to see if there was someone more important in the room. Someone, perhaps, with money or influence who could keep his Formula 1 team on the go. But with mounting debts, poor results and fifteen years of trying to keep the show on the road, it eventually all became too much for Eddie. In order to protect himself, his family and his ailing team, Eddie Jordan decided it was time to sell and get out. He sold Jordan to Russian billionaire Alex Schneider of Midland Grand Prix at the beginning of the 2005 season.

Formula 1 had lost one of the most enigmatic characters ever to grace a pit lane, and, with his departure, the craic pretty much disappeared from the sport. No longer were there welcomes in his garage and motor home at race weekends. Gone were the infamous parties at the British Grand Prix. Gone were the last vestiges of the independent Formula 1 team, swallowed up by the big car manufacturers and their teams of PR nobodies.

Born in Dublin on 30 March 1948, Eddie Jordan went to school on the southside with the Christian Brothers of Synge Street. He professed to the fact that he 'wasn't particularly academic' but liked sports and played Gaelic football, hurling and soccer as well as golf, where he quickly got his handicap into single figures.

He had intentions to become a dentist, but he quit college and found himself working for the Bank of Ireland as a clerk while selling cars on the side to make a little extra money. In the late 1960s, during a bank strike in Dublin, Jordan was posted to work on the island of Jersey, off the south coast of England. It was there that he came across kart-racing. Jordan purchased one, and his first race was on Jersey at Bouley Bay in 1970 at the ripe old age of twenty-two. The following year, he entered and won the Irish Kart Championship.

After leaving karting in 1973, Jordan began his progression through motor sport's junior formula when he raced in the Formula Ford 2000 series in a Crosslé 30F, in which he competed for two years, winning the famous Leinster Trophy at Mondello Park in 1975.

He suffered a bad crash at Mallory Park, breaking both his legs, which forced him out of the 1976 season. When he recovered, he raced in Formula Atlantic in 1977 with an ex-Alan Jones March chassis and won three races before winning the Irish Formula Atlantic Championship in 1978.

As with any branch of motor sport, it cost money, and Jordan did everything he could in those early days to get it.

'I can now look back at some of the crazy things I did, whether it was at rugby weekends selling smoked salmon on the side of the street or selling carpets or taking out a stall in the Dandelion Market

Above: Derek Daly's first racing machine, a stock car at Santry.

Right: Derek Daly being interviewed by Robin Rhodes, the self-proclaimed 'voice of Irish racing'.
Photo: Con Connolly.

Below: Derek Daly raced not only in single-seat racing cars but in sportscars as well. Pictured here at Le Mans in the Silk Cut Jaguar. Photo: Michael Chester.

Left: Rosemary Smith emerges from the Hillman Imp in 1966, the car that became synonymous with Ireland's number-one lady driver.

Right: Rosemary Smith in a glamorous pose at Monte Carlo, with the Hillman Imp.
Photo courtesy of www.imps4ever.info.

Below: Rosemary Smith on her way to victory in the 1964 Tulip Rally in the Hillman Imp. Photo courtesy of www.imps4ever.info.

Above: Michael Roe at Mondello Park in his Formula Ford days. Photo: Con Connolly.

Below: Michael Roe (inside) in a battle on the main straight at Mondello Park with P.J. Fallon. Photo: Con Connolly.

Above: Michael Roe's winning CANAM Car which swept all before him during the 1984 season.

Below: Michael Roe raced in the Hemelgarn Racing IndyCar in the USA for four races in 1985.

Left: Michael Roe is helped to his car at the Dallas Grand Prix where he set a new outright lap record, despite a broken foot.

Below: Robert Dunlop on the 125 Honda at the Mid-Antrim 150 races. Photo: Harry Havelin.

Above: Joey Dunlop sweeps into Dublin Corner, Skerries, ahead of Paul Cranston.
Photo: Chris McLoughlin.

Right: A picture of concentration.
Joey Dunlop on the grid with his
famous yellow helmet and lucky
number 3 on his bike.
Photo: Harry Havelin.

Above: Joey Dunlop at Bell's Crossroads during the Tandragee 100. Photo: Chris McLoughlin.

Below: Stefan Johansson (left) and Eddie Jordan, team-mates on Team Ireland in British Formula 3. Photo: Con Connolly.

Above: Eddie Jordan turns at the first corner (Mountjoy) during a Formula Atlantic race at the Phoenix Park. Photo: Con Connolly.

Below: Team owner Eddie Jordan at a press conference during the 1998 Formula 1 season.

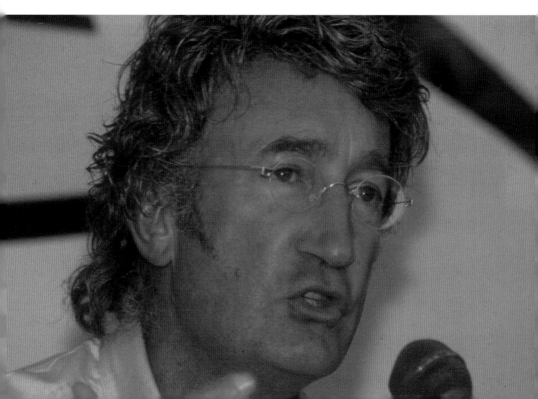

(at St Stephen's Green in Dublin). That place has become somewhat of a cult. To be there you had to be in a band [U2 famously played in the Dandelion Market] or have a stall. You were part of the 'in crowd' then, and I did it primarily for money. I remember I also used to go to Ashbourne selling rugs and carpets with the Traveller families.

'If I could sell something to somebody and make a profit, so be it. I never had any shame. For years I had the Carpet Mills sponsorship on the car – all the way up to my Formula Atlantic days – and the owner and I came to a deal: I could have all the remnants and all the pieces of carpets that he was no longer using, and I would sell them. That money went directly towards the racing team, and he got advertising space on the car, so everyone was a winner. I never had any inhibitions about going out selling cars, selling fish, selling anything to keep racing.'

In 1979, Jordan moved to Silverstone and teamed up with Stefan Johansson at Team Ireland to race the Chevron chassis in the British Formula 3 Championship and in the same year not only raced in Formula 2 but also got as far as testing for the McLaren Formula 1 team run by Ron Dennis. He also married Marie McCarthy, a former Irish international basketball player, and she went with Eddie to begin their new life in the UK.

'What percentage of people have ever driven a Formula 1 car? A few people are fortunate enough to realise what a machine that thing is. A Formula 1 is a special car, and to have driven one was something special. McLaren, in particular, at the time was a very strong car. Other cars were probably quicker in out-and-out speed, but the mobility of a Formula 1 car, how it is constructed, its pure raw aggression and speed were amazing.

'There's no doubt that I wasn't the quickest driver of all time. I'd started late. I had my mind set on the business side of it rather than the actual driving, but that didn't happen until later on – until I'd gone away and left Ireland to pursue a career as a professional driver. McLaren needed to test a car, and I tested their car with other drivers, but you could not put Eddie Jordan on the same level as the likes of John Watson, Eddie Irvine or, indeed, Martin Donnelly or some of these really high-quality drivers.'

At the beginning of the 1980s, and at over thirty years of age, Eddie Jordan made a decision that was to affect the rest of his life and set him on a path to Formula 1. He retired as a racing driver to concentrate on running Eddie Jordan Racing (EJR).

'When I got the chance to do the McLaren test, I'd already made up my mind to set up a team. I was beginning to put people together to design a Jordan car. I was also in my early thirties at this stage, and it's not the time to be starting planning a big driving career in Formula 1. Now, of course, if you haven't made it by twenty-one or twenty-two, it seems as if you've missed the boat.'

In 1981, E.J. started his own management team, running cars for paying drivers in the British Formula 3 Championship, and brought in British driver David Sears. Sears took pole position for EJR in his first race in a Ralt-Toyota at Thruxton and finished second. Like Jordan, Sears also went on to manage motor-racing teams and to become the boss of the Supernova Formula 3000 team as well as running the New Zealand and German teams in the A1 Grand Prix Championship in the 2006/7 season.

Times were tough then for Eddie and Marie. They had gone to the UK with a couple of thousand pounds in savings and were cooped up in a one-bedroom flat near Eddie's base at Silverstone. But the Dubliner was resilient and clever. He drove the team truck himself to save money and began to bring in sponsorship deals to keep the wolf from the door. EJR raced in the British and European Formula 3 series in 1982, and James Weaver won for the team at Donington Park, Nogaro and Jarama.

Jordan also gave a certain young Ayrton Senna da Silva his first run in a Formula 3 car.

'At the end of the summer I gave da Silva a test in our Formula 3 car at Silverstone, and he blew my mind he was so quick. He changed his name very soon after that to Ayrton Senna, dropping the da Silva. I lost him because he went off to drive for another team – Dick Bennett's – and Martin Brundle was with us in 1983. It was a titanic battle that season, one of the best years ever in Formula 3. It was a battle from the very start in March until the end of October, one that Senna won.'

EJR ran Brundle and Allen Berg in British Formula 3 and Irishman Tommy Byrne in the European series as the number of race drivers in his stable continued to rise. Brundle took six wins but finished second overall to Senna. Jordan had also started his own driver-management company at this stage, insisting that the drivers who drove for his team also became part of his management set-up. Brundle was one of the first to sign up with E.J., who set up the company with a lawyer named Fred Rogers.

Canadian-born Berg stayed with the team the following season and also won six races in the UK as the team finished second again, this time to Johnny Dumfries. Berg was joined by Jordan's old team-mate Stefan Johansson at EJR.

In 1985, the Fédération Internationale de l'Automobile (FIA, the world governing body), replaced the European Formula 2 and Formula 3 Championships with the all new International Formula 3000 series, which, up to 2005, became the main support category and feeder class to Formula 1, before it was replaced by Gp2. The international Formula 3000 class used cars with a 3-litre rev limited engine, quick in a straight line but slower than Formula 1 cars when it came to cornering. EJR was one of the fourteen teams who entered the new series. It wasn't the most auspicious of starts, with only one car, a March-Cosworth driven by Belgian-born Thierry Tassin. Budgetary constraints meant they only raced in six races that season, picking up a solitary point at the Österreichring in Austria. It didn't get any better in 1986 and 1987 in Formula 3000, as the team failed to score any points. There were two cars in the 1986 series, but it was back to one in 1987, driven by Sweden's Tomas Kaiser.

While the team were struggling in Formula 3000, back in the UK success came at last. After yet another second-placed finish in Formula 3 in 1986 for Brazilian Sandro Sala behind Andy Wallace, it was Johnny Herbert who won the 1987 series, giving Eddie Jordan his first championship success as team manager. Paul Stott was

Herbert's team-mate that year, and the team also delved into France, running Joe Ris in *their* Formula 3 campaign.

'I've had some good times with some good drivers. I was always focused on the key elements of the ladder to Formula 1, and they were, at the time, Formula Ford, Formula 3 to Formula 1, and if you could miss out on Formula 2, that was a bonus. I never actually ran a car in Formula 2, although I'd driven it myself. I won't say it was a graveyard, but it was a formula for parking people up until an opportunity arose. The really quick ones, like Mansell, Senna and Piquet, went straight from Formula 3 to Formula 1.

'I wanted to stay in a category until I'd won the Championship, and that happened in Formula Ford earlier on, with David Hunt and then Johnny Herbert. I decided to stop Formula 3 after 1987. I moved up to Formula 3000, although I was reluctant to do so. I never really felt that Formula 2 was the right category, but Formula 3000 seemed to be, and it had a lot of good drivers in it.'

In 1988, with a Formula 3 championship under its belt, EJR ran five cars – three in British Formula 3 and two in Formula 3000, with Herbert moving up in class, teaming up with Tomas Danielson. Herbert won the opening round at Jerez in Spain and picked up a third-placed finish at Monza. But the season ended horribly for Herbert after a horrific race accident at Brands Hatch.

Irishman Martin Donnelly was now also racing for Jordan, having come into the team to compete the rest of the season, starting with that race at Brands. Donnelly was leading when Herbert's car, which was third, kinked sideways and slammed into a concrete wall, wiping out most of the field and smashing both his legs. It's been described as the worst crash in Formula 3000 history, and many of those involved were lucky to be alive, including Herbert, whose legs were left sticking out of the end of his smashed car when it finally came to a stop.

The race was restarted some two hours later, but only six cars made the starting grid, including Donnelly, who took the race win. Donnelly also won the last race of the season at Dijon in France, which helped EJR and Donnelly to take third place in the 1988 series behind Brazilian Roberto Moreno and Olivier Grouillard of France.

'I had probably the best two drivers at the time in Johnny Herbert then Martin Donnelly. I was managing them as well, and that was probably the heyday of Jordan where I was able to put as many drivers as I had into Formula 1. Donnelly won races for us, and Jean Alesi won the Formula 3000 Championship for EJR.'

French driver Alesi had finished tenth in the 1988 season for Oreca Motorsport, but when EJR signed up to run the Reynard Mugen-Honda cars, who were making their Formula 3000 debut, Alesi came on board, not only as a driver, but he also signed to Jordan's management company. Donnelly was retained after his excellent end to the previous season. In racing terms, at twenty-five, Alesi was getting on in years. He had won the French Formula 3 championship in 1987 and was in his second year in Formula 3000, but he had yet to drive in Formula 1. That was about to change.

Alesi won the 1989 Formula 3000 title, taking three wins at Pau, Birmingham and Spa-Francorchamps, winning the series with a race to spare. Donnelly only managed to pick up points at two races but won at the sixth round at Brands Hatch, the venue of Herbert's appalling crash the previous year.

Also in 1989, Alesi and Donnelly took their first steps into Formula 1. Jordan farmed his drivers out, with Alesi going to Tyrrell and Donnelly to Arrows for the race at the Paul Ricard Circuit in France. Alesi became only one of a handful of drivers to pick up points in his Formula 1 debut, finishing fourth in his Tyrrell – just over a minute behind race winner Alain Prost in a McLaren. Donnelly was twelfth on that July day in France. Alesi finished out the season in both Formula 3000 and Formula 1. He ran in seven of the remaining nine Formula 1 races while still chasing the Formula 3000 championship, which he won with a sixth-placed finish in the penultimate round at Dijon, giving EJR a then unique British Formula 3-International Formula 3000 double.

Eddie Jordan put other drivers in the thick of the action in Formula 1 that year, including Bertrand Gachot who would later become Jordan's first Formula 1 driver, and he now had it in mind to go to the pinnacle of his sport, Formula 1.

'I was able to place my drivers in Formula 1 and, particularly, Jean at Tyrrell.

'The thing about coming from Ireland in those very early days was that you had to build up a confidence factor. We had no history of international motor-racing in Ireland. It was always either horse-racing or football. Motor-racing was a completely new sport, and you often felt a little touch inferior to those other sports. Those inferiority complexes, thankfully, have dissipated now, but it was around in my day. I really believed in myself enough to want to tackle Formula 1.'

After their successful 1989 season, Eddie Jordan set up Jordan Grand Prix with the intention of running in the 1991 campaign. He left the British Formula 3 series and only ran in Formula 3000. With Alesi gone to race in Formula 1 with Tyrrell, Eddie Irvine had come on board and was partnered by Heinz-Harald Frentzen. Both would later become Formula 1 drivers with Jordan Grand Prix, and Irvine finished third in the 1990 season with French driver Érik Comas taking the title. E.J. would later sell Alesi to Ferrari for an undisclosed fee, thought to be in the region of $5 million, of which Eddie received around 20 per cent.

In 1990, Gary Anderson, from Coleraine in Northern Ireland, joined Jordan Grand Prix. Before hooking up with E.J., Anderson had a long career in motor sport, which included working as a mechanic with Brabham, McLaren and Ensign Formula 1 teams. In the 1980s, he branched out on his own and founded the Formula 3 race-car manufacturer Anson, and, by the turn of a new decade, he found himself working alongside Jordan as their technical director, his job being to design the first Jordan Formula 1 car. Anderson would stay with the team for eight years before an acrimonious falling out between the pair meant his leaving to head the design team at Stewart Grand Prix in 1999.

'I'd left home in Dublin to be a racing driver. I made a career change after about eight or so years pursuing that, and now the move to Formula 1 was not a problem,' says Jordan. 'I could put up with the bad hours; I could put up with working seven days a week;

but I needed somebody to have a shoulder to lean on, because Formula 1 was such a different game, and even now, looking back, I'm not even sure I realised how big a step it was. Without Gary Andersen, I don't think I would have embarked on that step, because he took all of the technology away in terms of me not having to be overconcerned about the structure of the car, the layout and how it was going to be developed, engineered, raced and tested. In those early years, Gary was just fantastic. I did the commercial side, the deals with the drivers and all of the financial aspects, and Gary put the finishing touches to the design and the concept itself.'

Ireland was going though an unusual sporting revolution at the beginning of the 1990s. An Englishman, Jack Charlton, had taken the Republic of Ireland football team to the European Championships in 1988 in Germany and followed that up with qualification for the 1990 World Cup in Italy where they lost in the quarter-finals to the hosts. Suddenly the Irish, living in a country with high unemployment, corrupt politicians and massive financial emigration, moved from a feeling of inferiority and insecurity and finally began to believe in themselves. In fact, some like to trace Ireland's Celtic Tiger economy back to the Charlton era where Ireland could now take on the world.

And into that new self-belief came Eddie Jordan and Jordan Grand Prix. On 27 November 1990, at the Silverstone racetrack, the first Jordan 191 was unveiled. A black sleek unpainted carbon-shelled machine, driven for the first time by John Watson. There were no sponsors on board the car that day as Camel, who had backed Jordan Racing in Formula 3000, didn't follow E.J. to Formula 1, going, instead, to Benetton. The car was powered by a Ford Cosworth V8 engine, and, after that initial shakedown, Jordan hired the Luxembourg-born Belgian national Bertrand Gachot as the team's first official driver, with Brazilian Andrea de Cesaris arriving later as the second.

The car was tested by Gachot in Portugal and France, but it was still without a sponsor until Eddie tied up a deal with Pepsi who agreed to give the Irish team a green livery with the 7UP brand on the car.

'We didn't have enough money to paint it, so we left it in a carbon. Actually, I think it worked out because when polished, it came up brilliantly and it photographed well. John [Watson] was the first to drive the car. I remember one journalist I used to have huge respect for called Jabby Crombac – a Frenchman working with *L'Équipe* – he was one of only six journalists, including RTÉ's Michael O'Carroll, who came to have a look at the car when we launched it. That will give you an idea of the credibility we had. They just did not believe that we could, in a short period of time, go out, design and construct this car. Crombac wrote, "Why do they bother?" Actually, he was saying what most people thought, and I was saying I'm going to prove them wrong. Watson tested the car, and we thought, maybe he's just being nice to us, but he said, "Look, the car is nimble, it responds, everything is right with it but what we need to do is to get some speed." We really didn't realise that within a couple of races we'd be running fourth and fifth in the Canadian Grand Prix, and when you think back how hard it is to get to the fourth and fifth now, it was a huge moment. They were fantastic days.'

The 7UP deal wasn't a big one by Formula 1 standards, and it was based on performances. Jordan hassled and harried money out of just about everyone he could. Fuji Film got the top half of the car, which was painted blue, and both drivers brought individual sponsors. There was no Irish sponsorship, much to the country's shame, although Jordan did eventually get a small amount from the Irish Government through their tourist agency Bord Fáilte. The Jordan 191 was visually stunning with its green and blue livery, and in 2007 was voted by *Motoring News* as the best-looking car to ever race in Formula 1.

Eddie brought in a host of Irish personnel to his grand-prix set-up. Outside of Anderson, there was Mark Gallagher who ran the press office (an office of one), John Walton as chief mechanic and Bosco Quinn as general manager; and they headed off to Phoenix, Arizona for the opening race of the 1991 Formula 1 season.

Formula 1 still had pre-qualify those days, and Jordan joined the likes of Scuderia Italia, Colini and the Fondmetal teams in a session on the Friday of the race weekend in Phoenix, Arizona, looking for two of only four available places to go forward for qualifying.

'Pre-qualifying. If ever you wanted to have a recipe for a heart attack then that's it. It was so stressful. At 8 o'clock on a Friday morning, you had one hour to get four cars from those that were allowed to run, and unless you made it through, you would have to get out and be gone by the Friday evening. It was hideous, and of all the races that we had to pre-qualify, only one driver missed once, and that was de Cesaris at the first race.'

The Brazilian was known as De Crasharis after eight very eventful seasons prior to his signing with E.J., and it didn't go well for him first time out in Phoenix when the engine blew. Gachot did at least get his car through to the race where he qualified fourteenth and was classified tenth despite a non-finish.

'It was an incredible and stressful weekend, but to actually be out on the track at the time with such unbelievable drivers like Senna and Piquet was great. I had some very close friends there, but you don't have that many friends when you're competing at that level. People are inclined to stay on their own, even though they will come privately and say, "Look, I wish you well," but not publicly. Formula 1 can be a very selfish place most of the time.'

After that opening race, 1991 was an outstanding debut year for Jordan Grand Prix, as qualifying became easier. After eight races, the team no longer had the indignity of having to run on the Friday morning, and at the Canadian race, round 5, both drivers finished in the points for the first time, with de Cesaris fourth and Gachot fifth. By the mid-point of the season, they were in sixth place in the constructor's championship with ten points.

De Cesaris drove the No. 33 Jordan-Ford Cosworth 191 for the rest of the season, but Gachot did not. After ten rounds, the Belgian was convicted and sentenced to four months in prison for spraying CS gas during an altercation with a London taxi-driver the previous year.

It was then that Jordan sat Michael Schumacher into a Formula 1 car for the first time at the Belgian Grand Prix on a wet weekend at Spa-Francorchamps in 1991. The German was contracted to

Mercedes, for whom he drove sports cars. Jordan needed a replacement for Gachot and contacted Schumacher's manager Willy Weber. The Silverstone test went well – Weber told Jordan that Schumacher knew Spa intimately; however, Schumacher had only cycled around the track on one occasion. He put in a stunning qualifying session on his debut and started the race ahead of de Cesaris, seventh on the grid. Unfortunately, Schumy burnt the clutch out on the start line, ending not only his race but his association with Jordan as well – Tom Walkinshaw, the owner of Benetton, snatched him away from under Jordan's nose.

For the next two races, Roberto Moreno, who ironically had lost his seat at Benetton to Schumacher, took over, while Italian Alessandro 'Alex' Zanardi raced in car number 33 for the last three races of the year.

Jordan ended up with thirteen points and fifth place among the eighteen competing teams in 1991, with de Cesaris finishing seventh in the World Drivers' Championship and Gachot eighth. The debut season was a dream, but it was all too good to be true.

'You get cocky, and I was cocky at the time. I thought, well if I can do this in my first year, then I can win this championship quite soon. And then, of course, the reality sets in. I found out that Formula 1 was easier the first year because we had a couple of years to prepare for it. The biggest and the most difficult thing was that while we were racing I had another crew of people behind the scenes developing, designing and creating a car for the second year. To do both takes a huge amount of organisation, and I didn't realise at the time how much resources were needed both in human and financial terms, and it was a very big task. Maybe I underestimated the amount of quality people that were needed to be in place to build the second year's car, and we suffered as a result.'

After a stunning debut season, it all went pear-shaped for Jordan Grand Prix in 1992. They ditched their fine Cosworth V8, for which they had paid some $6 million, and, as a result of their successes in the 1991 season, Jordan persuaded Yamaha to come in as a free engine supplier to the Sasol-backed Jordan 192, with Italian Stefano

Modena and Brazilian Mauricio Gugelmin as their drivers. But the engine proved unreliable, and the other teams were now fore-warned. In the sixteen championship races of 1992, they only picked up a single point in the very last race at Adelaide, where Modena finished sixth.

It didn't get much better in 1993 when Rubens Barrichello signed up, driving in all sixteen races that year. The Brazilian had a succes-sion of team-mates: Italian Ivan Capelli for the first two races; Belgian Thierry Boutsen for the next ten; Marco Apicella for round thirteen in Italy; and another Italian, Emanuele Naspetti for the fourteenth race at Estoril. Jordan then persuaded Ireland's Eddie Irvine to leave Formula 3000 in Japan, and he raced in the final two rounds, including that now-infamous race at Suzuka where he un-lapped himself from Senna, finishing sixth and receiving a smack in the mouth from the great one as a result.

Jordan and Yamaha's brief partnership ended at the end of 1992, and it was a return to customer engines again, this time spending $5 million of money he didn't have for the Hart V10. The return? A mere three championship points. Jordan had also invested in new premises at Silverstone. It didn't look good for a For-mula 1 team to be run out of two sheds, so he bought a purpose-built factory on the site which was home to the British Grand Prix.

However, lack of success put a drain on finances. Jordan had made a considerable amount of money during his Formula 3 and Formula 3000 days. He bought a villa in Spain and was providing well for his family. After the success of 1991, the failure of the next two years meant he began to dip into his own money to keep the team afloat.

'Yes, that true. I think what happened was that the second year was just a chasm. We just went right into this huge big hole, and you didn't know whether you were going to get swallowed up or not. I could have been swallowed up because we were very friendly with the bailiff. He was always trying to take things from us, but he'd tell us when he was coming, so we managed to escape him and the VAT officer.

'They were hand-to-mouth times, but we had some decent sponsorship, and we had to juggle figures and juggle money to try and keep banks and various other people away to keep the team in business. It took a while to recover from the 1992 season, and you had to build up a belief and get drivers to say, "I would like to drive for Jordan." It did happen, but it did take two years to recover from the 1992 season.'

In 1994, still with the Hart engines, Barrichello and Irvine were the team's two drivers, although in the very first race at Interlagos, Irvine was involved in a massive incident with the Benetton of Jos Verstappen and the McLaren of Martin Brundle. Irvine was found guilty of causing the crash and banned for the next three races. Aguri Suzuki came in for the Pacific Grand Prix, while de Cesaris returned to the team for the next two before Irvine's return. The year also saw the death of both Senna and Roland Ratzenberger at Imola, while Barrichello survived a monster when his Jordan cleared the tyre wall in qualifying in San Marino.

Jordan finished fifth overall, with twenty-eight points, nineteen of those to Barrichello, six from Irvine and three from de Cesaris. They also got their first pole position when Gary Anderson sent Barrichello out on slick tyres on a drying track catching out the rest of the paddock.

There was more progression in 1995. The team had stabilised in terms of its driver line-up, retaining both Barrichello and Irvine, and, helped by a second and third place in Canada (their first time on the podium), Jordan Grand Prix finished fifth in the Championship with the Peugeot engine now powering their cars.

They would also finish fifth in 1996 and 1997, now one of the most consistent points scorers in Formula 1 and with the distinctive Benson and Hedges sponsorship, brokered by another Dubliner, David Marren of Saatchi & Saatchi. Barrichello was joined by Brundle in 1996, while Irvine scampered off to join Schumacher at Ferrari. Barrichello ended his association with the team in 1997 as Italian Giancarlo Fisichella and German Ralf Schumacher (Michael's brother) came in to score thirty-three championship points between them.

Jordan Grand Prix were well ensconced in the Formula 1 paddock, but, despite picking up regular points and podium place, a
win eluded them. Fisichella had come close in 1997 when he was
second in Belgium, and, ironically, it was Spa-Francorchamps that
had provided Jordan with many outstanding moments in the year
that finally gave Eddie Jordan his first win in Formula 1.

It was all change for the 1998 season. Mugen Honda was now
the engine suppliers, and Damon Hill, the 1996 World Champion,
was in the Jordan-Mugen Honda 198 with Ralf Schumacher as his
team-mate. It was another outstanding year as they broke into the
upper echelons of the sport to finish fourth in the constructors' table
with thirty-four points, only four points behind the mighty Williams. Sixteen of those points came from a wet day at
Spa-Francorchamps at the Belgian Grand Prix on Sunday 30
August.

It was an incident-packed day. On only the first lap, a massive
accident wiped out most of cars, with many drivers having to race in
their spare cars after the restart. The Jordans somehow survived,
and, in a race of attrition, Damon and Ralf lay second and third,
before Michael Schumacher, who was seemingly strolling to victory
in his Ferrari, emerged from the mist just before the Bus Stop corner
and slammed into David Coulthard's McLaren on its way back to
the pits, ripping off his front wheel.

Suddenly, the Jordans were one and two, with Ralf in second –
the quickest of the pair and closing in on Hill. Jordan told the
German over the team radio to hold position, to ride shotgun for
Hill and not risk an accident, which would have taken out both cars.
Ralf apparently did not initially reply to Jordan's team orders; there
was silence from his car. Jordan repeated himself, asking Ralf did he
understand. The German replied with a simple yes when he eventually replied.

'A lot of motor-sport fans, I think, will always remember that race
in Spa-Francorchamps – maybe not because Jordan finished first and
second but because of that huge crash. It was full of excitement, and
Michael Schumacher punched David Coulthard after blaming him

for his accident. Many thought we were lucky, but I have to challenge them a bit because we did qualify Hill third, and Ralf was eighth, and Damon led the race from the restart. Sure, he got passed by Michael Schumacher, who then made a mistake and Hill took up the lead. I think it was one of Damon's best races to be honest.'

Hill eventually finished the 1998 season with twenty points and in sixth place in the driver table, while Ralf took fourteen points for tenth.

While 1998 was good, 1999 was even better. Hill was joined by German Heinz-Harald Frentzen, but the Englishman was getting tired of Formula 1. He wasn't as competitive as he should have been and bowed out with only seven points to his name in a very competitive car. Frentzen, though, helped to take the Jordan-Mugen 199 to third place in the both the drivers' and constructors' championships.

Frentzen registered two wins in France and Italy, three second places, three thirds and four fourths in an outstanding season. After the win in the Italian Grand Prix, Jordan was asked by RTÉ's Declan Quigley about the championship, and Jordan replied that it was between Ferrari and McLaren. He seemed unaware that Frentzen could actually win the title; such was the euphoria surrounding the win.

As it was, Mika Häkkinen won it that year for McLaren, with Irvine second and Frentzen third, but there would be an acrimonious end to the relationship between Jordan and Frentzen in 2001.

In 2000, Frentzen was joined by Italian Jarno Trulli and gaining sixth place in the championship, with the German on the podium twice at Brazil and the USA, but cracks in the owner–driver relationship were beginning to appear. Jordan denied there had been rows, but he was clearly not happy with his German driver who he fired in 2001 just before his home Grand Prix, making Jordan the most unpopular man at Hockenheim.

According to Heinz-Harald, 'In 2001, everything should have been better. It was not. Following intense quarrels a few days after the British Grand Prix, Eddie Jordan dismissed me by means of a fax sent to my home. Suddenly, in the middle of the season, I was reduced to being a spectator at the German Grand Prix.'

Jordan said, 'I suppose what happened towards the end of the 2000 season probably spilled over into 2001 with Frentzen. In the second last race, we'd done two pit stops, and we were going out on our final run, and Frentzen switched the car off by mistake. Partly our fault for putting a switch in a place that he shouldn't have been able to get to, but he did, and he brushed against it, and we didn't find out. The car expired and stopped, and that's a race we should have won. In retrospect, he was our most successful driver. He scored more points for us than anyone else. It was remarkable what he had achieved.'

The team was also haemorrhaging behind the scenes. Technical Director Mike Gascoyne left for Stewart in 2002 and was replaced by Egbahl Hamidy from Arrows, and Jordan also brought back Gary Anderson as Director of Race and Test Engineering. But Jordan was standing still as the manufacturers took hold of Formula 1. By 2002, they were running out of money, and Managing Director Trevor Foster and engineers Tim Holloway and David Brown left. Jordan was also now very much in the background as sponsorships agreements failed.

He had already sold a 40-per-cent shareholding in the team to venture-capitalist company Warburg, Pincus & Co, securing his own future but not that of the team. In 2003, he lost a high-profile case against mobile-phone company Vodafone. Jordan claimed that in the course of a telephone conversation in 2001 between himself and David Haines, at that stage the Global Brand Director of Vodafone Global, they agreed he would become title sponsor of Jordan for three seasons, 2002–4, for $150 million including bonuses. Jordan claimed damages for breach of the alleged contract. Vodafone denied that any such agreement was made, and Mr Justice Langley of the British High Court found for Vodafone saying that Jordan's claim was 'demonstrated to be without foundation and false.'

Justice Langley described Eddie Jordan as an 'a wholly unsatisfactory witness' and his evidence, 'in many instances, in stark conflict with, and indeed belied by, the documents, often of his own making.' Not only that, he ordered Jordan to pay around £1.5 million of Vodafone's legal costs. It not only hurt Eddie Jordan's pocket but the case also soured the relationship that he had with the Gallagher Group, who had backed his team through their Benson and Hedges brand. The winter of 2002 was tough for Jordan. But, once again, they scrambled a budget together and took on what proved to be their penultimate season with Giancarlo Fisichella and Ralph Firman.

There was one more win for the team as Fisichella gave Jordan a surprise victory in Brazil. In a race full of accidents, which was finally red-flagged, Fisichella was initially placed second behind Kimi Räikkönen's McLaren, but an FIA inquiry led to Fisichella being declared the winner as he was leading on the lap before the red flag appeared.

But their fourth Formula 1 win wasn't enough to stop the decline. In 2004, another new driver, Nick Heidfeld, was joined by Giorgio Pantano and Timo Glock, who were paying for their drives, and in the close season, Eddie Jordan sold out to Russia's Midland Group, owned by Alex Schneider.

'For us to have finished on the podium in the World Championship, to have won grands prix was fantastic, but the whole business had changed since 9/11. There wasn't the availability of private funding that there used to be. Entrepreneurs were more cautious, more careful. There wasn't enough money to go around, and any big corporate money was staying with the big manufacturers and the big teams, and, as a result, it was much more difficult for us to survive as a going concern. There's no secret that motor-racing is one sport that is fuelled by money, and without the right sort of money, you can't survive.

'I was facing a situation where the previous year had been a massive financial struggle costing a lot of money, and I felt this was an opportune time whereby I could leave with dignity. It was not necessarily what I wanted to do, but I felt that it was too risky. I am a risk taker, but this was a very big risk. To leave it another year when I wasn't sure that we could continue would have been wrong.'

Jordan Grand Prix is still revered in Formula 1 circles. At one stage, Jordan merchandising outsold everybody else except Ferrari, and they included some strange items such as an E.J.10 sports drink and even a tie-up with Waterford Crystal.

As he bid farewell to the sport at the beginning of the 2005 season after fourteen years in Formula 1, Eddie Jordan had used twenty-eight drivers, scoring 279 points from their 231 races, with four race wins. Schneider's new team retained the Jordan brand for one campaign, but it was Jordan in name only.

Eddie Jordan emerged from the sport financially secure, no longer wanting to put his own wealth into his ailing team. Since he sold the team, he has worked on various charity projects, making a reality-TV programme for Channel 5 in the UK called *Eddie Jordan's Bad Boy Racers,* and he has even caddied for his good friend Paul McGinley at the 2005 BMW International in Germany. His autobiography, *An Independent Man,* hit the bookshops in May 2007.

Paddy Hopkirk

orn on 14 April 1933 in Belfast, Northern Ireland, Patrick Barron Hopkirk or 'Paddy' was the first Irish motor-sport superstar. He reached the height of his fame in 1964 when, along with his co-driver and navigator, Henry Liddon, their British-built Mini Cooper S, Reg. No. 33 EJB, won the Monte Carlo Rally.

The win was dramatic enough after the pair's long and difficult drive, which had started in Minsk in the then Soviet Union, but what really catapulted Hopkirk onto the world stage and into the consciousness of the British and Irish public was his appearance with the car and the erstwhile presenter Bruce Forsyth on *Sunday Night at the London Palladium* on ITV, which attracted over 20 million viewers. It was a staggering audience figure, and the sight of Hopkirk and, indeed, Liddon on top of the Mini on stage at the Palladium in London threw the Irishman into the limelight, and to this day he is still revered as one of Ireland's top sportsmen and drivers.

Hopkirk used his celebrity to good effect. He should have won Monte Carlo in 1966 as well, but the French organisers, shocked at a potential British Leyland Mini one-two-three that year, threw out Hopkirk and the other Cooper S drivers because of 'illegal headlight beams.' The same fate befell Rosemary Smith, who was leading the

Ladies Trophy in the 1966 Monte Carlo, before her Hillman Imp was also thrown out at the behest of the organisers. 'Victory' went, instead, to a very embarrassed Citroën team after it was decided that the Minis and Smith's Imp were guilty of a dipped-headlight infringement. It was a shocking and outrageous decision.

Nevertheless, the Belfast boy showed, on numerous occasions, that he was not just a flash in the pan. His first win was in 1955 on a St Patrick's Day trial in a VW Beetle. His last was in 1990 on the Pirelli Classic Marathon from London to Italy. In between, he also won the Acropolis in Greece and the Circuit of Ireland five times, as well as many circuit races in which he competed when he wasn't rallying. He is a Life Member of the British Racing Drivers Club (BRDC), having been elected in 1967.

Hopkirk wasn't a man who was fearful of driving; in fact, he positively revelled in it and wrote a book on his experiences in the London-to-Sydney rally in 1968, driving an Austin 1800 for British Leyland. The book was titled *The Greatest Drive of All*, recounting his drive across 10,000 miles of some of most dangerous territories in the world along with team-mates Alex Poole (also an Irish-born driver who won the British Saloon Car Championship in 1969, along with being inducted into the Motorsport Ireland Hall of Fame) and Englishman Tony Nash.

It was all a far cry from his youth growing up in Belfast.

'I was born just off the posh Malone Road – but we weren't very posh – in a house called St Claire. It was a happy childhood, which, unfortunately, was interrupted by the Second World War. During the war we moved out to Whitehouse, on the north-east side of Belfast, and I grew up there really. I went to school in Belfast. After the war, we moved back into Belfast, a place called Summerton Road. But I did go to Clongowes Wood College in the South. They call it the Eton of Ireland, and I kept telling everybody in the UK that, but nobody'd ever heard of it. Those Jesuits left a very strong impression in my mind, and then I went to Trinity, scraping in by the skin of my teeth.

'By the time I was in college in the South, I was already into cars. At a young age, I had a car given to me – a thing called a Harding, with a motorcycle engine in the back. I remember my father got permission for me to drive it round an estate next door to the house in Whitehouse, and so I presume I got the driving bug into my veins at a very early age.'

That Harding belonged to a local clergyman.

'I'd better not say which denomination. He left it to me, and I've still got it. Well, put it this way: I lost it, but I did a radio programme in London one day, *The John Dunne Show* on the BBC, and some guy from Dulwich rang up and said he had a Harding in pieces. He was a motorcycle restorer, and I went down to see it, and there it was, with the registration number IJ 9670, same plate. It's in pieces, and I was going to restore it, but I'm afraid it's still lying in tea chests in my barn. But it's in good nick if somebody has the time to do it one day.

'I used to go up and down to Trinity and back to Belfast every weekend in it. It was a great little car, very reliable, did my first courting in it; I think I kissed my first girl in that car as well.'

And why did he get into motor sport in the first place, an era then of gentlemen racers but not as organised as it is now?

'Circumstances led me into it. I had this car given to me when I was nine, and I just got very interested, and my father was interested in driving cars too. He was a good driver and he liked good drivers. I joined the Trinity Dublin University Motorcycle and Light Car Club, which is no more. I wasn't much good at anything else. I wasn't very academic, but I was quite good at driving cars, so I found my niche.'

Hopkirk had caught the bug, and he learned car control in the Harding, giving him the urge to become a professional racing driver. He also drove motorcycles (one with a sidecar when he was fifteen) before getting his full licence at seventeen, and went auto-testing where he learned how to reverse, brake, spin, handbrake – all the skills that would later hone his rallying skills and rallying career.

'Saturday-afternoon trials, as we called them, consisted of events both North and South. You went out and you did a bit of plotting on the map into the Wicklow mountains and then they just closed the roads, took a crossroads covered in dirt and put some chalk down, a few pylons and then there was a guy there timed you. So we all learnt that, we were good at it, and, of course, the Harding only had brakes on the rear wheels so I already knew that if you lock the rear wheels you go sideways, so it was a good training.'

The first time that he came to the Irish rallying public's notice was in 1954 when he won the now-famous Hewison Trophy, driving a Volkswagen Beetle which his father bought for him.

'Well, it got me noticed. There was a chap called Matt McQuaid in Dublin, who was brother of the Archbishop, and he was running the Standard Triumph Assembly Plant in Dublin, and he mentioned my name to an English guy, a competitions manager called Ken Richardson. Ken got stuck for a particular event and asked me because he couldn't get anybody else. I couldn't take part in the event because they wouldn't allow a change of driver, but I reminded him of that, and I hounded him, and he eventually gave me a drive in the RAC rally.'

That was in 1955. Unlike rallying of the present day, the event started with driving tests at Blackpool, and, as a result of his autotesting in Ireland, he was much faster than anybody else. Indeed, it looked as if Hopkirk might actually bring the car home to victory until the sump broke.

'That's right. Ken was in a bar somewhere in Blackpool, I think, and he heard on the BBC that a young unknown Irish driver was leading RAC Rally.'

Hopkirk was pitting himself against the good drivers of those days, ones he describes as 'pretty posh' – Sidney Allard and Ian Appleyard were serious guys with serious cars too, so it was quite a shock to their system. They were people with money and background, and here's this upstart from Belfast jumping in and taking the lead in the RAC Rally in 1955.

It was also the era that rallying, in particular, started to become organised. Hopkirk's career started to take off, and in 1958 he won his first Circuit of Ireland in a Sunbeam Triumph run by Richardson before he switched it to the Rootes Group Team and drove the Sunbeam Rapier, winning two other circuits in 1961 and

1962, the days when the event started in Belfast and circumnavigated the country.

Now he was with the Rootes Group, Hopkirk was finally a professional racing driver, but he wasn't exactly getting paid the enormous sums that top-class racers can attract nowadays.

'I think we got £30 or £40 a day or something. If you stayed in a really cheap hotel and ate potatoes all day, you saved money, so we made a profit out of the expenses, and all the flights were paid for, of course. Yeah, it was a job, and you were able to make a profit on it, and then, of course, the oil companies started to pay a little bit in prize money, and it got better and better.'

After the Rootes Group, there was another switch to the British Motor Corporation (BMC) outfit, partnering a couple of Finnish drivers, including the great Timo Mäkinen, while driving an Austin Healey 3000.

'The Healey was hard to drive, a very quick car, but I won a few rallies in it, including the Austrian Alpine. To be honest, I actually joined BMC to get my hands on the Healey, because it was an outright rally winner, but it was hard to drive. The Finns were very good at driving a car like that. Mäkinen and Rauno Aaltonen were a very hard act to follow, and I must say they kept me on my toes.

'I suppose internally I hated them, because we were all dog-eat-dog, but they taught me a lot. I knew nothing about racing on those roads until later on, and they could drive cars like the Healey much better than me really. But, you must remember, those boys were superstars. If you're a good rally driver in Scandinavia, it's like being like Beckham – I mean, it's got as much following there as football. I've done a few rallies in Scandinavia, and you get everybody out in their mum's car on a Saturday night and they're upside down in the trees wrecking them. They really go quickly, and it's because it's very important to them. Mäkinen, I think, was given the keys of Finland by the King at one stage.'

All that was a prelude to the greatest era of Hopkirk's career and his much-vaunted association with Mini Cooper S. Few rally cars have fuelled the imagination like the giant-killing Mini Cooper as the combination of size, road-holding and power often ran rings around the opposition.

The Mini, when it first came out, was a district nurse's car, and then John Cooper came along and put the Cooper S engine into it. Although it was cheap, with the installation of the Cooper engine, it became a very high-performance machine, light and very fast, and the front wheel drive and the transverse engine were quite new in those days.

Following the original 997-cc launch in July 1961, Pat Moss won the 1961 Tulip Rally on only the car's second outing, and the following year John Love won the British Saloon Car Championship, also in a Mini.

In 1963, the 1071-cc version came on the market with a much higher specification engine than the original and more efficient front-disc brakes. Rauno Aaltonen won the 1963 Alpine Rally in one. And then there was Hopkirk's association with the car with which he became synonymous.

'Stuart Turner was a very clever guy to work for, and he was our competition manager. He hedged his bets, you know. He'd start with one car here and one car there in case there was a wipe-out in the snow and the car didn't get through – that could happen some years.'

Hopkirk acknowledges that he had a wonderful team of mechanics from BMC in Abingdon.

'They'd do anything for you. The cars were immaculately prepared; drivers were well prepared; and we all practised our guts out. Turner always ensured that we had the right tyres and the right set up with the car.'

For Hopkirk and Liddon, the Monte Carlo Rally started in Minsk just after midnight on 18 January 1964 in freezing conditions in the depth of the Russian winter. The story goes that Turner asked his drivers who would like to go to Russia to start the event in Minsk. Hopkirk, quick as a flash, said he had never been to Russia so he put his hand up. According to *The Paddy Hopkirk Story*, co-written by Bill Price and Paddy himself, the most difficult aspect of the run was, outside of the cold, when they crossed from the Soviet Union into

Poland. There they were met by the heartbreaking experience of people dropping notes into the car pleading with the pair to take them out of the rule of Stalin.

'It was a very sinister place, the Iron Curtain, and you never knew when some policeman was just going to stop you and keep you sitting there for eight hours at the border crossing. I remember the soldiers looking under the car with mirrors 'cause people were trying to get out – swim across, parachute across, anything – and here we were, coming out of a foreign land that nobody in the West knew what was going on. I made a documentary in 2004 with the BBC, and that was good fun. We went back to Minsk and retraced the steps over the route and brought back a lot of memories.'

The Monte Carlo Rally started in different countries and headed for its finish in Monte Carlo where the winner was declared on aggregate (starting times, engine size), etc.

Hopkirk and Liddon faced a 3,000-mile drive in January of that year, through one of the harshest winters Europe had ever experienced. However, the Mini obviously was suited to it because some of the heavier cars like the Mercedes, the Volvos and the Citroëns just weren't suited to their particular routes.

'Well, it was the top rally in the world because we got so much publicity by starting all over Europe. It got journalists from every country to come down to Monte Carlo, and it got a lot of publicity. It was front-page news. You were driving for your country.'

Minsk may have been the starting route for Hopkirk and Liddon, but drivers also started from the likes of Paris, Oslo, Glasgow, Lisbon, Athens and Monte Carlo. They all got together in Rimes in France and then had a common route down.

This is where the rally began in earnest. There was a lot of special stages up over the mountains which were covered in snow, and it suited the Mini. There was no such thing as pace notes back in the 1960s, which are used extensively by co-drivers in modern-day rallying; instead, Liddon was forced to use maps to guide Hopkirk through the special stages, but he was, perhaps, ahead of his time when he used phrases like 'medium left' or 'fast right' to guide his driver.

'Liddon was a wonderful co-driver and a wonderful note-reader, and I could really go flat out and rely on the fact that he wasn't going to make any mistakes, and so it was all done and dusted before we got to Monte Carlo.

'We nearly lost it in France when I went up a one-way street. It was very snowy in Colmar, and I went up a street the wrong way as the signs were all covered with snow. This very nasty policeman stopped us. There were coupons in the rally book, for which if they were removed, you got penalty points, and Henry, being a good honest English gentleman, was about to hand one to him. I couldn't let that happen, and I interfered, hid the book and told him we were out of the rally and on the way home having had a death in Ireland. He almost started to cry, silly git, and as soon as we got round the corner, we were off again. I think I pulled a real "flanker" on a French policeman. I remember stopping on the way down, and Stuart Turner asked how we had done, and I said, "I don't know, we've done our best, we haven't gone off the roads and we haven't had any problems." But I was lying. Christ, we were nearly late into Monte Carlo. Anyway, we got to Control on time.

'Of course, we were all on Dexedrine to keep awake. Capsules of Dexedrine – I'll never forget them. One half pint of beer and you were falling over. The cheapest way to get whistled. Anyway, we had a meal, and then went to bed, and about four o'clock in the morning Bernard Cahier, a very well-known European journalist, called me up, and I thought I was dreaming. He said, "I think you've won the rally."

'There were no electronic results, and they had to wait until they had your start time, the stages' finish times. They all came into Monte Carlo, and somebody had to sit down with an adding machine and work out the difference with the handicaps.

'I had no idea how important the Monte Carlo rally was, and I remember getting a telegram from the Prime Minister, and *Life Magazine* came over and did an article with me, and I thought I was a real superstar. It's funny now. I went up to get the prize from Princess Grace and Prince Rainier, and she shook my hand. I had

worked out what I was going to say to her, you know, "I'm from Ireland, and I know your name's Kelly, *blah blah*." But I didn't say a
bloody thing I was so dumbstruck. She was a good-looking bird, I'll
tell ya.'

Sunday Night at the Palladium was one of the biggest television
programmes in those days, and both Hopkirk and Liddon appeared
on the show with the Mini Cooper. It was international fame for
Paddy Hopkirk. Fame, though, by his own admission, perhaps got
to his head at that time.

'I must have got very cocky and ghastly. I apologise to anybody
who remembers me when I was like that. But *Sunday Night at the Palladium* was good fun. Millions of viewers, because there wasn't much
else on television, and Bruce Forsyth did it the year I won it.'

They were heady days for the talented Belfast driver. Success kept
coming. In 1966, the Minis were leading one, two, three in the
Monte Carlo Rally until they threw them out because of irregulari-
ties with the headbeams in the car to facilitate Citroën. It was a
scandalous decision. The regulations for the rally were sent to the
RAC in London well beforehand in order for British entries to con-
form to the specifications laid down by the French organisers, who
were becoming increasingly annoyed that the British cars were
outperforming the marques. The specifications were in French and
were translated and copies sent out to all leading manufacturers in
the UK. The regulations were later amended and, in a glaring over-
sight, the organisers failed to send the amended copy to the RAC.
The new amendments included the banning of halogen lights and
were not relayed to the British team or to the Rootes Team in particular. Thus, Hopkirk and the rest of the British entries who were
using the relatively new lighting systems were disqualified. Indeed, the amendments also affected Rosemary Smith, who had,
until the officials overturned the results, won the Ladies Cup. It
was a fiasco reflecting more upon the French organisers than on
the likes of the Rootes Team who ran the Minis and the Imps. Hopkirk and Smith were the moral victors but had victory snatched
from beyond their grasp by officialdom.

'That was awful, and it became an international incident; in fact, it gave the rally a lot more publicity for us losing rather than for Citroën winning. I remember being interviewed from Monte Carlo on television by Ludovic Kennedy. Here was I on a current-affairs programme! I was terrified I was going to say something wrong or incorrect. When we got back, we went to the Palladium again, Timo Mäkinen, Rauno and I were there, and Jimmy Tarbuck was the compère. They played 'Rule Britannia', and everybody stood up, and if there'd been a Frenchman in sight he'd have been garrotted.'

Undaunted, Hopkirk won the Acropolis Rally in 1967 and, in between, took his number of Circuit of Ireland wins to five with victory in 1965 and 1967 – in between attempting, in 1966, the London–Sydney 10,000 miles rally, taking the competitors across Europe into Turkey, Iran and Afghanistan, down to Bombay in India before being shipped across to Australia.

A trio of them set out from Crystal Palace in London with Hopkirk and Poole sharing the driving and the late Tony Nash as the navigator. They were squeezed into the BMC 1800, which was chosen as the entry for the Abingdon team. Not the quickest of cars compared to, say, the Mini, but its road-holding was good, and the bodywork was strong enough to complete the journey, helped by a Hydrolastic suspension.

All seemed to be going to plan when they arrived in Bombay lying in fourth place.

'P&O had been persuaded by the organisers to divert the ship *The Chusan* to Bombay (it didn't normally go there) to take these cars down, and they'd done a great job. But we were a long time on the boat, about eight days or something, and it was pretty boring really. So, when I got to Fremantle, some BBC2 cameraman stuck a camera in my face and said, "What do you think of it so far?" and I said it was "the best advertisement for air travel ever." P&O were absolutely furious. Luckily I wasn't working for them, because I'd have been sacked instantly.'

And how did the three, cooped up in a car, get on over 10,000 miles? Hopkirk said there wasn't a cross word between them.

'Well, I remember Alec brought a gun, a revolver. I think he got it from one of the Garda in Dublin who lent it to him. We had a gun because we were quite nervous in East Turkey as there were quite a lot of bandits around. But I don't think there was one cross word, and I mean that. We were a great team, and it was good fun, you know. I mean, we were in it to win, but we were even good friends with our competitors. Andrew Cowan, who won it, and his team . . . he's still a great friend of mine.

'Alec was terrific. He was not only a good driver, but he was a fantastic mechanic as well, and he was very helpful because sometimes it was a long time between service points, in Australia especially.'

Suddenly Hopkirk's professional career took a nosedive. Despite a second-placed finish on the 1969 Circuit of Ireland in the Mini, a change was coming, especially with the introduction of the Escort Mark 1, which, in its Mark 2 guise became the quintessential rally car. The Mini's days were, basically, coming to an end, and Hopkirk decided to call it a day on his pro career.

'The trouble was that they couldn't get the power through to the road, and the car didn't handle very well on 12-inch wheels. The Escort was a fantastic car, and Roger [Clarke] was a fantastic driver, and Porsches were coming up then too. Lord Stokes took over the BMC and closed the competition department, so I used it as an opportunity to get out because I was already married three years to Jenny. I just got out. I did get offered a drive by Lancia. Cesare Fiorio asked me to drive for Lancia, but I didn't know that I would be able to understand the culture, so I just used it as an opportunity to quit. I'd had enough. I'd fifteen years as a professional, which was very enjoyable, and I don't think rallying is everything in life. I wish I'd been a brain surgeon or maybe helped people more because rallying is a pretty selfish sport.

'But I made that decision at that time in my life, and people say, "Would you make that decision again?" and the answer is yes, because I thought I was making the right move at the time. I liked the glamour, and there was nice money as well – it wasn't anything like today, but it was quite good – but it was time to quit.'

Hopkirk concentrated thereafter on his business. He had an ongoing cartoon strip in the *Daily Mail* called 'Drive', with a caricature of himself and Jenny giving weekly driving tips, and in 1969 he helped form the Mill Accessory Group supplying car parts to the industry. It wasn't all plain sailing. In fact, one of their shops in Belfast was blown up by an IRA bomb. Paddy Hopkirk Limited came into being in the 1980s doing something similar to the Mill Accessory Group, and the combination of his driving and business acumen has given Hopkirk a pretty decent standard of living and a stunning farmhouse property near High Wycombe in the south of England.

Hopkirk, though, didn't completely retire from motor sport. He repeated the London–Sydney Marathon in 1977 with Michael Taylor and Aussie Bob Riley, where they finished fourth in a Citroën CX2400. Hopkirk won the RAC Golden 50 in 1982 in a Mini before trying, along with Alec Poole, the 1989 Pirelli Classic Marathon from London to Cortina d'Ampezzo in the Italian Alps. The pair finished a distant seventy-second that year, but in 1990, they astonished the rallying world by winning the event in a Cooper S.

'Alec built the car for that; it was wonderful. He got an old 1965 Mini and redid it, called it the Hopkirk 1. We amazed ourselves because we beat MGs driven by Stirling Moss and Ron Gammon, and it was dog eat dog, but it was good fun.'

Hopkirk also decided to have one more crack at the Monte Carlo Rally in 1994, competing in a Mini alongside Ron Crellin, a former partner at BMC. He was able to get his old reg, L33 EJB, for the event, in which they finished a creditable sixtieth overall on the thirtieth anniversary of his 1964 win.

'Funnily enough, we did quite well. I did lot of practising. I couldn't see in the dark the way I used to. Ron was very professional and used the old notes, and we just practised and practised. On the last night, the fan belt gave up, and we lost our lights and water pump. But when we got to Monte Carlo, they made a real fuss of us and the Mini.

'Prince Rainier wasn't getting up to shake anybody's hands. They brought us up quite early, although we hadn't won anything as such, and he got up and gave Ron and I a gold watch each, and I said to him, "Does that mean you definitely don't want to see us back again, like the retirement gold watch?"'

Hopkirk's one real regret in life is that he couldn't work on *The Italian Job*, the movie, which, along with Hopkirk's win in the 1964 Monte Carlo Rally, made the Mini as famous as it is today.

'We were always very annoyed because when Michael Caine made the original *Italian Job*, we were going to be the stunt drivers, but because we weren't members of the equity union, we weren't allowed to do it.'

Nevertheless, Hopkirk still talks affectionately about the car that brought him so much success.

'It caught the imagination. Alec Issigonis designed the Mini as a district nurse's car, but when you drove up to the big house, the big mansion, there were two Minis there – there was a Mini and probably a Cooper S. One belonged to the lord of the manor and the other belonged to the cook. It was sort of a classless car, and when we won the Monte Carlo in 1964 in the Mini, it took off.'

Hopkirk was inducted into the Irish Sports Hall of Fame in 2005, his name alongside George Best and Olympic champion Mary Peters. Alec Poole made the Motorsport Ireland Hall of Fame, but Hopkirk, having run on an RAC licence, is not eligible to be inducted.

7

John Watson

ohn Marshall 'Wattie' Watson remains Ireland's top Formula 1 driver, winning five grands prix, one with the Roger Penske Team (their only Formula 1 win) and four with McLaren. He very nearly landed the ultimate prize in motor sport, the 1982 Formula 1 Drivers' Championship, only to be dropped by McLaren at the end of the 1983 season, ending his twelve-year career in grand-prix racing.

Watson exuded an air of aloofness, but beneath it all, it covered up an innate shyness. This, by his own admission, cost him drives and, perhaps, led to him being pushed around a bit in the Formula 1 paddock. In fact, three-times Formula 1 Champion Jackie Stewart said of the Irishman one time that he was 'too nice a chap to win races.'

But win he did, and, in his own quiet determined way, Watson has become one of the most respected Formula 1 drivers of his generation and a good one as well, as witnessed by his remarkable drive from twenty-second place on the grid to win the US Grand Prix in Detroit in 1983.

John Watson raced in a dangerous and exciting era that cost the lives of the likes of Canadian Gilles Villeneuve and his good friend Ronnie Peterson and almost ended the life of World Champion Niki

Lauda, who managed to somehow to survive his horror smash at the 1974 German Grand Prix at the old Nürburgring in Germany. Indeed, Watson was the man who cradled the Austrian in his arms after he had been pulled from his burning Ferrari.

Born in Belfast on 4 May 1946, he began his racing career in the late 1960s and raced in Formula Libre races as well as the now defunct Formula 2 championship, racing against many of those who would also ultimately become his rivals in Formula 1. Backed by decent sponsorship, he rose quickly to become a Formula 1 driver, and, by 1972, he was a professional in grand-prix racing. His Formula 1 career last twelve years until 1983 when McLaren opted for Alain Prost. (There was a one-off drive in 1985 for McLaren at Brands Hatch.) Watson then switched to racing sports cars, where he distinguished himself in the all-powerful Silk Cut Jaguar team, before calling it a day in 1990.

He then turned his attention to journalism. He's worked for Eurosport and Sky TV as a Formula 1 analyst and partners Ben Edwards as commentator for the A1 Grand Prix of Motorsport series. In addition, he runs the John Watson Performance Racing School at Silverstone.

There are only a handful of Irish drivers who have made it to Formula 1 and only two, Eddie Irvine and Watson, have ever won a Formula 1 race.

'I grew up in Belfast, and when I was seven or eight we moved. My father and mother found a wonderful house on the shores of Belfast Lough which became the family home where I lived until 1970. In terms of the Troubles or sectarianism, I wasn't aware of them particularly. As I grew older, certainly, then you became more aware, but I think one thing that motor-racing did was that it transcended all that.

'I've had friends motor-racing both in the South and in the North. Gerry Kinane was a great racing driver and entered his own cars, prepared them along with Fred Smith, and they were based up in Beechmount Avenue, off the Falls Road. I spent half my time up there with Gerry and Fred and others talking about motor-racing. They would sometimes assist in car set-up or engine builds.

'We raced together, and we didn't think about it as being any-thing to do with religion or sectarianism. The first time I raced at Dunboyne, I realised what being a racing driver was all about. Re-ligion had nothing to do with it whatsoever. I think that is one of the advantages that sport brings to communities. It cuts through all that rubbish.'

John Watson's father, Marshall Watson, is credited with having won the first saloon-car race to be held in Ireland, driving a Citroën Light 15, and was successful in the motor trade in Belfast. He subse-quently bankrolled his son's racing up to Formula 2, in which the young Watson competed for three years in both Lotus and Brabham cars purchased by his father.

He raced in various categories in Ireland in the late 1960s and early 1970s and won the now famous Leinster Trophy twice in 1966 and 1971. The trophy has been won by the likes of Mike Hawthorn in the past, and Watson took the first of his two wins at Dunboyne in County Meath when he raced in a Crosslé. His second win in 1971 was at Mondello Park in Kildare in a Formula 2 Brabham.

'When I started racing, Formula Ford hadn't even been invented. Karts, which kids start in today, were called go-carts, and they were sort of fun things. When I started, I raced in an Austin Healey Sprite, which was my road car and had been tuned up to become a race car. After that, I eventually got into single-seaters, but there was no infra-structure in motor sport anywhere in the world as we have today.

'When Formula Ford became properly structured in the middle or late 1960s, there started to be a proper stepping stone for a young driver to follow. The career path in my day would have been For-mula 3, Formula 2 and Formula 1. I bypassed Formula 3 and went into Formula 2, and that was a big advantage. I think one of the great shames of modern motor-racing is that there is no equivalent of Formula 2 today.'

With his father's backing, Watson was one of the dominant driv-ers on the Irish scene, competing and winning in Formula Libre races. By the late 1960s, John Watson felt he needed to move abroad, leav-ing Ireland to step up his career. He had raced a number of times in the UK, by his own admission 'for fun' and 'during holiday periods', but he persuaded his father to back him in his first real championship season in European Formula 2 in 1970.

The European Formula 2 Championship was introduced in 1967 when Belgian Jacky Ickx, driving a French-built Matra MS5, won the inaugural series, and it was a championship that saw many drivers take part in both Formula 2 and Formula 1 throughout the early seasons with the likes of Clay Regazzoni, Ronnie Peterson and Mike Hailwood all winning the Formula 2 series from 1970 to 1972, the years in which Watson also took part.

'In 1969, I persuaded my family to support my racing more. A Formula 2 Brabham was acquired in 1969 for the 1970 season, and I started out in international Formula 2. We went to some proper race tracks like Barcelona, the old Nürburgring, even Zolder in Belgium, as well as going to Thruxton for the opening round. Gerry Kinane had acquired two Lotus 48s, and he took one car for me and one car for John Pollock to take part in that event, the opening Formula 2 race of the 1970 season. I had had a cracking race in the final, but sadly I went off and damaged the car, but that actually was the moment that I realised I had enough ability to be able to race at a level against established and named drivers.'

However, Watson didn't go through the 1970 season unscathed. He had a very big accident at Rouen in France when a rear tyre, which had been deflating, separated from the rim in a flat-out right-hand corner at about 140 miles an hour. The car bounced off the barrier like a ping-pong ball and resulted in Watson fracturing an ankle and breaking a leg and arm – almost costing him his life. It ended his 1970 season but not his love of motor-racing.

'I suppose the fear that my family had was that that accident was a warning sign. Nonetheless, I wanted to continue, and we rebuilt the car for 1971 and carried out a full season. But the car was effectively a year old by that time, and racing against a factory March team with Ronnie Peterson and Niki Lauda, as well as the factory Brabhams, was quite difficult. We weren't competitive at the front. We ran quite strong in midfield, but that was about it. At the end of 1971, the realisation was that my family were not able to continue; with new engines and new cars, costs were escalating, and there's only so much a family can do, and it looked like the dream was over.'

It was beginning to look as if Watson would not get a drive in Formula 2 in 1972, and by May of that year, he was still without a seat. But just when it seemed that he might have to sit out that year, he got a call from a New Zealand team owner, Allan McCall, who had built his own Formula 2 team and a car called a Tui, named after a New Zealand bird. McCall had also worked as a mechanic for the great Jim Clark and for the McLaren Formula 1 team.

After racing in Formula 3, McCall entered Formula 2 in 1972 with the Leda-Tui AM29, but they sadly lost one of their drivers, Bert Hawthorne. Hawthorne, who was born in Northern Ireland but who had immigrated to New Zealand at an early age was killed in a race in Hockenheim earlier in the year, and McCall turned to Watson to partner English driver Dave Morgan. The 1972 season proved to be something of an up-and-down period for the Tui team, but there were some bright moments as Morgan put the car on pole position at Albi in the south of France, and Watson took fifth at Rouen, the scene of his big accident two years before.

McCall was to work with Watson again when he managed the Hexagon Brabham Formula 1 team.

With three years in Formula 2 behind him, Watson made the step up to Formula 1 in 1973, but he only managed to take in two races that year, making his championship debut in the British Grand Prix at Silverstone where he drove a Brabham BT37, but he ran out of fuel mid-race, and in his only other race that year, he retired from the US Grand Prix at Watkins Glen.

It was another year blighted by a bad accident.

'I was driving for Bernie Ecclestone, who had acquired Brabham at the end of 1972. I'd had a strong end to that season in Formula 2 and signed up to drive for Bernie and also signed up to drive for the Gulf Sports team with Mike Hailwood.

'At the start of 1973, at the Race of Champions at Brands Hatch, I was in the BT42, a totally revolutionary car by Formula 1 standards – the first car designed by Gordon Murray, probably one of the most innovative designers in Formula 1. In the race, I had a sticking throttle, and I thought, well, I'll get by. But coming into Stirlings, it didn't fully close, and it went off the track and hit the barrier. The front of the car wasn't actually quite as strong as it maybe ought to have been, and it turned through 90 degrees and so did my right leg.

'I had a compound fracture, which, again, was a major setback and meant that I missed half the season. I made a comeback just prior to Le Mans with the Gulf Mirage Team and then had my first Formula 1 World Championship Grand Prix in 1973 at Silverstone in the predecessor to the BT42, the BT37, and that was entered by a young guy named Paul Michaels, who owned a business called Hexagon at Highgate.

'The high point of that race was that I had the sixth quickest race lap, whereas in qualifying, we were nowhere. But it fired up Paul, and it made him realise he wanted to be a Formula 1 entrant, and it allowed me to get a drive in Formula 1.

'At the end of the year, Bernie generously ran his third car in the US Grand Prix at Watkins Glen for me, and it led to Paul acquiring the ex-factory BT42s, and we set off on our World Championship crusade in Argentina in January 1974.'

The team, initially named John Goldie Racing with Hexagon, had one season in Formula 1 and managed to see out the entire 1974 championship with Watson their only driver. It was one of the better midfield teams, even though they had outdated customer Brabhams, and Watson finished in the points for the first time ever when he was sixth in Monaco, fourth in Austria and fifth in the USA, giving him and the team six championship points.

Goldie Racing folded in 1975, and Watson, having previously driven in a few Formula 2 races for former World Motorbike and Grand Prix Champion John Surtees, joined his Formula 1 outfit for the 1975 season. He didn't pick up any points but did get a second place in the non-championship Race of Champions and a fourth in the International Trophy.

Overall, it was a frustrating season for Wattie. The Surtees-Ford was unreliable and underfunded, and Watson saw its demise coming. He drove one race for Lotus before Surtees called a halt to their 1975 season after the Austrian Grand Prix, leaving Watson without a drive. He missed out on the Italian Grand Prix but did at least get another seat, this time with the Penske team at Watkins Glen, where he finished ninth and was offered a contract for the 1976 season.

American Roger Penske, who was to become one of the real powerhouses behind IndyCar Racing in the USA, entered Formula 1 in 1974 and had originally sponsored the second McLaren in the 1971 Canadian and US Grand Prix, backing Mark Donohue.

Donohue, also from the USA, took part in two races in 1974 and stayed with the team in 1975 as Penske had its first full season in Formula 1. However, Donohue crashed and died while practising for the Austrian Grand Prix in Zeltweg in August 1975. His death saw John Watson race for Penske as his replacement.

Watson's first full season for Penske, in 1976, proved to be a fruitful one and included his first visits to the podium when taking third-placed finishes on consecutive race weekends in France and Britain.

There was also a seventh-placed finish in the following German race at the Nürburgring, when Niki Lauda crashed at the fast right-hander at Bergwerk. It bounded his Ferrari, now in flames, across the track, and it took the bravery of Brett Lunger and Harald Ertl to pull Lauda out of his burning car. Watson stopped at the scene a short time after. Thankfully, Lauda survived, and in the following race, Watson earned Penske their first, and only, grand-prix win at the Austrian Grand Prix at Österreichring on 15 August.

'What I remember of 1976 was the summer, a fantastic summer. Ironically, it was the Austrian Grand Prix, where one year earlier Mark Donohue was killed in a Sunday morning warm-up, which was my first grand-prix win. Actually, the reality was that throughout that grand prix I had the realisation that I was going to win this thing, but nothing felt any different. I didn't seem to do anything different in the car. Obviously, the car was performing well, and I was doing a good job, but not any better than I might have done in other races or on other occasions.

'I took the chequered flag . . . but I thought, where's the eureka, that sort of mystical emotion – it just wasn't there.'

The win cost him his beard, which he promised Penske he would shave off after the team's first win.

'Roger Penske's team were very clean-cut, a bit like McLaren would be today. I had a beard at that time, and I could tell that Roger would have liked me to shave it off, but he couldn't quite bring himself to do it. During the negotiations, I brought the subject up, and I said, "Listen, Roger, I know you are probably not terribly happy about the beard, but that's me, that's what I am. But if we win our first grand prix, I'll shave it off."

'We won the Grand Prix, flew back to England, and on Sunday night got into the hotel, and I exposed myself, my face, for the first time, I think, in about eight years, to natural light, and because 1976 was such a cracking summer, my face was quite brown but, of course, the bit under the beard was lily white, almost nipple pink.'

Although the first high point of Watson's Formula 1 career was 1976 and winning his first grand prix, in the remaining five races, he only managed a single point, that in the USA, because James Hunt won the title in a dramatic finale in Fuji in Japan, claiming third place in the wet for McLaren to give the Englishman his only championship success.

'In all respects, Niki Lauda would have been World Champion by a country mile, but his accident at the Nürburgring precluded him from a number of grands prix, and he made an extremely courageous and heroic return at Monza.

'James ought to, by rights, have had more points up to that accident in Nürburgring, but for a variety of reasons he found himself running a long way behind Niki. But James saw the opportunity [after the accident in Germany]. He had a very competitive car; it suited him. He had a team that enjoyed the sort of air that James brought to the team. He got his head down and did a fantastic job.

'He won that race at Nürburgring, but we went to Austria, and I won it, which was a big setback for James. He was upset that I would have deemed to take away maximum points from him. I remember ringing up Niki after the Austrian race, and he was delighted I had beaten James.'

But Hunt wasn't to be denied. He won three of the next four races, while Lauda, who incredibly only missed two grands prix after Germany, made a remarkable return to finish fourth in Italy and third in the USA to set up that grandstand finish in Japan.

'That day in Japan, James drove with total commitment and was very positive, very strong mentally. It was a tragedy for Niki because it was run in, virtually, flood conditions; it was appalling. He had a major problem with a tear duct in one of his eyes, and in the very cold damp conditions, his eye was flooding, and, frankly, after an accident like he'd had at Nürburgring, he wasn't about to toss it off into the barriers, and he retired. He took a gamble, knowing that James needed to finish third or higher to win the Championship, which he did.'

Watson himself spun off in Japan, and that ended his relationship with Penske, who decided to pack up Formula 1 and instead concentrate on racing in the USA.

'Sadly, Roger was committed to motor-racing in three forms: IndyCar, NASCAR and Formula. At the same time, he was in the process of building up his business empire, and he felt that he couldn't continue. On top of which, Formula 1 was going through a period of revolution where we were just about at the beginning of the period of ground effects, and budgets were going to go up yet again. The idea of running a single car was becoming less attractive. Running a two-car team was going to be the way to go, and I remember I got a call from Roger at about 1 o'clock in the morning, and I never heard a man's voice so broken as Roger's was, to say that he had decided to wind the team down, and he wouldn't continue in 1977.'

Watson was, once again, left without a drive, and virtually every seat had been filled by that stage. He felt he was left with very little choice, but the immediate point of contact was Bernie Ecclestone, with whom he had started his Formula 1 career. Carlos Reutemann had one of his many head throws and had left in a fit of pique to go to Ferrari, leaving the seat vacant.

Ecclestone had the late Brazilian Carlos Pace as one driver, and they were in negotiation with Clay Regazzoni to drive the second car. However, within the space of twenty-four hours, from losing a drive in a team in which he was extremely happy, Watson was back with Bernie in the Martini Brabham Alfa Romeo Team, and poor Regazzoni arrived at Heathrow airport thirty-six hours later to find out that the seat he had expected to sign for had gone to Watson.

Watson stayed with Brabham for the next two years. He picked up nine points in 1977 and took his first-ever pole position at the Monaco Grand Prix but subsequently retired from the race. He should really have won the French round at Dijon, but a fuel problem let him down on the last lap, and he finished second to the Lotus of Mario Andretti.

The year 1978 was to prove more productive. He was joined at Brabham by Lauda and managed three podium finishes in South Africa, Britain and Italy, where Brabham had a one-two with Lauda beating Watson to the line by just over a second. Watson went on to claim twenty-five championship points, helping him to sixth in the drivers' standings, and the pair combined to give Brabham second place in the constructors' rankings.

But the long shadow of death continued to haunt Formula 1. Welshman Tom Pryce had died in South Africa when his Shadow ran over a marshal, who also lost his life, and later in 1978, Watson's good friend Ronnie Peterson died hours after a pile-up involving his JPS Lotus at the Italian Grand Prix at Monza.

The race was started too early as some of the cars on the back of the grid were still getting into position. At the first chicane, Riccardo Patrese's Arrows hit Hunt's McLaren, and it caused carnage, which led to a massive fireball engulfing Peterson's car. The Swede had multiple leg injuries, and it took some time to get him medical attention. Italian police even denied Formula 1 doctor Professor Sid Watkins access to the scene at one point. The delay was fatal, and during the night in the Niguarda hospital in Milan, bone marrow seeped into Peterson's bloodstream through the many fractures in his legs, and he went into full renal failure, dying a short time later of a lethal brain embolism.

Peterson was in his last year at Lotus and had held contract talks with McLaren with a view to racing with them the following season. Watson, in his second year with Brabham, was devastated at his friend's demise but found that Peterson's death led to *him* signing with McLaren instead for the 1979 season.

'Again, I was the beneficiary of somebody else's tragedy. At Monza, Ronnie had that major accident, and, within an hour of so of the race finishing, I was having discussions with McLaren about a possibility of driving for the team because it was apparent at that stage that Ronnie's injuries were quite severe and he certainly wasn't going to be in a position to drive, certainly in the early part of 1979.

'Hours later, the news came through that Ronnie had died. It was appalling, one of the biggest shocks of my life, because we were friends – there was a group of drivers who were friends. Ronnie was amongst those. He was a genuinely nice guy, no sides to him, just a racer through and through.'

Formula 1 was a world unto itself in those days. Drivers raced against each other, but, more often than not, they also hung out together, and there was a set that included the likes of Watson and Peterson who wined and dined not only themselves but their wives and girlfriends as well.

Motor-racing, a dangerous sport, was also glamorous, and the best-looking women always attended grands prix. There was never a shortage of ladies for Formula 1 racers.

Watson, who at one stage had a relationship with Jochen Rindt's widow Nina, had befriended Peterson's wife Barbro Edwardsson, a top model, whom the Swede had married in 1975, and, after Ronnie's death, they became an item.

Barbro and John moved in together and also helped to raise Ronnie's daughter Nina-Louise, who was also born in 1975. They were due to get married in 1981, but it fell through, even though the trio continued to live together. She never really got over Ronnie's death, and their house was a shrine to her late husband, despite Watson also living there. Barbro suffered major depression in her latter years, and, tragically, on Saturday 19 December 1987, Watson, having broken down a bathroom door, found her dead in the bathtub, having taken her own life. She was just forty years of age.

Nina-Louise and John Watson attended Barbro's funeral in Örebro in Sweden, where she was buried with her late husband, and their daughter, now aged twelve, stayed in Örebro with her grandmother and grandfather, apparently against Watson's wishes, before she eventually moved in with her uncle Tommy.

There were even more repercussions from Peterson's accident and subsequent death. James Hunt, who had helped to pull the Lotus driver from his burning car, was also badly affected. It's been said that it led to his retirement in 1979 on grounds of 'self-preservation' and may have helped to contribute to the many years of depression that followed for the ex-World Champion before his untimely death in 1993 aged just forty-five.

After Peterson's death, Watson failed to finish the last two races for Brabham in Canada and in the USA, and in 1979, he moved to McLaren, where he was to spend the next five years. It started well for the Watson–McLaren pairing, and, in the opening race of the 1979 season, Wattie, partnered by Frenchman Patrick Tambay, was third in the Argentinean Grand Prix in the McLaren-Ford. But it was a car he didn't like, and two fourth-placed finishes at Monaco and Britain gave him a total of fifteen championship points and ninth in the drivers' standings. Tambay fared worse, not able to pick a solitary point all season.

'McLaren, who had a reputation of building outstanding grand-prix cars, were building their version of what was a Lotus 79, a ground-effect single-seater, and what a disappointment it was; frankly, I think, one of the worst grand-prix cars ever made by any team, and I don't know how McLaren ever allowed themselves to build such a bad car. It didn't have the level of aerodynamic efficiency of the teams around us, and, eventually, the car that stole a march on everybody mechanically was the introduction of the new Williams. It was the 007 car, which was a Lotus 79 built properly with a rigid chassis and very good aerodynamics. It was light, nimble and a fantastic little car.

'As a consequence of that, we then had a revision: a McLaren M29, which came out for the British Grand Prix and which was our version of the Williams – but still it hung to the tried and tested philosophies of McLaren. They didn't understand, at that point, what aerodynamics were all about. As an example of it, we had aluminium underbodies for rigidity and lightness, whereas Williams had carbon-fibre underbodies, which were much more sophisticated and had much more down force.

'In fact, it wasn't until 1980 that we got round to making carbon-fibre floors for our cars, and it was really only when John Barnard and Ron Dennis became a part of McLaren and, ultimately, became the owners that they started to move forward with the introduction of the MP1, which was the first full carbon-fibre chassis Formula 1 car as well as being the first one to win a grand prix – Silverstone in 1981.'

After the 1980 season, which produced a return of just six points for Watson, courtesy of fourth-placed finishes at the US West and Canadian Grand Prix, 1981 saw a turnaround in fortunes for driver and team. While team-mate Andrea de Cesaris returned just a solitary point, Watson picked up twenty-seven. The campaign had started poorly enough, but by mid-season he was right in the thick of the action: third in Monaco, second in France, and the second win of his career came at the British Grand Prix at Silverstone.

It was a tough race and a brilliant drive by Watson. Starting fifth on the grid after qualifying, he slipped to as low as tenth at one stage after an engine stall, having just missed the collision between Gilles Villeneuve and Alan Jones. But he gained places hand over fist after that, and on Lap 17 he was suddenly second when the engine of Alain Prost's Renault blew.

At one stage, it seemed as if Watson was destined for a creditable second, but Prost's team-mate René Arnoux, who was on the way to victory, slowed over the final laps with engine problems, and Watson roared past to win in front of an ecstatic Silverstone crowd.

'In terms, I suppose, of pure emotion, winning at Silverstone in 1981 has got to be the high point, simply because it was an unexpected victory. Early in the race, Villeneuve lost it and spun the Ferrari in a cloud of smoke and was hit by Jones. I was just behind but managed to avoid hitting anybody. The engine had stalled because I hit the brakes so hard, but I managed to put the fuel pump back on again, put it into gear, bump started and off I went.

'As the race unfolded, it seemed that day that something was shining on me, and we picked up speed, got past people, and others had problems. Both Renaults struggled, and I found myself in the lead at the British Grand Prix and took the chequered flag.

'The high point, in a way, apart from the obvious emotions, was that my family were there in the grandstand at Copse Corner. It was also the first grand-prix victory for a carbon-fibre car and for the really newly constituted McLaren team. In those days, you did a lap of honour on the back of a flat-bed truck, and there'd be a crowd invasion. British crowds are, by and large, very reserved. They applaud, but they don't have an outpouring of emotion as, maybe, Italians or other Europeans might do, but as we exited Copse, there were people on the track applauding, cheering and waving flags.

'In later years, you saw it with others like Nigel Mansell and Damon Hill, and, to some degree, you got a bit of a jingoistic element going, a bit like with football crowds when they expect a team to win. I felt what I got was totally spontaneous, totally natural, and, because of that, it remains in my emotions as being the high point of my grand-prix career.'

Watson came close to another win later in the year when he came second to Jacques Laffite's Ligier in Montreal.

For 1982, de Cesaris was dropped, and Watson was joined for a second time by Lauda. The Austrian had retired in practice at the 1979 Canadian Grand Prix and had set up Lauda Air. But he ran into financial difficulties and returned to the cockpit of a Formula 1 car in the Marlboro McLaren and set about trying to prove that he still had something to give to the sport.

Prost won the opening two races for Renault in 1982, while Lauda won the third one for McLaren. Neither contested the San Marino race due to a dispute between the non-works teams and the world governing body, and Watson then won the next race in Belgium, a race that saw the death of Gilles Villeneuve when his Ferrari crashed spectacularly in qualifying.

'It was one of those races; somebody had to win the race. I took the nine points and walked away comfortable with that, but motor-racing had lost somebody who has become iconic in many ways. Gilles Villeneuve was an outrageous talent who was probably squandered in many respects by Ferrari because he needed some element of not, say, control, but maybe more guidance. He was a bit like a petulant child, an out-of-control hyperactive child. Winning a World Championship was very much within his grasp, but I felt he needed to do that in a team outside of Ferrari because they didn't capitalise on his potential.

'Ultimately, in 1982, the rivalry between Didier Pironi [Villeneuve's team-mate], who was very ambitious and, maybe, two-faced, didn't help.'

Pironi and Villeneuve were one and two in San Marino and were advised to slow down to conserve fuel by the Ferrari team. Villeneuve was leading and had expected to stay there, but the Frenchman had other ideas and passed the leader on the last lap, breaking what the Canadian had perceived to be a gentleman's agreement. Villeneuve was furious and vowed not to speak to Pironi again. His words were prophetic, as he was dead by the next race at Zolder.

'The agreement that they had for the Grand Prix at Imola, which was not supported by the non-factory teams, set a poison in Gilles's mind, and in the qualifying in Belgium, Pironi had established provisional pole position, and Gilles decided in a minute before the session finished that he was going to go back out and take pole away from Pironi to show who was the quickest driver.

The Dirty Dozen

'He, I felt, was so blinkered when he came across Jochen Mass, who was coming in on his in-lap. Mass thought he was doing the right thing by moving from the left, which is the racing line, to the right to give room. He misjudged the closing speed, but I think the bigger misjudgement was on the part of Gilles who went around the outside of Jochen so as not impede his lap. He wasn't prepared to give up the lap; he took a calculated risk, which, I think in retrospect, certainly was a very bad calculation.

'He went over the back of Jochen's car, cartwheeled, barrel-rolled and was flung out of the car and landed up on the catch fencing some 50 or 60 feet away. I was maybe the third or fourth car around after the accident, got out of my car, walked across and saw his body lying there without a helmet on, looked in his eyes, and there was no life. Got back in my car, was pushed out, came back to the pits and said that Gilles Villeneuve was dead.

Another win followed Watson's victory on that saddest of weekends in Belgium. Watson took the chequered flag at the US West Grand Prix in Detroit, having started seventeenth on the grid, and suddenly he was in contention for the World Championship. But retirements in Britain, France and Germany cost him his title aspirations, and, despite a second-placed finish in the final race in Canada, the crown went to the Williams of Keke Rosberg.

Watson finished the year just five points behind Rosberg and tied for second with Peroni but was officially third on countback.

Lauda and Watson were again paired for the 1983 season, and it was to prove Wattie's last full season in grand-prix racing. He felt that he had shown the team what he was capable of and demanded a salary of $1.3 million, which Ron Dennis was not prepared to pay. Watson held out and, instead, ran on a race-by-race basis. He won his fifth and final race, again in the USA, when he took the spoils in Long Beach, California. Starting from twenty-second and twenty-third on the grid, the McLarens ended up, remarkably, first and second.

'You could say that Niki and I were fairly surprised to come first and second but not as half as surprised as the team was when we got back to the pit lane. They could barely bring themselves to say

"Congratulations, well done, what a fantastic drive." They were sometimes a little bit disingenuous.'

Watson finished seventh in the 1983 Formula 1 World Championship. His best results after that amazing win in California were two third places in the US East Grand Prix in Detroit and at Zandvoort, the seaside track that hosted the Dutch round of the championship.

The year ended in frustration when he was disqualified at the South African race at Kyalami when he was forced to use the spare McLaren. Instead of starting from the back of the grid, Watson put his car into its original position and was black-flagged, ending his race.

He didn't know it then, but things were about to get worse. Alain Prost, who had partnered Watson in 1980 at McLaren, had lost the World Championship that day in Kyalami when his Renault failed to finish. Brazilian Nelson Piquet won the series for Braham with *his* third-placed finish. Prost was under all sorts of pressure at the French team. He was blamed by the French media for helping to remove René Arnoux from Renault, and there were allegations of an affair with a wife of one of their senior-management team. When 'the Professor' failed to win the title in 1983, the media heaped scorn upon the little Frenchman, and he was sacked.

That decision was to have repercussions for Watson, who ultimately found himself without a drive as Prost became Lauda's team-mate at McLaren for the 1984 season.

'Yeah, the season in 1983 ended after the South African Grand Prix, and we were all heading back up to Europe. The team said, "Well, I suppose we'd better discuss what we do with you in 1984." We got back to Europe on the Monday morning because it was a Saturday race in South Africa in those days, and I got a call from Niki saying that he had heard that Prost had signed a contract to drive for McLaren.

'Prost had gone back to Paris, having lost the World Championship, and was summarily fired. He had contacted Marlboro because they were sponsoring McLaren and Ferrari. The situation was totally closed at Ferrari, but they said, "We've got a seat at McLaren. Niki's under contract, John's contract is up, so we'll want to talk to you".'

Watson was out but was offered the chance to go to the JPS Lotus team. He turned down the opportunity, apparently because he didn't want Barbro to see him racing for the same team that ran her late husband.

'I didn't particularly want to leave McLaren, and I'd no desire at the end of 1983 to find myself in the situation that I did. Had negotiations opened up at an earlier date, it may not have arisen. The Prost situation was purely circumstantial. Had he won the World Championship, he wouldn't have been fired. I can't put it down to anything other than the team hadn't or weren't prepared to negotiate or discuss the 1984 season any earlier for whatever reason. They were just being awkward, and there was arrogance on their side as much a lack of commerciality on my side.'

Watson also discovered that Lotus made a play for him because they were not anxious to sign Nigel Mansell who was pushing to get into the British team.

'I found myself effectively being replaced [at McLaren], having done the same to Clay Regazzoni some years earlier. There were discussions with Lotus, but, for a variety of reasons, they didn't actually want me; they just wanted anybody other than Mansell. Peter Warr, who was the Team Principal at that stage, was not a Nigel fan, and he had not established himself in the way that he would do in later years. So I took a deep breath and said, "Thanks but no thanks," which many people took to mean that I had actually retired, which wasn't the case, but that was their view.

'That led on to becoming involved with the Rothmans Porsche Team in a variety of events, then BMW in 1986 in the IMSA [International Motor Sports Association] Championship in the USA. I came back to Europe with Jaguar in 1987 and 1988, then in 1989 and 1990 I was doing a number of races for Toyota by which time I thought, Well, I'm not going to get the kind of drives I would like. Also, sports-car racing, as enjoyable as it is, wasn't my sort of thing. I like Formula 1, and I like single-seater racing. I didn't like particularly to share a car, and I don't like long-distance races. The Le Mans twenty-four hours to me is twenty-two hours too long.'

Watson did have one more Formula 1 drive during those years when he competed in sports cars, stepping in for Lauda at McLaren at the 1985 European Grand Prix at Brands Hatch, in which he finished a fine seventh.

By the end of the 1990 season, Watson finally retired from motor-racing. He had some decent results during his years in world sports-car racing, including winning in 1984 in Fuji with Stefan Bellof as his team-mate, and had three victories with Jan Lammers in the 1986 season in their Jaguar XJR-8. The pair finished runners-up to Brazilian Raul Boesel who raced in another XJR-8.

There was one more significant drive for John Watson when, in 1990, he became the first man to drive a Jordan Formula 1 car in its shakedown at Silverstone prior to its press unveiling.

'Being at Silverstone through the late 1980s and going into the local greasy-spoon café at the circuit, Eddie would be in there with his team having lunch, and we started a friendship. Eddie had committed himself to entering Formula 1 as a team owner, and he generously offered to allow me to be the first person to drive the car. The car was also designed by Gary Anderson, who I'd known from when he came into Formula 1 in 1973 at Brabham. He had worked in other areas and designed other cars, but this was his first Formula 1 car, and it was fantastic. I think it's the best Jordan ever.'

Unfortunately, E.J. and Wattie fell out a number of years ago, allegedly over one shopping the other to the British Racing Drivers Club over, of all things, a dodgy golf handicap.

'That's it: no more wheels, no more cars, no more driving,' is a quote attributed to Watson when his career came to an end, and he turned his attention to broadcasting and running the John Watson Performance Driving Centre at Silverstone.

He was part of the Eurosport commentary team in the 1990s for their coverage of Formula 1 and has also worked with ESPN in the USA and with Sky TV on both Formula 1 and the A1 Grand Prix series. He drove demonstration laps for the Team Ireland A1 outfit at Zandvoort in Holland in 2006.

'The broadcasting side is something I enjoy very much because I like to give a view of motor sport. I noticed in a monthly periodical that I've been called "notoriously opinionated". I think that's what experts are meant to do. You are meant to be provocative and controversial and not just to toe a party line.'

John Watson's Formula 1 career spanned twelve years and included 152 races, five wins, two pole positions and five fastest laps. He was also a race winner on the world sport-cars scene, but his real love and passion was for Formula 1. He was quick and tough but, perhaps, didn't have the force of personality or, indeed, the best cars to take him further and make him a world champion.

By his own admission, he should have won more races and been much more of a commanding figure on the Formula 1 grid.

'When I started in 1970, I was coming out of a community, and by that I mean Ireland, where there hadn't really been any great history of international motor-racing. There had been a number of drivers – and probably Desmond Titterington was the best known in the post-war era, along with the likes of Joe Flynn. They raced internationally, but they were, with the exception of Titterington, considered gentlemen racing drivers. I was setting off with a clear career path in mind of being a professional grand-prix driver, and I ended up racing against people for whom I had enormous respect and admiration.

'I remember one time seeing Graham Hill, for example, in 1972, carrying two churns of fuel down the paddock in a Formula 2 race, and I almost went up to him and said, "Graham, you shouldn't be doing that, you're a hero." So, maybe I had too much hero worship and too much respect for some of my competitors to feel that I was their equal or in some cases their better. Today's drivers look at reputations as being a target. There is no respect in motor sport today. I think maybe I was overly respectful of some of the people I raced with and maybe some of the team principals.

'You can imagine some of the negotiations that might take place today where you've got very sharp hard-headed businessmen and very astute bright young drivers. It's now a tough negotiation. There are some very sharp managers around, and by sharp I don't necessarily mean that they're dodgy, they just know the game. They know how much somebody is prepared to pay, and they know how much they can push for, and it works two ways.

'Eddie Jordan was a sharp negotiator, but on occasions he's paid too much for some people, and he's regretted it. Losing Michael Schumacher is probably the thing Eddie regrets most in his grand-prix career. The fact is that Eddie wasn't the master of that destiny because once Schumacher had done what he had done in Belgium, there was a move amongst the hierarchy in Formula 1 to get him out of there as quick as possible, because it was important for the future of Germany as an emerging Formula 1 nation with engine manufacturers as well as young drivers. It was too important for the sport to keep a talent like Michael Schumacher in a team like Jordan.'

John Watson lives in Oxford, England, and remains Ireland's top Formula 1 racer. He is surely destined at some point to be induced into the Motorsport Ireland Hall of Fame.

8

Billy Coleman

illstreet in County Cork is a small unassuming little town whose main claim to fame was hosting the 1993 Eurovision Song Contest. Ireland won again that year with Niamh Kavanagh's song 'In Your Eyes' topping the pan-European vote, and the event was reckoned to be a success for its organiser. The good people of Millstreet were up in arms before the contest when the BBC's Nicholas Witchell described the Green Glens Arena as a 'cow shed'. It was an off-the-cuff remark, but too many sensitive souls took exception. Millstreet's other claim to fame is its most famous citizen, Billy Coleman, born to parents Paddy and Peggy Coleman on 8 May 1947. Considered to be the best rally driver Ireland ever produced, he is the only Irishman to win both the British and Irish Rally Championships.

To the rallying fraternity, the Millstreet Maestro, as he was dubbed, is a god. Shy and introvert, Coleman had the common touch, and, rather like the late great Joey Dunlop, a man whom Coleman greatly admired, the Irish public took to him in their droves. To ask any rally enthusiast to name their number-one driver of the past fifty years, invariably one name will spring from their lips: Billy Coleman.

Born into both a farming and motor-trade background, Billy divided his time between the land and driving, always claiming that farming was his first passion despite the many rally victories he took in his illustrious career.

It was his ability to get the best out of any car he drove that brought him the adulation of the rallying public. The outward shyness belied a steeliness inside that decreed that the County Cork farmer would be a winner.

'At no point in my career did I give all my time to the driving. My interests were always split between my life on the land and the rally driving. I think to get to the very top in any sport, even at that time, you had to be totally dedicated. When you look at somebody like Roy Keane or, another fellow Corkman, the late Christy Ring, who was actually a friend of ours, those men were absolutely living for the game and they're totally professional. There wasn't a day that Christy would not practise hurling and try to hone his skills. I was never quite of that mindset, and I think it was much to the detriment of my career ultimately.'

But it was because he *didn't* adhere himself to what was expected that endeared himself to so many followers of rallying. He set his own rules and, as respected motor-sport journalist Sammy Hamill put it, 'He loved the driving but he hated the fuss.'

His father Paddy was in the motor trade near Millstreet and was the main Ford dealer in the area. Billy's brother John, who played Gaelic football for Cork and rugby for Munster, has kept the business going since his father's passing. It's now a Fiat dealership.

In his formative years, Billy attended Millstreet National School for his primary education before going to Rockwell College in Tipperary from 1960 to 1965, where he played rugby for the senior team in his last two years. The highlight, he says, was kicking two penalties in a senior game against Blackrock College to tie up the game at 6–6. After secondary school, he went to University College Cork (UCC) to do a B.Comm. in accountancy, but it was a career path he never followed.

Billy's first introduction to rallying came in 1966 at UCC when he attended the Munster Motorcycling and Car Club evenings in

Vernon Mount, becoming friendly with one Dan O'Sullivan, an engineering student. In fact, the first time he met O'Sullivan, the man who was ultimately to shape his rallying career, was when Coleman picked up his fellow Corkman thumbing a lift to one of those meetings. Not long after the chance encounter, O'Sullivan had the idea of entering a rally, getting Billy to drive, saying he would navigate. The fact that Billy's father owned a car dealership helped.

'Dan came up with the idea at a meeting one night. So, the next week, I turned up with a Ford Anglia, threw off the hubcaps and suddenly Dan and myself were rally-driving. My father was probably suspicious of what was going on at the beginning, but in fairness, once we got going, he was very supportive.'

There was almost instant success for the Coleman–O'Sullivan pairing.

'The first rally I won was in a Cortina GT back in 1968, the Circuit of Munster. We actually beat Rosemary Smith, who was a big name those days, and it was fairly big news in Munster that time. It was also the weekend of the college exams, and I suppose some of the professors were wondering what was going on when I was supposed to be studying.

'At that time, the great thing about motor sport was that if you had a bit of money – maybe a thousand or two – you could actually do a great deal with it. Nowadays, if you have serious intentions about trying to make a career out of it, you're talking hundreds if not hundreds of thousands, if not millions.'

In two years rallying the Anglia and the Cortina, Billy and Dan did numerous night-stage events, and their first Circuit of Ireland Rally came in 1967 where they 'just about finished,' according to Billy.

It was in the 1969 Benson and Hedges Circuit of Ireland that Billy really started to make his mark. His brother John found a crashed Mark 1 Escort (Reg. No. TIU 250), and they set about repairing the car for the event which started in Larne.

'That Ford Escort was a cheap, simple car with a great engine, and it would run for ever. Absolutely ideal for a young driver. If you crashed it, it was relatively easy and cheap to repair.'

The first problem for the Cork crew was that the 1969 Circuit was oversubscribed, and Billy travelled to Belfast to plead his case for entry. It didn't look likely that the Escort would start at all, but at the last minute, there was a withdrawal, and Billy and Dan were in. Up at the head of affairs were the Escort of Britain's Roger Clark and Ireland's Paddy Hopkirk in his Mini Cooper S, but Coleman made a stunning start and, at one point, had worked his way up to third.

'That was an amazing weekend, and, again, one keeps making the contrast with the present day. At the time, I think, we started at 120 [it was actually 115] and we really had no idea what was happening up at the head of the field. We were driving hard, and we assumed that we weren't in any prominent position in the rally.

'It had started in Larne, but it was actually only coming into Killarney on the Saturday evening when somebody said they had seen the noticeboard that said that we were in third place overall. We immediately assumed, Dan and I, that there had been a major mistake and it was probably 103 or something instead of 3, but, in fact, it turned out that it *was* our position, and I think in a rally of fifty or sixty stages, we had eight fastest times, so we had a really good run.'

Their ageing, tatty Escort was third for much of the five-day event, but their rally was to end in disappointment in Donegal.

'Clark was leading the rally from the great Paddy Hopkirk. Then there was ourselves, and, as far as I remember, there was a considerable gap to fourth place. We got as far as Donegal on the final night, and we were almost on the home straight. But the manifold broke on the car, and suddenly there was a huge amount of noise and fumes in the cockpit. I was able to cope with that, but I lost my head – through inexperience I suppose – and the car slid off the road. I got a warning first because the crowd pushed us back on, but a couple of miles farther on, there was a blind brow on the Glen Stage, and, to my great regret, we ended up in a bog, 10 feet down off the road. That was the end of it. It was a pity really because we should have been a very solid third. But it was great experience, and I think I learned my lesson about keeping one's head.'

Despite his non-finish, Coleman had done enough to attract some of the big-wigs at Ford.

'The Ford Motor Company had begun to give us a bit of help during the rally, an event my late colleague and friend Roger Clarke went on to win. Their rally manager for Ford in Britain was Bill Barnett. And I got a letter from Bill following the rally saying that he was coming to Ireland in the summer and he would like to talk to me as he thought I had considerable potential as a driver.'

Unfortunately for Barnett, it was Coleman's final year in college, and he had planned to go to the USA for a year.

'I wrote back to Bill Barnett and said that unfortunately I wasn't going to be there. I often regretted doing that, even though my year in America was something I'll always remember and it was really a special experience for me. But I lost my first big chance in the rally world by forgoing the meeting with Bill Barnett, and when I came back from the States a year later, I had to sort of re-establish myself, which took quite a long time.'

It didn't take *that* long: Billy came back to Ireland in 1970, and he won the Cork 20 rally for the first time in the Escort with a new co-driver, Noel Davin. They repeated the win in 1971 and completed the hat-trick in 1972, again with Davin, in a rear-engined Renault Alpine. Coleman's Escort was also second in Galway in 1971, and the Alpine was second in 1973 when he was partnered by Frank O'Donoghue.

There was no Irish rally championship at that stage, with clubs organising individual events. Nevertheless, the cream of world rallying came to Ireland in those years, including Clark, Hopkirk, Timo Mäkinen, Ari Vatanen, Russell Brookes and Per Eklund. Billy was amongst a host of top Irish drivers in those days, which included Cathal Curley, winner of a hat-trick of Donegal titles; Adrian Boyd, the first Irish driver to win the Manx Rally; and Coleman's cousin Ger Buckley, who won five Cork 20s and who was runner-up in the 1981 Irish Tarmac Rally series.

The first official Irish championship only came into being in 1978 when Britain's John Taylor won in an Escort RS 1800, but the

British Rally Championship was in full swing, and Billy decided to enter the 1974 series with Dan O'Sullivan navigating the early rounds in a newly acquired Escort RS 1600 (Reg. No. MEV 36J).

'The British Championship was extremely competitive at that time, and the Ford Escort was still really *the* car. There were a lot of them about in the hands of some very good drivers. The decision to go over there was against the advice of a lot of people, including my late father, because he thought that we would have no chance. Michael O'Carroll of RTÉ TV was a great supporter of ours, and he encouraged us to go. We had a team of lads who were based in Dan O'Sullivan's house in North London, and I had some help from my father and my brother at home and the mechanics in Millstreet.

'Evan Hughes and Steve Mills from Limerick were also based in Dan's house, and they were the hub of the team. There was tremendous morale for the whole year, and it was a unique experience, a memorable year.'

Billy wasn't joking about the unique experience. The house was full of spares, tyres and bits of engines, with the Escort in the garage at the back. O'Sullivan, Hughes and Mills lived in the house during the 1974 season, while Coleman went back to the farm in Millstreet between events. He had to have an address in the UK as well to get his British competition licence.

Coleman began his assault on the British Championship in early 1974 and was second in Wales to Marku Alen, won the Texaco Rally based in Ulster (with Peter Scott co-driving), finished second on the Jim Clark Stages in Scotland and lost out to Roger Clark by only one second on the Burmah Scottish Rally.

'The Burmah was in Argyllshire in Scotland, and the conditions were very bad. There had been heavy rain, even though it was the month of August. But I revel in those conditions, and, amazingly, we found ourselves in the lead. It was a rally we should have won, but on the longest stage, the bonnet opened, and we had to stop. We probably lost fifteen seconds or more, and that cost us.'

Billy was now leading the British Rally Championship, and Ford was impressed. The top man in Ford was Stuart Turner, who went on to become Head of Motor Sport Ford Europe, the man who called the shots in the rally and Formula 1 teams. He summoned Billy to a meeting after the Burmah Rally.

'I was called to a meeting with Stuart on the Monday morning after the Burmah, and he told me quite plainly that Roger [Clark] had been their main driver for a long time and he thought it was time for a younger driver to hit the scene. He was impressed with the driving in Scotland and the fact that we were leading the Championship, and he wanted to look at the following year. But it was not a good time to be Irish in England because, sadly, the Troubles in the North were in full spate, and it was a really difficult time. To their credit, all the mechanics we worked with in England were absolutely fair with us. We built up a lot of relationships and good friends over there, but it was not the ideal time for a rising young Irish sportsman.'

Billy went on to win the championship, helped by fourth-placed finishes on the Manx and a third place on the Lindisfarne, which ran many of its stages in the Kielder Forest in Northumberland. Billy also tackled the Firestone Rally in Spain, where he and O'Sullivan finished sixth.

The following year there was to be another assault on the British Championship. He was now a Ford works driver and was at the height of his career. That season, Billy also won his first Circuit of Ireland rally with Paul 'Felix' Phelan as his co-driver.

'The Circuit of Ireland was an absolutely tremendous challenge, and quite a few of the roads were gravel as well. There was a lot of night-driving, especially on the first day, and that really gruelling final night going into the fifth day. It was an absolutely huge event and unique, in my view. I have done rallies all around the world, but the Circuit of Ireland was a very special event, and it was for that reason that it attracted a lot of the world's top drivers over the years. You had to be a very complete driver. You had to be able to read the road, as there were no pace notes. You had to able to drive in the dark, which was probably a particular strength of mine, and I was often more competitive in the night stages. Sometimes, there was fog, and there were even years when we had snow on the

Circuit. It was a tremendous test, and sadly it's not there as a real circuit any more. I think it is a great loss to motor sport that it isn't.'

After the success of 1974, Billy narrowly lost out to Roger Clark in the race for the 1975 British Championship crown. He won the opening round in Yorkshire with England's John Davenport as his co-driver in the Escort run by Thomas Motors of Blackpool. He was also leading in Wales before mechanical problems put him out, and Clark's victory in Scotland set in train a sequence of results that helped to give the Englishman the title.

'I was very disappointed not to win the championship in 1975. Again, we were leading, and at one point we had quite a massive lead. But around September, Clark, who was now my team-mate, began snapping at our heels.

'The second-last round was the Lindisfarne, which was held in the Kielder Forest, one of the biggest forests in Europe and a tremendous challenge. It was tailor-made for my style of driving because there was very little service on the event. You went into that huge forest, and there was stage after stage with very little break in between. But once you got a momentum, you kept it going.

'That event also reflected something in my career. Very often, I didn't take people's advice, and several people, including my father, used to say to me that I wasn't hard enough on the car. The Cosworth engine which was in that Ford Escort was a phenomenal unit, and you could really rev the daylights out of it. But I had a habit of changing up just at peak power, which was at about 8,000 revs. So I put the theory to the test to see if the extra revs would do anything, and what a difference it made. In spite of the fact that we had this experimental four-speed gearbox, we had a string of fastest times until the gearbox failed.'

Going into the final round in 1975, the Lombard RAC Rally, Billy had to beat Roger to claim the title for a second time, but he finished sixth while his Ford team-mate was second – enough for the Englishman to take his fourth and final British crown.

'I did several RAC rallies, a tough event held in the forests of Britain. It went all over the UK, up to the middle of Scotland, took in

Wales and even the south-west of England. There was some jinx on me in that event. Practically every year something really strange happened. It was also a world rally, and I actually had an outside chance of winning it on more than one occasion if everything went right. But we seemed to be jinxed for some reason. In 1975, Clark and the great Timo Mäkinen were going hammer and tongs for the lead, and Dan O'Sullivan and myself were dicing with Stig Blomqvist for third place. I remember the late Henry Liddon, who actually I'd done a couple of rallies with, was Timo's co-driver, and he said to me up in Carlisle at the service before we went into Scotland, that if I played my cards right, I could end up winning, because he reckoned that the pace that Clark and Mäkinen were going that neither of them would probably finish.

'The next stage after that was in southern Scotland, and the Escort suddenly stopped. I think we were nearly fifteen minutes parked on the side of the road, and all that had happened was that a small electrical connection under the bonnet had come apart. We eventually finished sixth, and Roger finished a few places higher, and it was enough to give him the Championship.'

In 1976, Coleman concentrated on many of the Irish events in his Escort, and he took victories in Cork (his fourth), a second Circuit of Ireland crown and his first win in Galway. He did a couple of British rounds as well and was third on the Isle of Man and sixth on the RAC. His career was progressing very nicely, and the works Escort was becoming synonymous with Billy Coleman. The public had taken to the little Corkman, who saw that their hero could now take on and beat the best that world rallying could throw at him.

Suddenly there was a change for the 1977 season, and Billy ditched the Escort in favour of a strange-looking left-wheel drive Ferrari-V6-engined Lancia Stratos, rallying's first supercar.

'I'd done a fair stint in the Ford Escort and, maybe, I just felt like a change. The late Tony Pond had been driving the Stratos, and he had moved on to Vauxhalls. I got in touch with David Richards, and we did a deal with the Chequered Flag Group in London (run by Graham Warner, who was Founder and Managing Director). They were the garage to drive for that year. The Stratos was a small car with a mid-engined Ferrari and a very good suspension layout.'

Richards later became known on the world rally scene as the Chairman of Prodrive who supplied world rally cars. He acquired the television and commercial rights to the WRC in 2000 and was also a former team principal at BAR and Benetton in Formula 1. He remains one of Billy's closest friends.

'Theoretically, the Stratos should have been the ultimate. But in actual fact, for a lot of the events we were doing, I felt the wheel base was a bit short, and I really had limited success with the car. We ended up winning just a single event over the year, and that was in Donegal with Austin Fraser. I enjoyed driving it, and I came second in the Circuit of Ireland to Russell Brookes, driving with no clutch for probably half the rally.'

During that year, another opportunity came up. The Fiat works team had been struggling in the World Championship against the Fords with their Fiat 131 Abarth, especially on the gravel. They approached Chequered Flag in London with a view to running a works car in three or four rounds of the British Championship, and Coleman and Richards were given the drive. It was a works car which came from Italy complete with the works mechanics, and the duo helped to develop the Pirelli tyres.

'I think the best result we got was fourth in the Scottish rally but, typical of my career, later in that year the head man in Turin, Daniel Audetto [later to became Super Aguri's Managing Director in Formula 1], offered us a works car for the San Marino rally, which was one of the big events in the World Championship, and I actually turned down the drive on the basis that it was a very busy time on the farm.'

Billy dabbled in the European Championship in the Stratos in 1977. He finished fourth in the Ypres Rally in Belgium, but his association with the Stratos was over by the end of the 1978 season, the first official Irish Tarmac Rally Championship year. It was a frustrating season, bedevilled with car problems. He did have one final run in Galway in 1979, but that too was a non-finish, and he was more than happy to say goodbye to the Lancia.

The following year, Billy felt the need to launch an assault on the European Rally Championship, a tough year for his team on a very small budget.

'In 1979, we were back in a Ford Escort, which was an ex-works car with backing from Ford of Ireland. We had quite a decent run, and it took us all over Europe, Spain, Italy, Poland, Germany. We did a lot of events that year and finished third overall.

'The European Championship was won by a German driver by the name of Jochi Kleint, and he was driving a works Opel. He was following in the footsteps of the great Walter Röhrl, who'd won it the previous year. Every round you went to, there was a very strong opposition, and in the Italian rounds, the Italian works teams were there, and it was quite competitive. It was a long series, and third overall wasn't too bad really with a restricted budget.'

Billy Coleman was now the biggest name in Irish rallying. By 1980, he had racked up a British championship win, numerous Irish victories and that incredible third place in Europe. He started a new decade with a win in the West Cork Rally and then moved on to the Circuit of Ireland.

It was ironic that his Escort expired on that event not far from his farm in Millstreet, because Coleman suddenly backed out of the sport.

'Through my farming, I fell into very bad health around 1980, and I actually couldn't drive at all whether I wanted to or not. The other failing I had was that when the rallies were over, frequently I would just head off home and close the door on the car or take off, which was most unprofessional, to say the least, and very bad for my career as well. But you are what you are. You can change yourself up to a certain point, but it wasn't really my forte, the public-relations side of it.

'People look at me and say I should have been certified for doing things like that and turning down drives. This is where the lack of motivation came in. I see how difficult it is for young drivers nowadays to get even the smallest works drive, but I was near enough the top at that time, and I was turning down drives. It was really just a lack of motivation.'

During the early 1980s, he overcame his health problems and did only one major rally over the next three years when, in 1982 he drove an Escort to fifth on the Circuit of Ireland before heading back to the land of Millstreet.

It was near the end of 1983 that the second phase of Billy Coleman's career began.

'I suppose I must have got itchy feet again. Con Murphy, who was married to my first cousin, said to me that we might enter the Rally of the Lakes, which was in December. Another old friend of ours, Sydney Meeke, gave us Bertie Fisher's car, an Opel Ascona. So, Con and I went down and, surprisingly, we won.'

The car almost didn't make it to Killarney, and the story behind its late arrival has now reached legendary proportions.

'It was typical of my career. Again, it was a last-minute job. Apparently, when Sidney was crossing the Border, a bond had to be paid because it was a British registered car, and it was a considerable amount of money at the time [reportedly £10,000]. It was a Friday evening, and there were no banks open. So, lo and behold, another friend of mine, Paddy O'Callaghan, from Kanturk, had a couple of bank drafts in his pocket, and they had to be deposited in the Port of Cork City with some customs agent, and at about three o'clock in the morning, the car was released from the Border. There were a lot of those stories over the years, a lot of incidents like that.'

Incredibly, Billy only stepped into the Ascona for the first time when the car arrived on the Saturday morning. It passed scrutiny just before the off, and the Millstreet Maestro showed that he had lost none of the flair and skill which had so endeared him to the Irish public when he won the Rally of the Lakes.

Thus ended a year that saw Austin MacHale crowned as Irish Champion for the first time. Their paths were to cross spectacularly the following season.

By the start of the 1984 season, MacHale had worked out a deal with Opel Ireland to run an Opel Manta but found out to his horror that Billy was to be part of the team on the insistence of the Munster dealers. Austin, who was based in Rathcoole, was the main instigator of that Opel deal, and he felt that Coleman was foisted upon him, reducing his budget as the dealers split the finance to run both cars for the 1984 Irish Tarmac Rally Championship campaign.

'That is exactly how it came about. Some of the southern dealers were keen to get me in a car that year, and I remember a meeting one day in the Opel office in Dublin with the late John Ritchie, the Sales Manager for Opel Ireland, and he wasn't too happy about the situation either. He said, "We had a budget for one car and now suddenly I have to find money for a second, because it seems, in Ireland, they can't resist a winner".'

Billy was hooked up with Ronan Morgan as his new co-driver. Morgan would make his name not only as Coleman's navigator but on the world scene as well, where he sat with the likes of the late British driver Mark Lovell and Mohammed Ben Sulayem from the United Arab Emirates. Morgan was lucky to escape with his life when a car in which he was competing caught fire on a round of the Middle East Rally Championship. He was also part of the consortium that persuaded the FIA to grant Ireland a slice of the WRC for the first time in November 2007.

The Team Dealer Opel Ireland Manta 400s, with their big and powerful 2.4-litre engines, debuted in Galway in 1984, and thus began one of the hardest-fought seasons in Irish rallying. It was set up for a head-to-head between Coleman and MacHale, who were run by two different outfits despite having the same sponsors – Coleman by Sydney Meeke with team manager Tom Walsh and MacHale by Mickey Eiffe.

The Opels, though, were usurped by the Vauxhall Chevette of veteran Brendan Fagan, who won the opening round in the west of Ireland as Coleman had to be content with second and MacHale crashed out in Galway.

Next up was the Circuit of Ireland, when Coleman took his third and final victory in the great event which included some of the biggest names in world rallying that year, such as Juha Kankkunen, Henri Toivonen, Jimmy McRae and top Irish competitors such as MacHale and Bertie Fisher.

'Toivonen [who died in a crash in Corsica in 1986] was a friend of mine and was leading by a mile in the Porsche when he suddenly got into difficulties around the Waterford area on the Easter Monday. I inherited the lead through driving consistently and making no mistakes. Austin, though, was chipping away at my lead and eventually got ahead of us. Coming into Donegal the final morning, there was probably less than a minute between us. I was really in very bad form, and I was beginning to regret that I maybe should have stayed in retirement. I said I'd better pull up my socks and give it one last go. After the breakfast halt, we took back a good bit of time, and then Austin's engine blew. In all fairness, I think he was unlucky not to win that rally because I certainly didn't deserve to win it.'

The win on the Circuit, though, was to be the catalyst to a championship-winning year for Coleman's Opel Manta 400.

'We had a very good dice with our late colleague Bertie Fisher in Donegal and with Austin as well. That was really where I refound my groove in Donegal that year, and I began to drive well again.'

Coleman began to dominate the 1984 series. He won Donegal for the second time and was also victorious in Killarney and on the Cork 20, and he claimed the Irish Tarmac crown, his first and only STP Irish Tarmac rallying title, which nevertheless was unique as it added to his British success of 1974.

MacHale had pushed Coleman all the way to the title, but Billy was the one who won events that year, and there were many who said that the Cork driver's relentless pressure told on MacHale, who suffered crashes and retirements. He denies that Coleman's driving was the cause of his problems in 1984, but the fact that he felt that Billy was pushed upon him at the start of the season did not help, and MacHale was perhaps more than relieved that their relationship in the Opel Team Dealership outfit only lasted one Irish campaign.

In 1985, Coleman began one of Irish rallying's most high-profile sponsorship deals when he was backed by Rothmans. The cigarette company had decided to get involved in a big way with Irish motor sport, backing not only Coleman but Joey Dunlop as well. In the 1990s, Rothmans also sponsored the Phoenix Park Motor Races, persuaded by John Morris from Mondello Park to bring the racing, ironically, into the lung of Dublin, back to something approaching its former glories.

'Actually, I knew Joey [Dunlop] well. I was in the car and he was on the bike. He was a man I had a lot of time for. He was quiet spoken, and we probably had a fair bit in common. It was a tragedy when he was killed.'

Coleman started the 1985 Irish season in the Rothmans Porsche 911, again with Morgan calling the notes.

'What happened there was that Ben Morrison and Rothmans approached me sometime in late 1984, saying that they had a budget and that they had acquired works Porsche 911s. We had a number of meetings that autumn, and we signed a two-year deal to drive their Porsche. It was really a new departure for me to do some Irish events and some foreign rallies as well with Ronan.'

Billy's first run in the Porsche was on the Circuit of Ireland, a rally also sponsored by Rothmans, where he finished fifth. By his own admission, the Group B 911 was a difficult car to get used to, and, after the Circuit, where his new team-mate, French driver Bernard Béguin finished fourth, the team headed to the Rallye de France Tour de Corse, the fifth round of the World Championship in May of 1985. Coleman finished fourth, the highest placing for an Irish driver on a world event. It would be twenty-one years before another Irish driver, Austin MacHale's son Gareth, would pick up WRC points when the young MacHale finished sixth in a Ford Focus in Mexico in 2006.

'Corsica was the second one in the car, and it was a most gruelling event, although it was held entirely in daylight over the three days. The roads were extraordinary – twisty. Physically, a very demanding event. But it was really what I needed to get to know the Porsche. By the end of those three days, I felt really confident in the car, and we came in fourth just behind our team-mate Bernard Béguin. It was a very satisfying result.'

Frenchman Jean Ragnotti won the Tour de Corse in a Renault 5, ahead of the Peugeot 205 of Bruno Saby with the Rothmans Porsches third and fourth.

Back in Ireland that year, Coleman won the Rally of the Lakes in Killarney in Sean Delaney's Escort G3, going through the event on only one set of tyres, showing that incredible ability to ease his car home.

Austin MacHale's Killarney ended when he put his Manta into a bog, but the pair renewed their rivalry in Donegal, and the somewhat acrimonious nature of their relationship was further deepened when Coleman's team protested that MacHale should have had a thirty-second penalty imposed on his Opel which wouldn't start leaving Parc Ferme on the last day. The protest was rejected, but Coleman reeled in MacHale over the last few stages to win by a mere one second to claim his third Donegal title. It was a stunning win and the fastest that the Corkman had ever driven as he threw caution to the wind in order to catch the Manta.

But MacHale got revenge in Cork and claimed his second Irish Tarmac title in the process.

In 1986, Billy started the year with a win in Galway in the Porsche but crashed out heavily on the Circuit, and there ended his association with the 911. Jimmy McRae had rallied the powerful MG Metro 6R4 on the Circuit that year, and, by Donegal, Coleman had switched to the MG Metro four-wheeled-drive, Group B supercar.

'The Metro was a fabulous car. It had four-wheeled drive and small enough dimensions. It had a Cosworth 3-litre V6 engine which was turning out 500-plus horse power, and it was the most exhilarating car. Considering I had very little experience in four-wheeled drives, I found the car super. In fact, when I was in the Isle of Man that year, Rothmans brought along Nigel Mansell, who was Formula 1 World Champion, and I had to give him a few spins up and down the road. He was just amazed with the power and the way the car handled. When he got out, he said he wouldn't do it for any bloody money because he felt it was so dangerous. My view would have been the reverse. I considered circuit-racing to be far more dangerous.'

Coleman showed once again that he could step into just about any car and make it a winner as he brought the Metro home to first place on the victory ramp in Donegal, his fourth win in the north-west.

He also won in Cork and was in contention to win the Irish Championship, but the Rothmans team didn't go to the final round in Killarney, and MacHale picked up his third Irish title as a result. As it turned out, that year's Cork 20 was Coleman's last international win.

Henri Toivonen, who had rallied in Ireland in the early 1980s, and his co-driver Sergio Cresto, were killed in a Group B Lancia Delta S4, which crashed and burst into flames in Corsica. The accident helped to focus the minds of the FIA in their decision to ban the cars from the world rally scene, although they were allowed to run in Rallycross events.

'Sadly, at the end of that year, Group B was finished because the FIA felt they were getting too dangerous and there had been a couple of serious accidents. The problem was with the turbo-charged cars which were generating too much heat, and some caught fire, and that was really the problem with them. They could have maintained the category by taking the turbo out and having more ccs.'

Another change of car came in 1987 for the Coleman–Morgan partnership. Coleman's new car for the 1987 season, which turned out to be his last, was a BMW M3 run by Prodrive, a car very much in its developmental stage.

'I was very disappointed in that M3 BMW. Frank Keenan and the people from BMW in Ireland had backed us that year. It had potential, but it was probably too early in its development when I got it, and we had problems with it. I think, though, that if we had it a year or two later, we could have had success in it.'

He had a couple of mishaps that year, and at the Cork 20, his full-time rallying career came to a sudden and dramatic stop when he ploughed the BMW into a bank on stage 3. Billy and Ronan climbed from the car unhurt, and Coleman decided enough was enough, and he called it quits for good.

'I was pushing on forty, and I felt that I had to attend to my family and Carmel my wife. We had three children at that stage, and I called it a day.'

For Billy Coleman, it was back to his land near Millstreet, where he still tends his 180-acre farm. He makes occasional trips back to motor-sport events, but his somewhat reclusive lifestyle has only added to his mystique.

'From time to time, I meet people from all walks of life. Some, you would imagine, wouldn't be remotely interested in motor sport, and they would say that they saw me driving in such and such a place – it could have been in the middle of Wales over twenty years ago!

'I probably do regret that I didn't give a lot more attention to the people who followed my career, but you can only do so much, and I was at a certain level of commitment. I had a reasonable innings, but it could have been a lot better, there is no doubt about it.'

His sons Gordon and Robbie have taken part in motor-sport events over the past few years; indeed, Robbie was the winner of the much-maligned Formula Ireland single-seater racing class back in 2002 before racing in Formula Ford in the UK, while Gordon has entered a few rallies.

Billy himself was at Mondello Park for most of that 2002 season, watching Robbie win the inaugural Formula Ireland Championship, which fizzled out after only a couple of seasons.

'Strangely, at the beginning, it's what I was going to do, and one point I had my bag packed to go over to Brands Hatch to their racing school, but I never actually got there. It was at the time when that Mark 1 Escort turned up, and I went on that route instead. It was one of the biggest regrets that I didn't do racing because I would say that I was more cut out for it. I was the right size. A lot of the problems I had with rally cars was motivating myself, but in the few races that I competed in, there was no problem, and I was going for the jugular every time. Having said that, the chances are I would have seriously injured or killed myself because it was so dangerous at that time. The tracks were treacherous, the cars were light and had I got into it, I don't think I would have lasted that long.'

Since retirement, Coleman makes the occasional guest appearance and has also put his name to the Motorsport Ireland Young Rally Driver of the Year award and the Coleman Foundation.

Former winners include Rory Galligan, Dessie Keenan and Shaun Gallagher, who is now on the world-championship scene.

'That scholarship is a help to young drivers, but really, when you see the stupendous amount of money that is required nowadays, I just wonder where the sport is going. It's so difficult to make it now because of the money. A lot of the better cars, especially in Ireland, are in the hands of much older drivers, and you very rarely see a young driver in a top car, which is an inverse of my day. I think that is a great pity. While the money that comes from the Coleman scholarship is useful, it only goes a limited way, and I just wonder is there any solution. My lads have been blessed with having a good sponsor in Gerard Kelly, who has been a very good friend of ours, but we need a lot more people like that. When you see the amount of money that some people have in Ireland nowadays, maybe they should consider young sportspeople – not just rally drivers but rugby, soccer, you name it. They can't take the money to the grave with them, so why not bloody well open up the purses and consider giving to sport, because corporate sponsorship is all very well, but private benefactors should get involved in sport.'

Billy did some events in the 1990s and into the new millennium, including a few historic rallies and the Punchestown Rally Experience (organised by Ronan Morgan during the foot-and-mouth outbreak in Ireland in 2001 that curtailed the rally season).

Not surprisingly, Billy Coleman was inducted into the Motorsport Ireland Hall of Fame in 2003. For the modest man from Cork, even the fact that his peers would recognise what he had done for rallying in Ireland caused some embarrassment.

'I was there to give out the Coleman Scholarship, and I was just swallowing a sup of tea, and, lo and behold, my name was called out, and I nearly fell off the chair. It was a nice honour to get, and it's something that I cherish.'

9

Jeremy McWilliams

eremy 'Jezza' McWilliams is one of a small band of Irish racers to have won a grand-prix motorcycle event when his semi-works Aprilia raced to victory in the 250-cc race at the 2001 Dutch Grand Prix at Assen.

Irish motorbike racing and its riders are seen as some of the best in the world. The onus and focus has been on road, as distinct from circuit, racing, where McWilliams plied his trade through Irish championship races and onto 500-cc and MotoGP rounds, where he raced with the top names in world motorbikes.

He began late for a rider and was twenty-four years old when he first started serious competition, taking part in the 1988 Irish Championship aboard a 350-cc production Yamaha. His first grand prix came five years later, when he was at the ripe old age of twenty-nine, and, since then, he has worked his way through the 250, 500 and MotoGP series. He has been one of the most consistent riders of the grand-prix series and has managed to get the best out of some pretty uncompetitive machines.

It hasn't been all sweetness and light for the Belfast driver. He had a disastrous flirtation with the British Superbike series in 2005 before landing a testing contact with Ilmor/BMW outift in 2006. Ilmor/BMW were preparing to launch into the MotoGP series the following season. Having secured a deal to compete in the 2007 season as one of Ilmor's two riders along with Australian Andrew Pitt, McWilliams had a bad accident while testing for his new team in Spain. To make matters worse, they pulled out of the MotoGP Championship after only one race. At the time of writing, McWilliams remains under contract to Ilmor along with Pitt, and the pair are continuing to develop the bike with a view to the company returning to the series in the near future.

McWilliams is a canny operator and has survived in the sport long after many thought he would. He still lives in Northern Ireland, in the village of Glengormley; his shop Racebase is the main Aprilia dealership in Belfast and specialises in new Aprilia motorcycles and scooters, along with spare parts and accessories.

Born to a Protestant family in Carnmoney on the outskirts of Belfast on 4 April 1964 and growing up in what were turbulent times for Northern Ireland, McWilliams fortunately found himself outside the conflicts that many of his fellow countrymen and women were suffering at the time.

'Well, I think everybody expects, with me coming from Belfast, a bit of a strange upbringing with bombing and shootings. Unfortunately, that's the first thing that people think of whenever you say you've been brought up there. I fortunately didn't see any of that. I had a great happy childhood and lived only about four miles outside Belfast. Mum and Dad were together, but they split up in the mid-1990s. My brother and I went to school in a place called Ballyclare, which is another six miles further out of that, and we had a great time really.

'I think most kids go through phases. I played a little bit of football at school and some rugby. Didn't really do much else, and motor sport wasn't really in my family. My father was a "horsey man", liked to go to the point-to-points, and I got dragged along against my wishes many times.

'Funnily enough, my brother Pat ended up becoming a jockey, probably against his wishes too, but he ended up as a professional jockey and is still working in Naas.

'I didn't really get to ride a bike properly until I was about four-teen or so; my parents were against it. It wasn't until many years later that I started persuading and coaxing them to get me a bike. So, I got a motocross machine and just played about with it.

'I've no idea why I got into motor sport, but it was something that a couple of kids in my class were into. Two or three of them were lucky enough to have motocross bikes, and they went racing at the weekend. Of course, they'd talk about it quite often. I was pretty en-vious of that, so I was hoping some day it might happen to me, and I think probably that's why I've raced and raced for so long because it didn't go out of my system. I didn't really get to ride motorbikes competitively until I was in my mid-twenties, so, for a bit of craic we used to go, when I was seventeen, up to the local circuit in County Antrim and get in there on a Sunday and race around it. I think I just found out by accident that I could ride a bike all right.

'I think you get into it, and you do it as a bit of fun. You know, it's like your rally drivers and F1 drivers, they didn't intend to be what they are. A lot of those guys started on karts. I just happened to start on two wheels and now I'm making a living at it. But I've really got no idea how, or what the difference is between somebody who's very good at it and the next person who can make it their profession. I'm not really sure where the cut of is, and I still can't work that out – how one guy can make a living out of it and the next guy can be pretty good and win multiple national championships but doesn't break into the big time.'

The amazing thing about McWilliams' career is that he was twenty-four when he won the Irish Production Class on the 350 Ya-maha. Most motor-racing drivers on four wheels start in karts at six or seven years of age, while bikers start in their teenage years. McWilliams started his competitive bike career when many guys were settling down and starting to raise a family.

'It's true, and most of the guys in the paddock would have been persuaded to race motocross from an early age and progressed through the ranks until they got into tarmac. I didn't actually start racing until I was twenty-four and didn't start racing professionally until I was twenty-nine because I raced for a bit of fun for a couple of years in Ireland. Won the Irish Championship in the first year of try-ing, then got a 250 ride and ended up winning the Irish Championship with Queen's University in Belfast (QUB).'

Robert Fleck ran the QUB Optimum team and started a near-decade-long association with McWilliams, beginning in 1991 where the Ulster rider won the Irish 250 Open Championship. Their part-nership lasted until 1999 when McWilliams took the plunge into the 500-cc World Championship.

After that early success in Ireland, McWilliams thought it would be a good idea to go to the UK and try his hand at their champion-ships, and in 1991 he raced in the British 250-cc Super Cup, where he had a couple of race wins, including standing at the top of the podium at Brands Hatch.

'I thought winning in Ireland was as far as my career would have gone at that time, but when you win an Irish Championship, you've gotta go win a British Championship. I went over and competed in England, and, although I won a couple of races in British Super Cup on 250s and got a ride on a 750 for part of the season, I didn't win a championship, but I ended up on the podium a couple of times.'

Joe Millar was the owner of the Millar Transport Company in Ran-dalstown, a small country village in County Antrim, Northern Ireland, and was a huge motorbike enthusiast. Millar backed Dubliner Eddie Laycock in the World Championship in the early 1990s as a single bike entrant before McWilliams got his chance with the team in 1993.

'Even though Joe had a grand-prix team at the time with Eddie Laycock, he'd been coming home to watch all the local stuff, and he offered me a ride in grand prix. I was so green, I really didn't know what that entailed, giving up your nine-to-five and walking away from it. I just asked him to match my wages, which I thought was very kind of him to do so, and walked into a professional career at twenty-nine years of age on a 500-cc two-stroke Yamaha, some-thing I'd never even ridden before.

'It was a big jump. At the time, I didn't realise how big a jump it was, but when I got there, I realised that I was struggling quite a bit to even to finish a race. I didn't have the fitness to race at World Championship level. I'd never experienced anything like it, and it took me probably six events even to finish a grand prix.

'Joe was just a total enthusiast and went to all the grand-prix races in his camper. He was a very successful businessman, and his transport company was one of the biggest in Northern Ireland until he sold it a few years ago.'

(Joe Miller has subsequently passed away.)

'When the team was running, he gave me a job as the number one rider. Unfortunately, Eddie Laycock then had no job, as he was only running a one-man team, so I took Eddie's ride and ended up going to the World Championship. To this day, if it hadn't been for Joe Millar, I wouldn't have got as far as I did. I don't think anyone else would have picked me up to do that. There were no British teams, never mind Irish teams, in grand prix at that stage.'

McWilliams was sent Down Under in 1993 to compete in his first 500-cc grand prix, which opened the new season at Eastern Creek in Australia. The Irish rider finished twenty-second in a race won by Kevin Schwantz on a Suzuki. The American also went on to claim the title that season for the Japanese works team.

McWilliams' recollection of lining up on the grid that weekend remains clear to this day.

'I think that anybody who says anything other than "petrified" would be lying. I only knew what I was doing in Australia when I got there. The reality of it starts hitting home when you go out in your first practice session. Then your qualifying session, and you realise that you're twentieth or twenty-first on the grid and not much sign of moving up. The reality of grand-prix racing is certainly very stark. It can quite quickly become apparent that you're not in any shape to race in grands prix because there's nothing prepares you for it.

'I had a gearbox break that had me off down on the track. We certainly had a few failures like that, but a lot of it was my own fault too. I crashed quite a bit after Australia.

'You go to the next one thinking, OK I just want to get it finished, don't really care where it is or whether it's in the points or not, I just want to get it finished. Fail to get a finish there, you go to the next one even more determined to do that again, and this is the way that grands prix that year went on for me until I got a finish, and even scoring a point was a major, major boost because there were a lot more riders back then, and the points went back to fifteenth place.

'That was just the start of Mick Doohan's long run of World Championship titles. There were some great riders around. I was fortunate enough to race against Wayne Rainey who was trying to win a title in 1993 when he had an unfortunate accident that ended his career. He's now wheelchair-bound.

'Kevin Schwantz won the championship in my first year – fine rider. Alex Barros and Loris Capirossi raced against me for a long time. It's quite strange to see those riders still there. I thought I'd a long grand-prix career.'

McWilliams stayed with the 500-cc World Championship throughout 1993. He was twelfth in the 1994 season, nineteenth in 1995 and sixteenth in 1996, while up at the head of affairs, Mick Doohan was stamping his authority on the championship series, winning the riders' title in all of those years.

Jeremy stayed in the 500-cc series until 1996 and then changed to the 250-cc class, making his debut in Malaysia.

'I think the main reason was because we couldn't be competitive at 500s. We were looking, as a team, to try and find a way to get to the front again, and we tried everything. When I was with Optimum, which was still part of the university, Robert Fleck had a sponsor from America, and it was called QUB Team Optimum, and they tried everything as well. We tried a Rock chassis with a 500-cc Yamaha engine in the French-built chassis, and we thought that'd be a bit more competitive than any of the other 500s that were available. I ended up racing the Rock in 1996, and I really couldn't get it anywhere near the front. Basically, there was a lot of money spent to go nowhere in 1996. So, in 1997, we had a rethink, and we looked at the 250 Honda kit bikes, and a decision was made to buy them because they looked like we'd get closer to the front. The gap in terms of lap times was smaller in 250, and it was the best move I think I ever made to go back on a 250 and become competitive on a bike with mechanics who really were also learning. We didn't have very much in the way of experience, but there was an awful lot of effort, you know, probably, I think, one of the best teams I rode for in my career was that QUB Team Optimum.

'In 1998, I remember beating Valentino Rossi and Capirossi at the Sachsenring in Germany on a 250, even after we had a minor glitch in the race when the fuel breather pipe had come off and the fuel was pissing out over the bike and over me, and I had to get it back on whilst trying not to lose too much time, but I still caught back up again and got through.'

McWilliams finished second that day on his way to ninth in the 250-cc standings, a race he still feels he should have won.

'Unfortunately, Tetsuya Harada had gone through, or it could have been the first win. Moments like that are what made my career. I've got some fantastic memories because of times like that. The 250 got us noticed again. I think we were a little bit unfairly done by as we didn't receive a works bike for the next year, and that's why we went to Aprilia.'

For most of his professional career, McWilliams has been a privateer's entry, racing semi-works bikes. It makes it all the more extraordinary that with over 150 appearances in the 250, 500 and MotoGP, most of his riding has come on older and underdeveloped bikes. It's to his immense credit that he has mixed with the big boys in his sport over the seasons.

'I think all my career was non-factory, except for the few times when I rode for Aprilia. That was full factory effort in the big class, 500 cc in 2000 and in 2004 on the three-cylinder four-stroke. When a team decides to go into and race in a championship, they can't just go and buy a factory bike, it doesn't matter who they are. The rider has to be the right one for the bike for Honda, Yamaha, Aprilia or whoever it might be. We raced in 1998 with a kit bike, which is only some trick parts that you add to a standard 250 Honda racing engine, and, luckily, those kit bikes were quite close to the factory ones, closer than they had been before or since, and that was probably why I was able to finish tenth in the Championship and on the podium a couple of times.

'When I wanted the full factory bike, at least I wanted one that was going to be run by our team, Team Optimum, and we decided to go to Aprilia because we thought we were getting a better deal. Obviously, it was the decision of the team financially. We did OK again in 1999 and did well enough that Aprilia chose me to race for them on their full factory V-Twin 500 cc.'

After four seasons in the 500 championship and another three seasons with the 250 class, the beginning of 2000 saw McWilliams get the break he was looking for: he got a full factory ride with the Italian Aprilia team, and it was back to the 500-cc class on their V-Twin partnering Harada. He admits he had a tough enough season, despite podiums in Italy and Great Britain and pole position in Australia. McWilliams was fourteenth overall in the championship.

'In 2000, it all went a bit pear-shaped. I was supposed to race for a 250 team again, but that fell through. Luckily, Aprilia came in and gave me a kit bike, and I raced out of one of their Aprilia Italian teams. Not a bad year, but not a great year. The Italian team failed to find sponsorship, and I had moved back to the 250s with a German Aprilia team and won my first race in 2001.'

The Dutch Grand Prix at Assen was the biggest moment of McWilliams' career. After nine years of racing in the World Championship, a race win had eluded the Irish rider, despite many podium or top-three finishes. Joey Dunlop had taken race wins in the old Formula 1 series, and Ray McCullough had done likewise at Dunrod (home of the Ulster Grand Prix in Lisburn, County Antrim). Ralph Bryans had also tasted victory in the now-defunct 50-cc Fédération Internationale de Motocyclisme (FIM) World Championship, and, on the 30 June 2001, McWilliams became yet another Irishman to take a grand-prix victory.

That year, before his race win in the Netherlands, McWilliams' return to the 250 class saw him take points in Japan (eighth), South Africa (sixth), Catalonia (eighth), France (tenth) and Spain (sixth). The race, on a drizzly afternoon at Assen, was McWilliams forty-ninth start in the 250 series. After the first warm-up lap, McWilliams took a massive gamble on tyre choice. The team wanted him to race on full wets as the other riders were doing, but Assen is a weather conundrum. Sometimes it rains on different parts of the circuit while other parts can be bone dry. McWilliams reckoned that while it was wet on the main straight, the skies were starting to clear elsewhere, and he took the decision, against the advice of Jan Witteveen, the Team Director, to race on hand-cut Dunlop slick tyres.

'Well, we used to go to Assen even before I started grand-prix racing. It was always one of my favourite circuits. It's probably one of the most difficult tracks you'll ever drive or ride, I'm sure. There's so much to it, and you never really seem to get a break anywhere. There's not really a straight even – the straights have kinks in them, and they're flat-out kinks. It's also the sort of place where you know it normally only rains on half the circuit, so only half the circuit ends up really wet and half ends up drying. So unless it's absolutely raining cats and dogs, you don't put wets on, you put anything else but wets on, and that's exactly what I did. I just looked and thought, Half the circuit on the far side is going to dry quickly. It's raining where we are sitting on the start/finish line, but I'll take the chance anyway.

'I've got to say that I made a few mistakes since then. One year, in Mugello, I did exactly the same thing on the Aprilia. Everyone else decided to take slicks, and I took wets and, of course, it dried out, and I was left behind. I had to pull in before my tyre disintegrated. But Assen was one of those places where I just got it right. It wasn't a smart thing, and it was just luck, to be honest.'

McWilliams changed his tyres from wets to a cut slick and felt his luck was in when he completed his warm-up laps. The back of the circuit was drying up, even though it was still raining on the main straight, and when he returned to line up at the start of the eighteen-lap race, he felt confident.

'I started from front row, and when I looked left, I could see all the wet tyres. Everyone had wet tyres, and I thought, This is easy, because we'd just done the second warm-up lap, and I realised there was a dry line coming already. I looked behind me, and there were a couple of other riders like Emilio Alzamora on slicks, and I thought, Well, he may struggle for a lap or two, but he could be a danger man.

'From the off, Marco Melandri led, but I went past Melandri and got away in the first lap. People still ask me to this day, "Why did you keep making such a big gap? Why did you want to win by sixteen seconds?" I knew that there were other riders on slicks out there, so I kept my head down. Funnily enough, Alzamora did close down, and he would have closed a lot further had I not kept my head down. He would have beaten me to the line as he was doing much faster lap times in the last couple of laps than I was.'

In the end, McWilliams eased home to win by seventeen seconds from Alzamora, who had also gambled on his choice of tyres but, unlike McWilliams, who had gone with an intermediate set; the Spaniard had dry tyres on his Honda.

Williams said about the win, 'I think it's probably one of those things that happened, and you wish it happened more often. You know, there were other times that I probably had as much elation from the pole positions as that win. Of course, winning a grand prix is fantastic, but sometimes they were such hard-fought races that just to get on the podium was as good as winning the race. That happened in Donington in the wet in 2000 when the tar started breaking up. Rossi had his first win, and Kenny Roberts pipped me for second place, which I was a bit disappointed about. But just getting on the podium was good because there were so many times that I was nearly on my arse.

'I think the biggest difference was that just after the race win how much the media want to speak to me and that is the one thing that I'm not that good at. I went away, turned my phone off for a couple of days and actually went to Bournemouth, of all places, stayed down there with my wife and kids on the beach and just drove home at our leisure. (We actually drove to Assen in the camper van.)'

Although McWilliams won at Assen, it wasn't a springboard to greater things in 2001. He fell at Donington Park and in Germany and broke his collarbone in the Czech round in Brno. He broke it again before the season's end – not racing but while on a break at home in Antrim when he was pitched from his trials bike. A broken bone is not something that ever stopped a professional rider. McWilliams returned and posted points finishes at the likes of Portugal, Valencia and Motegi in Japan where he was third. Harada, his team-mate, was second in the championship, while McWilliams was a battling sixth.

By the end of the 2001 season, the 500-cc championship was no more. While the 125s and the 250s remained as part of the grand-prix package, in 2002, the MotoGP series was born, and McWilliams went back to the premier class riding for the Kenny Roberts team on the Proton KR.

Traditionally, there are several races at each motorbike grand-prix event. At one time or another, there were races for 50 cc, 80 cc, 350 cc and even sidecars. In the late 1970s and early 1980s, 50-cc and 80-cc bikes lost their grand-prix status. Germany's Anton Mang was the last 350-cc champion in 1982, while the last sidecar series which was part of the grand-prix package was in 1989.

Up through the 1950s and 1960s, four-stroke engines dominated all classes, but the two-stroke engines began to dominate, and by the 1970s the four strokes were all but gone, and, until 2002, the top class of grand-prix racing was restricted to four cylinders and the 500-cc class, which ran primarily with two-stroke engines.

However, it was all change in 2002 when the FIM allowed manufacturers to choose between running two-stroke engines for bikes of 500 cc or less or four-strokes, which were for bikes of 990 cc or less. The 500 cc proved to be much slower than the near-1,000-cc machines, and, by 2003, the class manufacturers decided to dump the slower machines for the near-1,000-cc bikes. Valentino Rossi proved to be the class of the MotoGP series. Having already won world championships on a 125, 250 and 500 (in 2001), the prolific Italian then won the MotoGP series for four straight years for Honda and Yamaha, before being dethroned by American Nicky Hayden on a Honda. There was a further change introduced for the premier class in 2007 when it was decided to have MotoGP bikes have their maximum engine-displacement capacity reduced to 800 cc.

McWilliams got the offer from Kenny Roberts, the three-time World Champion, to join the Proton outfit for the start of the new MotoGP campaign in 2002, and he jumped at the chance. He joined up with another Irishman in Tom O'Kane who was Chief Mechanic for Kenny Roberts Jnr.

'Well, it was a really easy decision. Team Roberts is still, I think, to this day, the best team I ever rode for. In terms of their efficiency as a team, they were incredible. Tom O'Kane was my chief mechanic and, unbeknownst to me, they told me that they tried to sign me the year before.

'In 2001, I'd signed to ride with an unknown Italian team on an Aprilia because Aprilia had decided not to run the V-Twin 500-cc bike again in the Premier Class. I was really disappointed about that, and I think that's why they signed me up that year. After that, the 250 deal fell through with a guy, a waster, who decided that he may come along and run a team with no money whatsoever – lots of lies, lots of promises, and it fell through. Aprilia put me on the 250 for 2001. It wasn't until 2002 that I realised I could have signed for Team Roberts in 2001, and if I could turn the clock back, that's the only difference I would have made in my whole racing career because I think we could have won races in the Premier Class in 2001 and not just one race on a 250 with Aprilia.

'If you look at the lap times and stuff that we produced in 2002 and overlay them on the times in 2001, they were massively better, much, much better. They would have been pole positions, and I really think they'd have been race wins.

'In saying that, 2002 was still a great year for me. I have some very good memories there. A fair few front-row starts, but, unfortunately, no podiums on that bike – but I think that we were very unlucky not to have any. There were a few times when the Proton, over the two years that I rode it, was right in the hunt and something went wrong – a seizure or a gearbox break. I had a gearbox break in Assen and a seizure in Brazil the year after, and I was lying third. I also broke my collarbone again. But there's certainly great memories of that team. The team were the best and the nicest team to work for and I'm still very good friends with them.'

And what was McWilliams' overall impression of the MotoGP series and the move away from two- to four-stroke engines?

'We were all very sad to see the two-stroke thing going away because in 2003 we set some records that will never be beaten. The Proton was the fastest two-stroke motorcycle around, but the fact was that we were probably a year out of date. We were just a year past the possibility of getting that bike onto the podium and maybe getting race wins. So when they decided to go four-stroke, a lot of riders thought it was the end, even for me. Going back from two-stroke onto four-stroke . . . well, my style was built around a two-stroke and I struggled.'

McWilliams and the Proton KR team had a two-year association in MotoGP. In 2002, the Irishman was teamed up with Bridgestone test rider Nobuatsu Aoki of Japan. Despite the fact that he thought it was a great team to work for, both riders really struggled on their underpowered three-cylinder two-strokes against the four-strokes, but McWilliams did take an impressive pole position at Phillip Island in Australia and finished the year fourteenth in the standings.

In 2003, the team introduced the V5 Proton to the MotoGP series, but it was another season where the team failed to mix it with the leaders, and McWilliams was eighteenth overall in the rider's standings. And there his association with Proton and Kenny Roberts ended, and it was back to Aprilia for McWilliams for the 2004 season, joining up with former British Superbike champion Shane 'Shakey' Byrne as his team-mate, but he was still sad to leave.

'The KR team pleaded with me to stay, and they offered me more of a contract to stay with them than Aprilia were offering me, but you've got to weigh up what you know and how competitive your whole package is going to be. The KR Team were a more competitive package than Aprilia, except that they weren't running Michelin tyres, and the Michelin tyres were the only tyres working at the time.

Had the KR Team had a Michelin deal, I would have signed there and then. I wouldn't even have been speaking with Aprilia.

'It was a strange situation for me. I had two offers, and both were great, to stay in grands prix, and I thought, it's great. Some people might not consider those two offers as being the greatest offers, but to stay in grands prix on semi-competitive machinery and do what other riders weren't capable of doing is still a good offer, and grand prix is the premier class. It's the World Championship, and whatever offer you get, you have to consider it over all other offers.

'I walked away because of the tyre choice of Team Roberts, but if I were getting the same choice again, I'm not sure I would have done that, because the Aprilia was a really difficult bike to ride, and it certainly didn't get any easier. It was the same bike that Colin Edwards had ridden the year before. Everybody else had moved on, and we struggled. We had the same bike the whole year, and it was a year-old machine at that stage, and it had all the same traits and all the same problems. Every time that Shakey and myself told them what the bike was doing, they pulled the notes out from the year before and said, "Look, we know." We were saying exactly the same thing as the riders before like Haga and Edwards were saying. We did what we could do with the bike. We changed some aspects of it, but, you know, the old traits that it had were there and couldn't be fixed.'

McWilliams endured a tough 2004 season in MotoGP and was placed nineteenth overall. The season was remarkable for the fact that Valentino Rossi had jumped off the all-conquering Honda and had gone to Yamaha, which, up to that point, wasn't a competitive machine. Lo and behold, the Italian goes and wins the World Championship. He's a rider that McWilliams admires greatly, but does he think he is the best grand-prix racer he has ever seen or ridden against?

'Without a doubt. I think anybody that's raced against him will say that. But it's funny, when you talk about riders from different eras, you know, they'll say, "Oh, Doohan or Rainey was the best, and it goes on. It's funny, but I've ridden in the Wayne Rainey era, and I always looked up to him more so than anybody else in motorcycling racing until Valentino came along. I don't think there's any, any doubt that he is the best rider in the world. He's got the best race craft, and I think he'll continue to win as long as he wants to.'

The 2004 season then ended acrimoniously for McWilliams because there was talk that he was going to go back to stay with the MotoGP Series for 2005, but of all people, the organisers apparently didn't want him to go back, and Shakey Byrne got the ride with Aprilia, leaving him out in the cold.

'I think I've got closure on it now, and I don't have to worry about it anymore. At some time, you've got to decide what's best for yourself. I could have gone down and started arguing with organisers and causing a scene, but those organisers had been good to me in the past too, where they'd supported me whenever I'd gone to Aprilia when they were looking for riders. There's always lots of different riders available, and it depends on what the organisers see as important aspects for TV coverage. They then try to place those riders with teams. I can say that I was probably pushed towards Aprilia, or Aprilia were pushed towards me when I raced for them in the grand-prix class, and, for that, I'm eternally grateful.

'What I didn't like and what I heard, was that a TV company in mainland UK was pushing to have Shane because of their viewing figures, and, of course, it was very obvious to me that I had to take a back seat, walk away from it, understand the politics of the sport and go and do something else, and that's why I moved to the British Superbike Championship (BSB) in 2005.'

Paul Bird, owner of the MonsterMob British Superbike Team said at the time that he made McWilliams 'an offer he couldn't refuse' for two seasons in BSB. Bird, who had previously won the BSB title with Steve Hislop and Shane Byrne, switched from Ducati to Honda for 2005 and wanted McWilliams to join fellow Ulsterman Michael Laverty for MonsterMob's assault on the British series.

The BSB Series at that stage was considered to be perhaps even better than the world series, with the regulars beating the world stars quite comfortably when the two series would link up for races in the UK.

'Yeah, guys like Leon Haslam had been in that situation, and he had his ass kicked both ways, but whenever riders are racing on the same circuits they're capable of winning, it's just the nature of your championship at that time. The circuits that you're testing and racing on are the circuits you shine on, and you can't take anything away from the BSB boys when they beat the world championship racers.'

However, the BSB turned out to be a disaster for McWilliams in 2005. Partly due to shoulder injury, the season proved a disappointment, and he missed many races that year. He also raced in a one-off ride for Team Roberts in MotoGP at the Czech Republic Round, but 2005 and, indeed, 2006 will not be remembered fondly in terms of his motor-racing career.

In 2006, he ditched the BSB, or rather it ditched him, and he pretty much sat out the season doing occasional outings for AMA Formula Xtreme outings for the Buell team in the USA, where he raced in the Daytona 200 and the Mazda Raceway at the famous Laguna Seca as well as testing for the Ilmor BMW team at the end of that season.

There was talk of a surprise return to MotoGP with the WCM Bimota team in 2006, but it fell through, and McWilliams, speaking in 2005, said he thought that the BSB would be his last championship before he finally retired.

'I don't think you can hop back in and out of MotoGP. I'd be kidding myself if I thought I could go there and get back on a grand-prix bike and be competitive again. When I was there, things were moving on ahead of me because the lap times were just unbelievable when you look at them. I think the only thing that I could do for Grand Prix again is maybe help Proton set the bike up, because they seem to be having an enormous problem getting what I thought was a competitive bike. You never know what's around the corner, but I can't really see myself signing for MotoGP at forty-two years of age. I can see myself in BSB, and, once I've learnt these circuits, maybe I'll look forward to staying.'

After his ill-fated 2005 and his occasional races and testing in 2006, did he think his career was coming to an end?

'I thought so, yeah. I cannot do this for ever, you know. I'm doing it for the love of it, but the body is starting to tell, and I've had a few problems this year. I had one injury (with BSB) that certainly was one of the most serious that I've had in my career. I had some nerve damage in my shoulder and was in and out of hospital trying to get it diagnosed. Unfortunately, there was nothing they could do except wait, and if it didn't get any better it could have spelt the end of my career.

'I've always looked from day to day and never from year to year – never even really from week to week. All my career was always, Well, let's see what turns up, you know. I've got kids and a wife and a mortgage, so I can't race for ever and hope that it's going to pay the bills, but I will have to do other things.'

With the BSB behind him and his career seemingly petering out, McWilliams got perhaps his last chance in the Premier Class when he began testing for the Ilmor team in 2006. There was a hint that they were preparing to race in the MotoGP class in 2007 with McWilliams as one of their riders.

McWilliams attended the final race of the 2006 season in Valencia when he held discussions with the team run by ex-Formula 1 designer Mario Illien, who designed Formula 1 championship-winning engines for McLaren in 1998 and 1999. Ilmor engines also won the Indy 500 on eleven occasions and he began testing with their new bike team in the latter part of 2006.

But the year ended with mixed fortunes. In November, McWilliams suffered multiple injuries in a crash during the final MotoGP test session of the year at the Jerez circuit in Spain. He was taken to hospital after fracturing the femur in his left leg and breaking his collarbone, breaking it for the umpteenth time in his career. McWilliams, who was riding the Ilmor 800-cc bike, also suffered injuries to the fingers of his left hand and actually lost the tip of one.

In December of that year, Joe Millar, who had given McWilliams his first ride at world-championship level, passed away. The Randalstown businessman, who backed many of the best riders in Ireland on roads and circuits throughout the 1980s and 1990s, was gone. It was not only McWilliams and Laycock who raced for Millar;

he also backed Eugene McManus, Alan Patterson, Johnny Rea and Adrian Coates at national and international level. British rider Michael Rutter also rode in the Millar colours, as did Isle of Man TT winner Con Law and the late Gene McDonnell.

'Joe's passing was a big loss to the sport. I raced for him at world-championship level from 1993 to 1995, when I took over from Eddie Laycock. It is doubtful whether any of us would ever have been racing in grands prix if he had not set us on our way.'

But there was some cheer for McWilliams for, despite Millar's death and recovering from his injuries, Ilmor was more than happy with the work that he had done, and, three days after Millar's passing, the team confirmed McWilliams and Australian Andrew Pitt, an ex-world superbike racer, as their riders for the 2007 season.

'I was very pleased to be part of a new team, and, obviously, I'm delighted to be back in MotoGP. With Ilmor, it's a very different situation. Having spent some time with him and the team, his passion and dedication were evident, especially at the facility in Northampton – he's not a man who's used to coming second.'

At forty-two, McWilliams was apparently back in the big time, until Ilmor pulled the plug on the MotoGP programme after only one race of the 2007 season. Both McWilliams and Pitt were retained as engine-development riders, but the Irishman's racing career, at the time of writing, looks to be all but over. It was a career that began in 1988, and McWilliams raced at the top level, between the MotoGP, 500 and 250 classes. He remains a respected rider and has harboured thoughts of moving into either management or team ownership.

'It would be a lovely thought, but, you know, there's plenty of great team managers out there with lots of sponsorship, and to walk in and do something like that competitively, you'd need a lot of backing. I would like to start at the lower end of the scale and help out with a team first and see how it went, maybe manage one way or another. But, you know, as I say, I've been very lucky. Let's hope that luck holds up and something else turns up in the future. It would be even better if it's with two wheels and not back to a nine-to-five.'

10

Martin Donnelly

H ugh Peter 'Martin' Donnelly was born in Belfast on 26 March 1964, a top-class racer who made it all the way to Formula 1, but who is unfortunately best remembered as having survived one of the biggest shunts ever in the history of Formula 1 racing. In 1990, his Lotus-Lamborghini slammed into an unprotected section of Armco barrier in practice for the Spanish Grand Prix at Jerez, ending a promising career. The impact destroyed the car and flung Donnelly's body, still strapped to his seat, across the track where he lay motionless with multiple injuries, blood seeping from his body and his leg jutting at a crazy angle.

A marshal Felix Muelas, who was working at the race that September weekend in 1990, was one of the first on the scene of Donnelly's accident.

The first abnormal thing that left us speechless was the noise. A horrendous bang so close that instants after that, it seemed like all the noise surrounding us had stopped. We looked at each other and started running. It was obvious that an accident had happened, and it had happened quite near to us. We saw the track marshals running too (they were wearing their bright green overalls) on the exterior of the track – we were on the inside, running on the grass and on the track itself. There was a cloud of smoke up there, at the exit of the Enzo Ferrari corner, a flat-in-sixth 160 mph leading onto the small straight downhill where we were.

We got there in something like a minute, and the sight was appalling. Carlos was shouting 'Don't touch him!', as he knew the ambulance would be arriving any moment – and I was paralysed. A body was lying on the track, motionless – I was convinced he was dead – with the seatbelts attached to a piece of the car, the bulkhead, and he had one twisted leg pro-truding at an angle. Of the car, well, there were bits and pieces everywhere distracting us for a moment. One of our du-ties had been for years to reconstruct the accidents on the track, so I remember that this algorithm took over our minds for a couple of seconds. But as soon as the answer [sic] came out of the brain, 'What the hell happened here?', we were back to poor Martin Donnelly.

I stood there watching whilst the body was being taken care of by the medical team, and later we heard with relief that, al-though very seriously injured, Donnelly was alive. But I had made a decision, and I have not regretted it since. It was time to quit. Not that I was not aware of the risks, I had been living with them for years, but up to that day it always seemed like if, come the moment, we could help. Not that day. I was so para-lysed in front of what I was convinced was Donnelly's final moment in life and felt so stupid not being able to know what to do that I just concluded my time was over.

Source: Forix.com

Muelas quit marshalling after Donnelly's accident, and even Ayrton Senna questioned why he should continue, having seen the Irishman's twisted and motionless body lying on the track minutes after the impact. Senna blew the radiator on his McLaren early in the race that weekend in Jerez, as Alain Prost took the victory for

Ferrari. Senna's decision to carry on came after a lot of soul-searching. The great Brazilian's life ended just four years later after his crash at the San Marino Grand Prix in Imola.

Donnelly somehow managed to survive the impact, despite multiple breaks and blood loss. He credits the outstanding work of Formula 1 doctor Professor Sid Watkins for keeping him alive. However, the crash ended a promising Formula 1 career. Donnelly was left with a permanent limp and, although he recovered, he wasn't allowed to drive a Formula 1 car again.

FIA rules state that a driver only has a certain amount of time, literally seconds, to extricate themselves from a Formula 1 car after an accident. Donnelly tried to convince the governing body that he could do it in the time allowed when he went for a test with Jordan in 1993, but the injuries meant that he was unable to do so, and his Formula 1 career was at an end. He spent a long time recovering and eventually was able to race again at a much smaller level. Donnelly went on to run teams in Junior Formula in the UK, but he fell on hard times, and in 2004 he filed for bankruptcy over the non-payment of taxes, mainly due to disputes over driver contracts.

Donnelly, though, as he showed after his crash in Spain, is a survivor, and he has since gotten involved with the Comtec Racing team in the World Series by Renault where he became Driver Development Manager. Motorsport Ireland also co-opted him onto their panel to choose the Young Racing Driver of the Year, and he is the overall judge for the final three participants in their skill test assessment.

But it's a case of what might have been for Martin Donnelly. From his debut in racing in Ireland in 1980, he rose through the ranks of Formula Ford through Formula 3 and on to Formula 3000 before getting one Formula 1 race with Arrows in 1989 and then his first full season with Lotus, which was so cruelly ended by that accident in Jerez in the latter part of the season.

Donnelly's career began on a small-time basis, helped by his father, the late Martin Donnelly Snr., a tough, hard-drinking, uncompromising man who backed his son's early forays into the sport.

'I was brought into motor sport through my father. He was a boy racer who liked his beer at the weekends and who liked sports cars. He had a lot of cars like MGBs, Hillman Imps and Sunbeam Rapiers, and he would go down to Kirkistown to race back in those days. He used to go to the track, have beers with his mates, and I would go with him.

'Those days, things were a lot more relaxed at the circuits with regard to insurance and people going out onto the track. So when Dad was in the bar getting hammered, I was on the track hammering his cars, and that's basically how I learned to drive. I started off on my dad's knee steering, and then he'd let me operate a pedal or a throttle, and then, bit by bit, over the months or years, he gradually taught me how to drive. I have fond memories of me and Alan McGarrity thrashing his Lotus Cortina E around the Kirkistown circuit late into the evening.'

Kirkstown race meetings would only take place on a Saturday due to local objections from the Protestant community who were anxious that Sunday racing would not intrude on their Sabbath. Saturdays would turn into nights, late nights, and his father refused to go home on occasions, leaving young Donnelly trailing behind him as they moved from the bar in the marquee in Kirkistown to the various local hostelries.

'After a while, it became a bit of a chore, because Dad and his mates got thrown out of the marquee at Kirkistown, and then it was up to the Mermaid Bar in Kircubbin. A few more hours in there, and then to the Wild Flower in Whiteabbey. By the time we were getting home, it could have been 2 o'clock in the morning, so it wasn't much fun because I was only a kid. On one occasion, I was left out in the car, and I found a head gasket on the pavement in Kircubbin. A head gasket is made up of lots of slices of aluminium, and, it being razor sharp, I slit my hands several times. So I thought, I'll cover my arms in blood and put a bit around my face. If I walk in there, the shock might hit him, and he'd say, "Let's get you home".

'So with blood everywhere, I walked into the back bar, and there he was with his mates, and all he did was turn to the landlady and say, "Take him upstairs, wipe him up, give him a bottle of pop and stick him out in the car again." That plan backfired.'

Nevertheless, there was a close bond between father and son, and, as his father's career in motor sport came to an end, the emphasis switched to Donnelly Jnr., and in 1980 his dad bought him his first Formula Ford, a Crosslé 32F.

To go racing in Ireland, drivers had to be at least seventeen years of age. At his first meeting at Mondello Park in the early part of 1980, Donnelly was still only sixteen, but he was not the first driver in Ireland to bluff his way onto the starting grid.

'I had a road licence before I had my competition licence. But before I was seventeen, we did two meetings. We headed to Mondello with no licence, but we thought, we'll blag this. We had a medical certificate, and a friend of Dad's filled it out in the bar at Mondello, signed it as a doctor. We went around into the scrutineering bay, and I went to sign on. The scrutineer said, "Where's your licence?" I turned to Dad and said, "I haven't got it, you've got it?"."You fecking eejit," he said, "Listen, in the rush in getting out, we left it on the kitchen table," and they said, "Ah sure, not to worry, bring it the next time, I know who you are." So, off we went, racing with no licence, and that was done for the first two meetings before I got my competition licence.

During his teenage years, Donnelly was at boarding school in Dundalk with the Marist priests and found it difficult to combine his racing and schoolwork. However, he found an ally in a priest named Tom Dooley who was the School Principal. Dooley was a motor-sport enthusiast himself, and he gave Martin special dispensation after study on Friday nights to go racing, unbeknownst to the others in the college.

'I would go over the wall, and my mates Ronnie and Martin were in the car outside waiting for me. Off we'd go to Mondello, test on a Saturday, race on a Sunday and come back on the Sunday night. One of my schoolmates, Brian McLean, organised to leave the artroom window off the latch, so up and over the wall, across the fields and through the window to bed. Up the next morning and back into class, and that went on for two years.'

Donnelly even smuggled his dad and his mate Ronnie McWhirter into the school to watch the highlights of a grand prix, only to be caught by Dooley in the recreation room, but, according to Martin, the Principal 'sat down and got a fag out and said, "How did you get on today? Did you get a result?"'

He began his first full season in Irish racing with the 32F in 1981, racing at Kirkistown and Mondello, but he also did sprints and hill climbs.

'It wasn't done as a serious occupation or anything like that; it was just a bit of gas, a bit of craic. It was my dad's excuse to get out of the house for the weekend – to get away from his wife (my mum) and have a few beers with the lads.'

Donnelly Snr. had run a few drivers before turning his attention to his son, amongst them Joey Greenan. Greenan ran the car, a Crosslé 16F, as well, and Donnelly Snr. was anxious to learn about gear ratios, tyres, engines and Formula Ford in general so that when Martin Jnr. came of age later on, they would know about the cars and Joey would be the mechanic.

Martin Donnelly Snr. bought a Royale RP24 in 1977 for Greenan, but that was a difficult time because more often than not the car was involved in big accidents, and that hurt the family financially. Nevertheless, they persevered, and they managed to acquire a Van Diemen RF81 chassis and an engine from Scholars before throwing themselves into Irish Formula Ford racing.

'I, quite stupidly back in those days, was trying to go out to qualify, maybe at the front of the C race and not try and go flat out. I would do the C race, and then I'm at the back of the B. Then I would get a good run and get into back in the A. On a good weekend, you have three races. Eventually, I did the job right and started getting in among the A boys.'

In 1982, Donnelly had his first big accident while racing at Kirkistown. He was challenging for the lead through Debtors Dip when he went over the top of the leader under pressure from his friend Alan McGarrity and barrel-rolled down the circuit, smashing all four corners of the car. Harry Johnson had offered him his 2-litre car to race that weekend, but the doctor at the circuit wouldn't let him race after the accident. The car was almost a write-off, but there was a silver lining as he went to England to rebuild the car at Van Diemen.

As with so many young Irish drivers at the time, Van Diemen-owner Ralph Firman took Donnelly under his wing, and, for the two weeks while the car was rebuilt, he stayed with Ralph and his Irish-born wife Angie. When Donnelly returned to Ireland, the first meeting he raced in was the Irish Formula Ford Festival at Mondello where Ralph insisted he do a test with new tyres.

'Joey [Greenan] was there, and he had a new RF82 car, but we went out and won it, we kicked ass. Derek Daly presented the trophy; I've got pictures in my office of Derek presenting me with the trophy for the Festival.'

Donnelly finished with boarding school in 1982, and he got into Queens University to do mechanical engineering. He also raced in the Formula Ford Festival at Brands Hatch with backing from a new sponsor, Frank Nolan, who handed over £500 to race at the Kent Circuit in England.

Frank Nolan lived in Lucan in Dublin and was in the construction business with his company Dwyer Nolan Developments. He didn't have a motor-sport background, but another Irish driver, P.J. Fallon, persuaded Nolan to back him in both Formula Atlantic and Formula Ford 2000 in the early 1980s. Nolan's association with Fallon ended in 1983, and he was looking to back another Irish driver, Paul Bishop, before a disagreement between the pair led the developer to Donnelly's door. Donnelly was to wear Nolan's colours of yellow and blue throughout the rest of his career, and it was Nolan who persuaded him to race in the UK. (Nolan had asked Fallon what colours he should run. They settled on yellow and blue after the Brazilian football team.)

'I had no plans for 1983, but, lo and behold, I got a phone call from Frank who said he wanted to help some young Irish kid to get into England and that I was one of four on his short list.'

Donnelly raced in the UK Formula Ford 2000 in 1983, taking his first win at Cadwell Park. However, his Zak engine was found to be illegal, and he lost all the points he had garnered that season in his Van Diemen RF83 with Frank Nolan's backing.

While he was setting out on a path that would eventually lead to Formula 1, it took some persuading for his mother to be fully convinced that her son was going in the right direction.

'I sat down with the family and we had a conference around the kitchen table, and my mum said she could see this as an excuse to go out, like my dad on the piss. They'd paid for me to go to the boarding school for seven years, so it was a major financial commitment. We spoke to the tutor at university, and they agreed to give me two years out, so I rang Frank back and said, "Right, fine, I'll go with it".

'He says, "That's good, because I've got a car being built at Van Diemen, and you've got to go over and collect it." Frank was a great man at reading people; he knew that I wasn't going to say no to the offer.'

Donnelly spent a couple of years in Formula Ford 2000, racing in the UK and Europe. He could have won the 1985 UK series, but he and championship leader Bertrand Fabi put each other off at the first corner in the final race at Thruxton, giving the Canadian the title.

'Frank was a hard taskmaster. At the end of each year, Frank would always write me a real nasty letter, threatening to drop me. The only logic I could put to that was that it was the rocket under my arse that I needed to go and get deals done. I remember at the end of 1985 going around to all the Formula 3 teams and asking them how much they were going to charge me. I came across a guy called Tim Stakes who ran a team named Swallow Racing, who was backed by his own company Rugby Finance. He also got sponsorship from British Telecom.

'I went back to Frank and said, "Swallow is going to offer me a half-price deal. We've got to bring half the money and they'll bring the other half." The deal was done, but, unfortunately for me, on 13 April that year Frank took a massive heart attack and died. The reason I remember that date is because it's the same date (although not the same year) that I got married to Diane [Ronnie McWhirter's daughter], which is ironic. It wasn't done purposely, but it just fell that way.

'Frank always wanted to see his car going through Casino Square in Monaco, and you know, we did achieve Frank's ambition to get

Above: Paddy Hopkirk and co-driver Henry Lidden await presentation of the awards for winning the 1964 Monte Carlo Rally.

Below: Paddy Hopkirk and Henry Lidden with their array of trophies after their Monte Carlo win.

Above: John Watson, like Derek Daly, was also part of the Silk Cut Jaguar Sportscar team. Photo: Michael Chester.

Below: John Watson raced sportscars for Jaguar and for Porsche. Watson won the Fuji 1000 with Stefan Bellof in Japan in 1984. Pictured here at Le Mans in the Silk Cut Jaguar. Photo: Michael Chester.

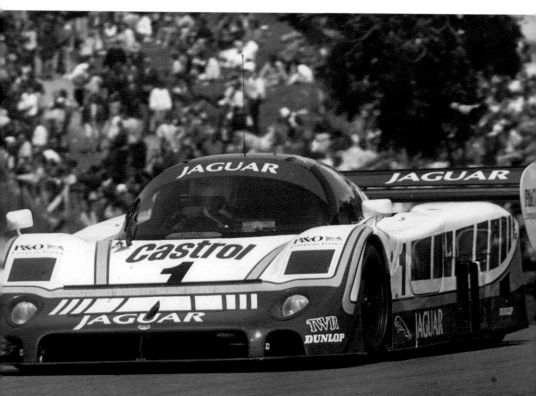

Above: Billy Coleman's Lancia Stratos, at the Galway Rally in February 1978. © RTÉ Stills Library.

Below: Billy Coleman gets into his car 'The Chequered Flag' Lancia Stratos, during the Galway Rally in 1978. Note the size of the television camera mounted on the car's bonnet. © RTÉ Stills Library.

Above: Billy Coleman was perhaps best known to his legions of Irish fans when he rallied in the Rothmans Porsche. ©RTÉ Stills Library

Below: Jeremy McWilliams, the only Irish rider to win a 250-cc grand-prix race, strikes a pose. Photo: Pat Donnelly.

Above: Jeremy McWilliams (Aprilia), French Grand Prix, Le Mans. Photo: Pat Donnelly.

Below: Martin Donnelly (left) is congratulated by Derek Daly after his Irish Formula Ford Festival win. Photo: Con Connolly.

Right: Martin Donnelly during his
British Formula 3 days.
Photo: Michael Chester.

Left: Austin MacHale, in a familiar pose
behind the wheel of the Toyota Celica.
Photo: Michael Chester.

Below: Austin MacHale and co-driver Brian
Murphy in the Toyota Celica during the
controversial 1998 AA Circuit of Ireland
Rally. Photo: Michael Chester.

Above: Eddie Irvine checks his mirror prior to racing in the Jordan Formula 1 in 1994.

Below: Eddie Irvine emerges from the Ferrari at the end of the 1998 Monaco Grand Prix, where he finished third.

Above: Eddie Irvine in the Scuderia Ferrari Marlboro, 1998.

Below: History as six Irish drivers compete in the Le Mans twenty-four-hour race in 1989. Back row: Derek Daly, Kenny Acheson, Martin Donnelly, John Watson.
Front row: Michael Roe, Larry Mooney (support, Irish Motor Sport) and David Kennedy.
Photo: Michael Chester.

some young Irishman out of Ireland and into Formula 1. I invited his wife Rita to see the 1990 Monte Carlo race, and it was an emotional day. OK, it wasn't his car, but it was his helmet colours. I always kept Frank's colours of yellow and blue, and I felt that we achieved what he set out to do.

'I'd never have gotten anywhere in motor sport if it hadn't been for three people from Ireland. First of all, my father, who got me started; second of all, Frank Nolan, who picked up the purse strings, got me to England and got me started in 2-litre racing and Formula 3; and Eddie Jordan.

'However, if Frank Nolan had been alive at the end of my Formula 3 career, we would never have gone to Jordan, because I think E.J. and Frank were very much cut from the same cloth. They're wheelers and dealers, and Frank wouldn't have spent his money with E.J.'

In 1986, Donnelly took three wins in his first year of Formula 3 at Donington, Oulton Park and Silverstone, finishing third overall in the championship, before repeating his third-placed finish the following season where he partnered Damon Hill in the Cellnet-Interscope team. He also won the prestigious Macau Formula 3 race in the ex-Glen Waters Ralt RT31-Toyota in 1987, and that win got him a Marlboro Formula 3000 test at Donington Park.

Despite a fine test session in the early part of 1988, there was no budget to go racing in international Formula 3000, so it was back to the Cellnet-Interscope team with Hill as his partner. But Donnelly wasn't happy with the set-up of his Ralt, and, despite a win at Snetterton, the Irish driver left the team to join up with EJR in Formula 3000. Cellnet were not happy and threatened to sue for breach of contract, but Donnelly did manage to see out the remaining five races that year for EJR where he won his first race at Brands Hatch followed by second places at Le Mans and Birmingham and a last-round win at Dijon in France which gave him a remarkable third place in the championship.

EJR now had a tie in with an Irish driver in an Irish team. Donnelly says it's a deal he had to take.

'I didn't really have much of an option. E.J. says, "There's the f***ing deal, take it or leave it." He had a six-year management contract attached to it, which was 15 per cent in those days, and my attitude was 15 per cent of nothing is a good deal. I remember talking to E.J. at Snetterton at the Formula 3 meeting, and Thomas Danielson, his driver at the time, had lost his competition licence due to an eye defect.

'E.J. was one driver down. He got backing from Q8 Oils, and the other car was driven by Johnny Herbert. But within forty-eight hours, Peter Waters of the Cellnet team rang to say, "We've changed our minds, we're not letting you go."

'Bear in mind having won the Cellnet award (for Best Young Driver of 1988), I had got a five-year personal sponsorship deal from them so well. So I went to see E.J. "Do you swear you're going to stick by me?" he says. "Yes, I'll stick by you," was my reply, so, sorry Cellnet, the contract's not worth the paper it's written on, and now I'm with Eddie Jordan.'

The relationship began with a bang in more ways than one when Donnelly won his opening race with the team at Brands in which Herbert had a massive accident ending his season, almost costing him his life.

'I went on to win the race, and it was a hollow win. I didn't spray the champagne on the podium that day, and afterwards I left and went to St Mary's Hospital in Sidcup to see Johnny. E.J. brought various drivers in to replace Johnny afterwards, and he then copped on about the finances after the second meeting, which was Birmingham when I finished second to Roberto Moreno.

'E.J. says, "Where's the f***ing money? You know, you're costing me a fortune." But I didn't have a penny. So really, in racing terms, he became my pimp, and he was just selling me to Japan or to whoever was interested. In fairness, he got me some great drives with Richard Lloyd in the Porsche at Spa, with Derek Bell, and in Group C in Japan.'

By the end of 1988, Martin Donnelly was suddenly big news. His win at Macau in 1987 and his fine end to the Formula 3000 season were making team owners sit up and take notice. Lotus were on the phone looking for him to be the second driver to former World Champion Nelson Piquet. It was a great opportunity, and he got into negotiations with the team. Satoru Nakajima though, came back with more money, and the Japanese driver got the second seat, as Donnelly signed with Lotus as a test and reserve driver.

Donnelly entered the 1989 Formula 3000 season with EJR, who had lost the Q8 Oils sponsorship, replaced by the Camel cigarettes brand and an all-yellow car for the Irish driver and his French team-mate Jean Alesi. Donnelly had a busy year racing in Formula 3000 and in sports cars. He very nearly got his first Formula 1 drive when Piquet broke a rib before the Brazilian Grand Prix after a slip on his yacht, but the three-time World Champion recovered in time. A trip to Ireland in the Jordan Formula 3000 saw him break the lap record at Mondello Park in 1989.

However, his big break in Formula 1 came at the French round later in the year at Paul Ricard, not with Lotus, but with Arrows as he replaced an injured Derek Warwick who was hurt the previous week in a karting accident. Alesi was pissed off with Jordan, as he felt he should have had first call with Arrows. After all, it was his home grand prix.

It was not the most inauspicious of starts for Donnelly when, having qualified fourteenth, a pile-up on the first corner meant he had to restart the race in the spare car, which was set up for the team's other driver, American Eddie Cheever. However, he managed a creditable twelfth place, despite a spin, while Alesi, who eventually got a drive through Eddie Jordan's dealing with Tyrrell, finished a stunning fourth in his first Formula 1 race.

'The car was difficult to drive as it was set up for Eddie – and I wasn't anywhere near fit enough. It was warm, the south of France, and normally at the end of a grand prix you'll do a slow-down lap. So I've taken the chequered flag, and I think, thank fuck for that. Put me head down, put me head back up again, and I'm going between two marshals not realising that I've got a lap to slow down. I almost wiped out those two lads.'

Eddie Jordan, while continuing his dealings by putting his

drivers in various championships around the world on a pay-per-drive basis, was putting the screws on Donnelly to give him a cut of his salary at EJR. According to Donnelly, during negotiations, E.J. and the Irish driver struck a deal for £50,000, but he was looking to take 15 per cent of that sum as part of his management contract.

'I said, "My fee of 50 grand has to be exempt from your 15 per cent. Why are you going to pay me the money in the left hand and take it out of my right? You can have everything else, the money from Lotus, the money from Nissan." I mean, we did a deal with Nissan for Le Mans, a one-off at $70,000. It was E.J. who did that as he had a good friend in Nissan at the time. There was good money coming in, and E.J. was getting a good whack of it.

'So, he relented. There was a massive dispute with Jean Alesi over who would sponsor his drive at the French Grand Prix. Both of us were under contract to Eddie Jordan, and one of Tyrrell's drivers was Michele Alboreto, who was sponsored by Marlboro. But Jordan had the Camel backing, and, somehow, he managed to get Alesi into Tyrrell with the Camel sponsorship, and the rest is history. Jean finished fourth, one of the very few drivers to ever get points in his first grand prix.'

Alesi raced in both Formula 3000 and Formula 1 for the rest of the 1989 season and was crowned the Formula 3000 champion, giving EJR the title. He also raced in seven more rounds in Formula 1 before signing a contract with Tyrrell for 1990, again set up by Eddie Jordan. Donnelly had wins at Vallelunga and Brands Hatch for EJR, but it was his team-mate Alesi who took the title. Nevertheless, Donnelly had done enough to convince Lotus to sign him up to partner Warwick for his one and only Formula 1 campaign which was to end so cruelly in Jerez.

'I felt very comfortable within Lotus. It was a good set of guys, and I formed good friendships.'

Donnelly had demonstrated in testing for Lotus that he could handle what was, in effect, an uncompetitive car, a midfield machine in the division-two ranks of Formula 1. In the first nine races of the season, Donnelly's car retired six times. He was eighth in San

Marino and Mexico, and in race 10 in Hungary had his best finish of the year, a seventh. There followed a twelfth place in Belgium, before further frustrating retirements in Italy and Portugal. Then Donnelly led the team onto the third last race of the year, at Jerez in Spain in September 1990.

'I remember some parts of that weekend, and it was back-to-back grands prix. We had the Portuguese race on the Sunday, and the following weekend we had Jerez. There wasn't much logic in flying back out of Portugal on the Sunday night to have to drive back down to London on the Thursday morning to fly out again.

'We had good friends that that time, Ed and Jenny Dillon. Ed was out in Spain looking at having a villa built, and we had decided that in between the two weekends, we would meet up with Ed and Jenny and have, like, a four-day break with them, and they would come with us down to the grand prix.

'We flew from Lisbon to Madrid and then Madrid to Alicante and met up with Ed and Jenny. We had four good days of relaxation before the four of us went to Jerez. At the track, we had two Vespa scooters, and myself and Diane went around on one scooter and Ed and Jenny on the other. As we got to the end of the circuit, I said, look, this is the best place to watch because you get the sensation of speed. It was one of the flat-out corners on the way back into the last bend.'

After that, Donnelly's recollection is, naturally enough, hazy to say the least.

'I don't remember much about restaurants or much about the hotel. That morning, the Friday, we had a warm-up, but I remember nothing about that at all. Then practice. I don't remember that. It must have been close to the end of practice, and lo and behold, where I had my accident is where Ed and Jenny were standing. Obviously it has been well documented that I got thrown out of the car and the car disintegrated.'

Donnelly was more than lucky to survive. His Lotus smashed into a section of the metal Armco barrier, which wasn't guarded by a covering of tyres, at over 250 kilometres per hour. The car fell apart, and Donnelly was flung clear onto the track with his seat still strapped to his back. He suffered massive leg injuries and bruising to his brain. He lost almost half the blood in his body. His life was saved by the Formula 1 doctor Sid Watkins.

'What actually happened was that the belt cranks were bonded underneath the bottom of the tub – most dampers these days are top of the tub; ours were bonded alongside the bottom. The belt crank was actually starting to come loose in the carbon fibre, and it's like most things, when you put heat and friction into it, like a coat hanger, if you bend it quickly enough through friction it will bend and break. The same thing happened to the car. The top of the damper broke off, the tub actually hit the ground, and all of a sudden it was on the tarmac.

'I was travelling at 165 miles an hour, and I had no steering or breaking control because the tub's on the ground. When I hit the Armco, the carbon fibre then disintegrated through shock, and I got thrown out. I think, realistically, it's fair enough to say that if the tub hadn't broken up, I'd have been killed instantly, because your body only has a certain amount of elasticity. I've still got a broken collarbone to this day and a limp, but Sid Watkins believes that the tub breaking up saved my life.'

The aftermath of the crash was seen on Eurosport TV, who were covering practice that day. A marshal is seen standing over the prone body of Donnelly, unsure of what to do as others run around, trying manfully to get the smashed Lotus off the track.

'It had an effect on a lot of people at that time. I've got pictures of marshals and a doctor stood beside me, and I'm lying on the track like a rag doll. But the rules stated at that time that nobody could touch me until Sid Watkins got there, and he was parked at the exit of the Formula 1 pit lane. He had to do almost a complete lap before he could get to me. When he got to the scene, he lifted my visor up and could see I was asphyxiated. I wasn't breathing, and my face had gone a pale shade of blue. So he got two tubes, stuck them up my nose and down into the back of my throat to clear my airways and then he cut the helmet off. While all of this was going on, Senna stood there watching.

'Obviously, it took a while, and Sid Watkins took his time to get me stabilised. He got me on a stretcher and off into the medical centre. My boys, my mechanics, were sent out with bin bags to go out to that part of the circuit and lift up all the debris. They were lifting up syringes, Fentanyl and fibreglass. I remember one of my good friends then was a guy called Crock, and he says that that just knocked the stuffing out of him. The mechanic on the car who worked on the part that broke, he was thrown out for quite some time afterwards. He had to have counselling.'

That ended the Formula 1 career of Martin Donnelly. The Lotus wasn't the most competitive of cars, but he liked the team and was anxious to stay with them for the 1991 season. There was also talk that Eddie Jordan was coming on board again for the following season, his first in grand-prix racing. It never came to pass.

'The morning of practice, Lotus took up their option and signed me for the following year, 1991. But there were three contracts on the table: Eddie Jordan's, Tyrrell's (because Alesi had already done his deal to move on to Ferrari) and Lotus.

'Lotus had the option of my services, and I got a cheque of $40,000. When I'd signed, I put a cheque into my phone book, somewhere safe so it wouldn't get creased and I knew where it was. After I had the accident, Diane then searched my kitbag, my briefcase, and she couldn't find the cheque. Fair play to Lotus, when I got out of hospital, the cheque had gone stale. I believed I was going to get back and so did they, so they issued a new one. Obviously, since then, I found the old cheque, so I got it framed, and it's on my wall in the office. A bit sad really, but I thought it would be a nice thing for my son Steffan to have in years to come.'

He never did race again with Lotus. The rehabilitation took a long time, and he still bears the scars today. He did try to get back into a Formula 1 car, but the problem was that he couldn't get out of one quickly enough in the case of an accident, and that's what really stopped him resuming his career.

'That's true. You had to get out of the car in five seconds with the steering wheel attached in its most awkward position, and I couldn't do it. I didn't have the mobility to get out. I drove the Jordan Formula 1 car in February 1993. E.J. stuck by his promise. I've also driven several cars for Clive Chapman, and I drove Senna's Renault Turbo.'

But, despite a near full recovery, his inability to get out of a Formula 1 car quickly mitigated against Donnelly, and he was forced to give up his dream.

After his accident, his marriage to Diane collapsed. He has since married Julie with whom he has two children. In between, he set up Martin Donnelly Racing (MDR) in 1992, and he raced himself in a few historic races. In the mid-1990s, Donnelly's team MDR raced in British Formula Vauxhall before he took the plunge into the British Formula 3 series in 1997, running Dallara-Opels with his two drivers, Brazilian Mario Haberfeld and England's Mark Shaw. It was a pretty good debut year in the unofficial junior world championship for MDR, with Haberfeld third in the series after two race wins at Silverstone and Snetterton.

The Formula 3 championship that year was won by another Irish driver, Jonny Kane, for Paul Stewart Racing.

In 1998, MDR ran two English drivers, Jamie Spence and Warren Hughes, but the team couldn't reproduce the form of their debut year, and Donnelly pulled out of Formula 3. In 1999, Donnelly himself got back behind the wheel of a car racing a McLaren M8D and won the International Supersports Cup at Silverstone.

Times have been tough recently for the Belfast boy. By the turn of the century, MDR ran into difficulties, and the creditors were moving in. In 2006, his beloved father passed away. In his memory, Alan 'Plum' Tyndall, who makes the *RPM* motor-sport programme for Irish national television, set up the Martin Donnelly Trophy races at Kirkistown, a Formula Ford 1600 shoot-out in honour of both Donnellys.

Despite the difficulties life has thrown at him since that day in Jerez, Martin Donnelly remains upbeat.

'I'm still involved in a sport that I very much love, and I've got a family – three wonderful kids, a wonderful wife in Julie – and life goes on. There is more to life than driving a Formula 1 car. But when you're in Formula 1, you're very much sheltered from the real world, and everybody does everything for you. But everyone wants a piece of you too, be it journalists, be it sponsors. The money is fantastic, and the lifestyle it affords you is great, but when that's taken away from you, you then realise that there is more to life than Formula 1, and I'm getting on with life.'

The crash at Jerez robbed Ireland of a driver who was looking at a long career in the world's top formula. But for that fateful day, who knows where it could have led.

'Life is full of hindsight, ifs, buts and maybes. When I see Johnny Herbert [who stepped in at Lotus after Jerez], I keep saying to him, "Where's that cheque? Are you sure you've got my home address?" Johnny was the test reserve driver for Lotus Grand Prix back then. But when I had the accident, Johnny stepped forward, and he got his second opportunity in the sport, and he went on to bigger and better things.

'Overall, though, the sport has been good for me. I suppose one of the mistakes I made was giving up on university because I went into Formula 1. Unfortunately, I didn't serve long enough in Formula 1 to get enough by to live comfortably, and by not completing university, I've got no qualifications. The best qualification I've got in life is motor sport. I know what makes a racing car tick; I know when drivers tell me what problems they're encountering, I've experienced them myself; and I know what it takes to run a team.

'I'm proud to say that in every year in motor sport that MDR has been involved since 1992, be it Formula Ford, Formula Vauxhall, Vauxhall Junior or Formula 3, we won races, including the Blue Riband Formula 3 event at the Silverstone Grand Prix in 1997 with Haberfield, and there's not many teams that can say that. And you know, if I can help young guys progress up the ladder and avoid the pitfalls that I fell into, sure wouldn't I have done a good job?'

Martin Donnelly still lives near the Snetterton racing circuit in Norfolk in England and was inducted into the Motorsport Ireland Hall of Fame in January 2007.

11

Austin MacHale

Austin MacHale is a five-time Irish Tarmac Rally Champion, winning the title in 1983, 1985, 1986, 1997 and 1998. MacHale finally brought the curtain down on his full-time rallying career at the end of the 2006 season to concentrate on bringing on his sons Gareth and Aaron, who have forged careers of their own on the international and national rally stages.

Indeed, the MacHales are becoming something of a rallying dynasty. Gareth, under his father's guidance, became the first Irish driver in over twenty years to pick up points in a WRC round since Billy Coleman's fourth-placed finish on the Acropolis Rally in 1985, when his Ford Focus took sixth place on the Rally Mexico in 2006. In 2007, Aaron MacHale became the National Rally Champion.

Although considered as one of best of his generation, Mayo-born Austin MacHale never had the charisma of the likes of other Irish rally legends such as the revered Coleman or Paddy Hopkirk, but his rallying skill was recognised, although perhaps grudgingly, by the rallying fraternity both here and in the UK, where he also competed on a regular basis. Indeed, MacHale came very close on more than one occasion to emulating Coleman's feat of being the only Irish driver to win both the Irish and British Rally Championships.

To those who don't really know him, MacHale wouldn't win Mr Popular. He has a rarely used smile, and there have been many occasions on which he perhaps felt, especially when he rallied in the North, that some were not altogether enamoured with a southern driver beating their boys. But with a record five Irish titles to his credit, the 'Rathcoole Ace' is a true exponent of a sport that, in spectator terms, attracts more people to its various Irish championships, be they tarmac, national or gravel, than any other sport in this country outside of Gaelic games and soccer. It's a well-known fact to those who live outside the Pale.

Even with his sullen demeanour, Austin MacHale is a true legend of the Irish rally scene. Five times its champion, he has steadfastly refused to believe that there are better national rally championships anywhere else in the world, and his aggressive and never-say-die attitude was the hallmark of a career that spanned four decades and three rallying eras. It included stunning fightbacks and two fantastic rivalries between himself and Coleman, three times an Irish championship winner, and the late Bertie Fisher, himself a four-time Irish Tarmac Rally Champion. Both rivalries are now etched in Irish rallying folklore.

A career that started with a creaking Ford Anglia lasted over forty years, and MacHale, who still competes in sporadic events, is as competitive and aggressive as ever. Since his humble beginnings sitting in the battered Ford Anglia on the Wicklow Rally in the mid-1970s, MacHale has amassed seventeen victories on Irish Tarmac Rally rounds which yielded five tarmac titles. He was also runner-up twice in the British Rally Championship.

'I was born in Louisburg, Mayo, just outside Westport, on 6 January 1955, but we moved to Kildare early on. I was brought up in a farming background, and I think that was the reason I got involved in motor sport. I was probably driving a tractor when I was six or seven years of age and took it from there. I started competing when I was eighteen. A guy called Fergal Allen, who was local to Maynooth at the time, and I built this racing Anglia out of Mondello, and we started to compete in that.'

MacHale admits that the spark that ignited his interest in the sport of rallying was seeing the late Roger Clark compete in the Circuit of Ireland in the 1960s and 1970s. Fergal, his brother-in-law Dermot O'Neill and Austin would make frequent trips to the Wicklow Mountains to see the British ace in action in the early hours of the morning over the Sally Gap.

Such was their enthusiasm that MacHale, with Allen's help, decided to have a crack at motor sport themselves. Allen became part of the MacHale backroom team that ran their driver for four decades. Over the years, Austin had the unstinting loyalty of those around him, and he amassed a crew that remained with him for pretty much most of his career.

'Yeah, the lads are together with me for probably more years than they care to remember. I suppose Noel Gilsenan is the one that goes back the longest. Noel was with me when we ran the RS 2000s, which would be back as far as the twin cams in the mid-1970s. Michael Eiffe, who is a brother-in-law of Noel's, took over the preparation of the car in about 1981, and Mick was with me up to 2002. He did all the cars from Mantas to BMWs to Toyota and the odd Group N car thrown in, the Starion and the Monza. Brendan Crinnion was the technician, and Willie Elliot was the panel beater. I've been lucky there that there have been a handful of lads who have been there from the start, and they're most loyal to me. They're into the sport and into the bit of craic, and that's great. There's nobody on the team who would not willingly do their best. Even with the Ford Focus, which Tom Gahan looked after since 2004, it's still mainly our own boys that are the back-up.'

MacHale built up his backroom team over the years, but it wasn't all plain sailing. The man who became one of the most dominant figures in Irish rallying, started his racing and rallying career humbly enough.

'The very first thing we got involved in was stock-car racing at Santry in north Dublin. It was an older brother of mine, Joe, who first got involved in that, and I started to compete there as well in the 1970s. Derek Daly started his racing career in Santry as well, but

I went into the rallying after that. I could have stayed circuit-racing, but the Anglia wasn't a great success, so we decided to try our hand at rallying. There was a guy called Sean Kelly who lived just outside Maynooth who did the early work on the car to get it ready to rally, and we were to go down to do the Circuit of Munster in Kenmare.'

Austin financed the car, and his friend Fergal Allen supplied the engine. But their first foray into the world of rallying in Kerry didn't last long. On a night stage, the Anglia had no lights, so Allen drove behind the Anglia in his own road car, using his lights to help MacHale to see where he was going.

'The first bend we came to, I got a shadow with the lights behind, went off down into a ditch and rolled. The car was damaged, and that was the end of my first rally.'

But it didn't deter MacHale, and he continued with Dermot O'Neill as his earliest co-driver. After a number of years competing in a Mark One Ford Escort, MacHale had a modicum of success, including a second-placed finish to Ger Buckley (Billy Coleman's cousin) in Wexford and an eighth place in Galway.

With the 1970s behind him and still struggling to put a decent budget together to compete, MacHale decided that he would compete in the 1981 Mintex Rally in Yorkshire, rallying an RS 2000 Ford Escort (Reg. No. 571 MYI) in the Group 2 or Group N category as it is now known.

The Irishman brought his Escort to face the mighty works machines of Jimmy McRae, Ari Vatanen and Hannu Mikkola, who became the 1983 World Champion, all competing in top-line factory cars. MacHale, not that well known in Ireland, let alone in the UK at that stage, would surprise them all that year.

'The first rally we took the Escort out in was the Galway Rally – I think it was 1975 or 1976, and we got an excellent run there. The car was reliable, and we finished well. That was really the start. It was just such a nice car and easy to drive.

'We changed from the twin cam in the late 1970s, and we did maybe two or three years in the RS 2000s before we decided to have a go at the Mintex, which was a snow-and-ice rally in the early part of the year up in Yorkshire. I felt it was easy enough to get a good result if you were lucky enough not to go off the road, and we got a third overall, which, I suppose, was something special for a Group 2 car.'

MacHale, who had John Magee as his co-driver, financed the run at the Mintex by digging the foundations of a house for a local garda sergeant and using the money to go rallying. He actually led the Group 1 section of the 1980 RAC Rally at one point before falling off. But it was the 1981 Mintex, the opening round of the Rothmans British Rally Championship, that really kick-started his rise up the rallying ladder, as only McRae and 'The Flying Finn' Pentti Airik-kala finished in front of the Irishman.

'That sort of started the ball rolling. That year, we did well in the Irish Championship as well, and we were lying around fifth or sixth in the Circuit of Ireland, which also part of the British Championship those days. [Swedish driver] Per Eklund was running ahead of us, and he was leading Group 1 by something like ten minutes. We were try-ing to catch Eklund, and we put it off into a field in Donegal. I think that's the year that Rosemary Smith came in on top of John Tansey's car. We were all on the same corner, crashed out at about 3 or 4 o'clock in the morning up in the Glenties in the Donegal Mountains.'

There was some success that year for MacHale, as he and new co-driver Christy Farrell won Group 1 on the Manx Rally; however, despite the class wins on the Mintex and on the Isle of Man, they weren't enough to displace British driver Mike Stewart at the top of the 1981 Group 1 standings. MacHale was also guilty of a wild driv-ing style that cost him in those early days.

By now, though, MacHale had well and truly caught the rallying bug and yearned to move up into the more powerful Group 4 cate-gory. In 1982, he purchased a Vauxhall Chevette HSR, and the wins started to flow. He won the Wexford Stages in 1982 and 1983 as well as the Cork 20, his first international win, and with it came the 1983 Irish Tarmac Rally series title, the first of five he would pick up in his career.

He may have been the champion by the year's end, but the 1983 season didn't start too well. MacHale failed to finish the Circuit of

Ireland and even managed to annoy the great Ari Vatanen, the 1981 World Champion, no end on the first Irish event of the year.

'We were delighted to get the car at the start of 1982. It was a car in which Jimmy McRae had won the Circuit the previous year, although McRae's car was not the one that we got. It was a sister machine. I remember Vatanen was behind us, and the first stage out, which was Moll's Gap (in Killarney) as usual, we got a puncture, and we stopped to change it. We were just pulling out when Vatanen came around the corner and clipped the front of the car, bending his axle. He wasn't impressed, and neither were we, because we only had the one spare wheel.'

However, after his non-finish on the Circuit of Ireland in 1983, things started to improve for MacHale and co-driver Christy Farrell. The pair finished second to Vincent Bonner's Escort in Donegal. It was a stunning drive to the runners-up slot as the Chevette at one point had dropped outside the top forty when MacHale lost time with a stuck gearbox which had to be changed by his crew. He actually fought his way back to lead with four stages to go before suffering not one but three punctures on the Atlantic drive stage.

There were some suggestions that the Chevette had been sabotaged to allow Bonner, a Donegal man, to take the victory, but it was never proven, and MacHale never questioned Bonner's win.

After his second place in Donegal, MacHale took his first international win on the 1983 Cork 20 and secured championship success in the final event of the series in Killarney, a rally that saw the return of Billy Coleman to the sport. Coleman won that weekend in his Opel Ascona, but despite the Corkman's remarkable win, MacHale had done enough to win the STP Irish Tarmac title for the first time.

'Nineteen eighty-three was our second year in the Chevette, and we got a couple of good results. Cork was our first international win, and we won the championship in Killarney. That year we went for the points rather than the outright wins, and there were some mighty battles. Bertie Fisher and Richie Heeley were competing in those days as well, and Richie was very, very competitive. He finished up second in the championship and also had some good scraps with Bertie.'

After his inaugural championship win, the following season proved to be a pivotal moment in MacHale's career. In 1984, the team ditched the Chevette, and Austin was instrumental in getting a deal together with the dealer team Opel Ireland, where he was due to drive a Manta 400. MacHale was the instigator of the deal, brokering it with the Opel dealers of Ireland, and he was all set to rally in his new car for the 1984 season. But there was a late twist. At the insistence of the Munster Opel dealers, a dual deal was done, and Coleman came on board in another Manta.

MacHale was more than a bit aggrieved that Coleman has been foisted upon him after he had made the initial deal with Opel. With the Corkman's arrival, the budget, which MacHale had worked hard to acquire for himself, was now split down the middle between the pair. At the time, it annoyed MacHale no end, although he downplays it now.

'I suppose it's water under the bridge now, but, yeah, we put the whole thing together with Opel Ireland and Basil Carr from Shell Oils. But just before we signed, when we looked to have to have everything sewn up, the Munster dealers announced that they were looking for Billy to get into the team, and they organised that. He'd obviously been around for a few years prior to me and was very experienced. It was something special for me, probably, to get him into the team.'

He may be a little more circumspect about the deal now, but at the time MacHale was hopping mad at the Munster Opel dealers' decision, and he blamed Coleman. For Coleman, it was his rallying comeback. He had been persuaded out of retirement in part by Ronan Morgan who went on to have a decent career as a WRC co-driver, mostly with United Arab Emirates driver Mohammad Bin Sulayem. Morgan, who also helped to bring the WRC to Ireland in 2007, navigated for Coleman in the Opel Manta in the 1984 season. Coleman had dropped out of the sport altogether for no apparent reason in the early 1980s. It was only in recent years that he revealed that the stress of running his farm near Millstreet in Cork had led to ill heath and his decision to quit.

'It was great to have him back and great to have him in the sport for the country's sake. Obviously, he had a huge support, and it was good for us because we had somebody to look up to and somebody to beat.'

The epitome of their rivalry came on the Circuit of Ireland back in 1984. Henri Toivonen retired his Porsche 911, which was left with only fourth gear while leading. After his withdrawal, the Opel Manta duo were in a position to battle for the overall win. At one stage, Coleman, who was leading on day four of the five-day event, pleaded with the MacHale camp to back off in order to give the Opel team a guaranteed one-two, but MacHale himself refused the pleadings and took the lead into the final day. He never finished the event as he hit a manhole cover on the run to Belfast, cracking the engine block, and Coleman took the victory, which was the spring-board to his overall championship success that year. To this day, there is a grudging respect between the pair, acknowledging each other's achievements in the sport, but neither would be top of the other's Christmas-card list.

Helped by the win on the Circuit of Ireland, Coleman was the dominant force in 1984, winning four of the five championship rounds and, with them, the tarmac title. MacHale, despite being the one who initially put the Opel deal together, won none.

'The Manta was a very hard car to drive because you had to be physically fit and strong as there was no power steering in it in those days. With the 10-inch wheels in the front and the 11-inch wheels in the back, it would really pull the arms and shoulders out of you, but it was a terribly reliable car.'

The tempestuous partnership, not surprisingly, lasted only one season. Coleman switched to the now-famous Rothman Porsche 911, and MacHale was back for the 1985 season with a Shell-backed, black-liveried Opel Manta. This time, it was Coleman who played second fiddle as MacHale took his second Tarmac Championship win, opening the season by winning Galway for the first time. Coleman beat

MacHale in Donegal by only one second, but a somewhat controversial win in Cork gave MacHale the series win. Normally, the cars were separated by thirty seconds at the stage start, but on the final day, MacHale asked for a one-minute gap (which he was entitled to do).The Rothmans crew at the end of the stages weren't made aware of what MacHale had requested, and they miscalculated the timings, believing that their man was quicker.

MacHale had outfoxed Coleman on his own territory, and the bitter rivalry deepened as a result. To this day, MacHale denies gamesmanship played a part in that 1985 Cork 20 win.

Coleman won Galway to open up the 1986 season in the Porsche, but he switched to the Group B Metro 6R4 Supercar by Donegal. MacHale crashed his Manta into a bank while leading in the north-west, which robbed him of a potential victory.

In between Donegal and the Ulster round, MacHale suffered kidney failure, collapsing on return from a visit to the Canary Islands. He was rushed to Jervis Street Hospital, where the kidney was removed, and, remarkably, three weeks later he was back in the Manta for the Ulster Rally, where he finished a stunning sixth in the non-power-steering Opel. It must have been hell to drive so shortly after his operation, but such was the bloody-mindedness of the man from Rathcoole that he refused to use his obvious discomfort as an excuse.

Another sixth place on the Isle of Man for MacHale, where Coleman was a non-finisher, gave the non-Group B car a chance of the 1986 title. But it wasn't the Cork driver who could stop MacHale: it was Cyril Bolton, in another Metro 6R4, who was the leading opponent. Coleman won Cork, but a first-placed finish by MacHale in the final round in Killarney gave the Opel Manta driver his third tarmac crown.

By the time the 1987 Irish Tarmac Championship came around, the Group B super-cars, which proliferated at world rallies and which had infiltrated the Irish scene, had been banned by the FIA, the world governing body, on safety grounds. Now, drivers at the top of the Tarmac Championship class had to use the slower Group A machines, and MacHale opted for an Opel Monza, a brute of a car.

On the Circuit that year, the heavy back window 'mysteriously' fell out, only to be replaced by his crew before final scrutiny.

'I think the back window just came loose, and the lads took it out. In those days, it'd probably be about two and a half hundredweight, and in the last stage we had to get it back into the car. I can admit it now: it didn't fall out. We took it out to make the car lighter.'

The Monza was ditched before the season's end, and championship success also dried up for the Opel driver. At the end of the 1987 season, he also lost long-time co-driver Christy Farrell, who had had enough and quit. He was replaced by Ronan McNamee, and MacHale's association with Opel ended on a high, winning the 1988 Rally of the Lakes after a very brief flirtation with an unloved Mitsubishi Starion.

The year 1989 saw a switch to another rather unloved car, the Sierra Cosworth, a make which was starting to dominate the Irish series. Indeed, British driver Mark Lovell upset the home-grown talent with back-to-back championship victories in a world rally Sierra in 1987 and 1988. Deprived of success, Austin then settled on the BMW M3 towards the back end of the 1989 season and, like the Opel Manta of a couple of years previous, it was to become a very distinctive, black-liveried car, sponsored by the Irish video-rental company Xtravision.

'We actually went to BMW M3 for two years, and we won several international rallies with that. It was another tough car to drive: 300 brake horsepower with a six-speed gearbox, and it weighed almost a ton. I suppose it was like going back to driving the Manta, non-turbo, but a friendly car to drive.'

The new M3 won the opening round of the 1990 series in Galway and was fourth on the Circuit. By the Donegal round, which he won for the first time, MacHale had a new co-driver in Dermot O'Gorman. A rival to his BMW emerged in the form of Bertie Fisher, who was also in a Prodrive-prepared M3. Coleman had now officially retired, this time for good, from the tarmac scene, and a second major rivalry, albeit a far less tempestuous one for MacHale, began that season. The MacHale–Fisher duels would last for the next decade, dominating Irish rallying before Fisher's untimely death in a heli-copter accident in January 2001.

MacHale's association with the BMW didn't start too well as the new decade began. It didn't finish in the 1990 Ulster Rally and was excluded from the Manx on the Isle of Man for using what were con-sidered by the organisers to be illegal tyres. MacHale got it together after that, picking up regular championship points and helped by his fourth Cork 20 win, the title decider went to the final round in Killarney, where MacHale started the event with a ten-point lead over Fisher's BMW. A fourth-placed finish would have been enough, but his car expired while leading on the Cod's Head stage with just 20 stage miles to go, putting the BMW out of the rally and enabling Fisher to take the first of his four championship crowns.

The following year, 1991, in his second year in the BMW, MacHale opened with a win in Galway, his third in all in the West, but crashed out on the Circuit while trying to chase down the Subaru Legacy of Colin McRae, and there the partnership with the M3 ended – as did MacHale's season.

He sold the car before the next round in Donegal, and his busi-ness and family commitments meant that he sat out the rest of the year, but behind the scenes there was a push to get a new machine, and by the time the 1992 season came around, Austin was back be-hind the wheel of a four-wheel-drive car for the first time when he introduced the left-hand-drive Toyota Celica GT4 to the Galway Rally, where it finished fourth. The car was converted to right-hand drive by the time that year's Circuit of Ireland had come around, but, although he was sitting in his preferred side of the car, MacHale failed to finish the event and, ultimately, third place in Donegal and second in Cork were his best results of the year, as Fisher won his second title in an ex-Colin McRae Subaru Legacy.

Fisher was starting to dominate the Irish tarmac rallying scene along with MacHale and Kenny McKinstry, who was also in a Leg-acy in the early 1990s. Fisher had won the 1992 title with wins in Donegal, Cork and Killarney and had his third championship win the following year, helped by wins in Kerry and Donegal as

MacHale struggled to keep pace. His crew worked hard on keeping the car on the road and close to Fisher, but budgetary problems meant that he was playing catch-up. Austin, however, was at least able to win his first Circuit in 1993 in the GT4.

'That [1993] was the last year of the long circuit, something around 500 stage miles and 1,500 miles in total, which was good for a Celica to have done. It was then the longest rally in the world, a real classic event.'

Despite his long-awaited win on the Circuit, MacHale didn't have a happy time for the rest of the 1993 season. This was epitomised by the huge shunt suffered in the Ulster Rally when the brake pedal broke on the Celica and he slammed it into a ditch at 100 miles an hour. A big moment, but, thankfully, he and Dermot O'Gorman were unhurt.

By 1994, Fisher had moved to a Subaru Impreza, and, in the MacHale camp, co-driver Dermot O'Gorman had been replaced by Brian Murphy in the navigator's, seat on the recommendation of Ronan MacNamee, who was now plying his trade on the World Championship stage with Pentti Airikkala. Murphy was actually a roommate of McNamee at one point and became MacHale's final navigator, the duo sharing their cars for thirteen years.

The pair had done sporadic events together before, dating back to 1988, but they became inseparable by the 1994 season, with the Killarney Rally of the Lakes, which had moved from its traditional December date back to an earlier start in May, the first for the new partnership of MacHale and Murphy.

The pair also had a new rival in Stephen Finlay as the Ulster driver won the 1994 title in his Ford Escort. Frank Meagher from Tipperary was also in the mix in another Escort, and it was he who took the 1995 crown, while Fisher remained a potent force, winning the 1996 title, his fourth – at that stage an Irish record.

Andrew Nesbitt burst onto the scene in the mid-1990s in a Celica, although his double championship success would come later in a Subaru Impreza, a car that was to dominate the Irish scene in the early 2000s.

MacHale was always there or thereabouts, but the Toyota Celica 165 was showing its age and wasn't as competitive as it should have been. As an amateur, MacHale was also conscious of the fact that he had to put bread on the table, as rallying was a hobby and wouldn't pay the bills, so work commitments – which meant a lot of time spent in Germany – meant that he wasn't as committed to the 1995 or 1996 championships as he would have liked.

MacHale had three tarmac championships under his belt by this stage, but he was now over forty years of age, and it looked like he wouldn't win another. That was until his Tom Hogan Motors team got hold of another Celica, this time the 185 version. It was a car that changed MacHale's fortunes and, with it, the Rathcoole Ace won two further tarmac titles.

'The 185 Celica was a very successful machine. It was a two-year-old car which was used in the French championship, and we won two Irish Tarmac Championships and had seven international wins and two seconds, which were probably the two best years that we had in the sport. Excellent results, and the reliability was there, so we were very happy with that. Didier Auriol [the 1994 World Champion] had raced it originally, and I think he had actually won Monte Carlo and the Portuguese rounds with it. The car then did a year and a half in the French championship, and we got it after that. But it was virtually unused. I would say it was the greatest Group A rally car ever made.'

MacHale felt energised by his new machine, and the Celica (Reg. No. KAM 703), backed by Ireland's national music station 2FM and oil company Castrol, began the 1997 season facing the likes of Nesbitt, Murphy and Eamonn Boland (both in Escorts), Liam O'Callaghan (Toyota) and Fisher, who were all hungry for success. Fisher won the Circuit that season, and, while he may have won the battle, it was MacHale who won the war, and, remarkably, he took his fourth tarmac crown, helped by another victory in Galway, his favourite event. Added together with wins on the Rally of the Lakes in Killarney and at the Donegal International, MacHale was able to wrap up the championship with three rounds still remaining in the series.

Fisher kept fighting for another title success and entered the 1998 Championship in his Toughmac-backed Subaru Impreza, and the pair were at the head of affairs again that season. MacHale won the opening round in Galway, making it win number six for the Celica driver in the West.

Galway remains MacHale's favourite rally.

'It is very well organised. It's at the start of the year, and the roads are very slippy, conditions are bad, and it puts a lot of pressure on the driver and the co-driver to make sure their notes are right and to cope with the different conditions. It's a bit like Monte Carlo, I think, for sheer out-and-out speed and a thrill. I like Donegal as well because it's the middle of June, and you have the crowds there, and it's nearly always very dry and very fast. For organisation and really good stages, I'd throw in Killarney.'

Although the Circuit of Ireland was no longer the classic round-Ireland rally it once was, it remained the jewel in the tarmac crown despite the Ulster Automobile Club's (UAC) decision to shorten the route.

The Circuit, which had originally circumnavigated the country, had its route cut because of the difficulty in marshalling the event, its growing costs and difficulties with road closures. For a few years, it ran from Bangor to Limerick and back, and by 1998 it was shortened even further, running from the seaside town of Bangor in Northern Ireland to Dublin and back again by the time the 1998 season had come around.

It was still run over the Easter Bank holiday weekend, and the 1998 version of the classic rally remains one of the best and most controversial in Irish rallying history. Fisher and MacHale began to dominate the event pretty much from the word go and traded fastest stage times over the three days at the head of affairs, this after the demise of early leader Andrew Nesbitt who went out on day one.

MacHale, Fisher and, indeed, Nesbitt rampaged through the opening stages. But by the end of the first day, Nesbitt was gone, and there was a problem for MacHale, as he was hit with a twenty-second penalty for apparently arriving a minute early onto one of the stages. Austin later claimed that a marshal had incorrectly beckoned the Celica forward to the starting position and then imposed the penalty when the car left the start. The imposition by a marshal of the UAC was to set up one of the most controversial finishes in Circuit of Ireland history.

'The controversy was with us and the motor club, not with the late Bertie. We had no problem with him or, indeed, he with us because it was the marshal that had beckoned Brian to come into the control at the wrong moment. Although we protested, they [the UAC] said they wouldn't do anything about it until the rally was over.'

It was a decision that would come back to haunt the organisers. By the end of day two, it had appeared that the penalty wouldn't have mattered, as Fisher was flying in his Subaru and led the Circuit by almost two minutes. But MacHale refused to throw in the towel and, spurred on by what he saw as an injustice, he began to gnaw away at Fisher's lead, which was cut to just over one and half minutes by day three, and, with two stages to go, it was less than a minute, still a considerable gap.

Fisher, though, picked the wrong set of tyres for the drying conditions on the second-last stage, and his lead was dramatically reduced to just twenty-five seconds by the hard-charging MacHale, with just the final stage to come. MacHale was also carrying that twenty-second penalty and was driving under appeal as they headed into the final run.

In a stunning drive, MacHale beat Fisher by twenty-six seconds. Without the penalty, MacHale would have been declared the winner of the 1998 Circuit by just one second. With the penalty still standing in the eyes of the UAC, it was his great rival Fisher who sprayed the champagne on the victory ramp back in Bangor on the bonnet of his Subaru, watched on by a grim-faced MacHale, clearly unhappy at the UAC's decision.

'He was running first on the road, and I was running behind him, and it was the greyhound after the hare, if you want. We'd everything to gain and nothing to lose, and he'd everything to lose, so we went for it. We got to it by twenty-six seconds, which meant we won the rally by one. Then, of course, the whole controversy started with the motor club, and they still wanted to penalise us the twenty seconds for the infringement that they reckoned that Brian had made.'

On appeal, the marshal, who had imposed the original penalty, eventually saw his decision overturned by the stewards at the meeting who ruled in MacHale's favour, and, days after the event, Fisher was stripped of the win.

Helped by that stunning come-from-behind victory, MacHale went on to take his fifth tarmac crown. He wasn't to know it then, but the 1998 Circuit of Ireland was to be his last victory in the Irish Tarmac Rally Championship.

Austin dropped the Celica 185 in 1999 for a left-hand-drive Toyota Corolla, his first world rally car. But a new crop of younger drivers were coming through, and, at the age of forty-four, he never got to grips with the new machine, even when it was converted from left- to right-hand drive. MacHale also had another big crash that year, this time in Donegal.

'The Celica was getting old. We were driving with Toyota Ireland then, and we got the Corolla. We won some national rounds, but we didn't win an international, and the 1998 Circuit was the last tarmac event we won in the Celica. The left-hand-drive thing, I think, didn't help. Spending so long in the sport and never having driven a left-hand-drive car took me a long time to get used to. But, in truth, by the end of the 1990s, I wasn't really dedicated enough and didn't have the interest, and there was a younger generation of competitors coming up.'

With MacHale struggling in the Corolla, it opened the door for Fisher, who went in search of *his* fifth title in 1999. It started well for his Impreza with wins in Galway and on the Circuit and, by the final round at the Cork 20, all that was needed to do to win the series and equal MacHale's haul of five series wins was to finish in at least third place.

But while lying second on the final day, he got stuck in a ditch, and Fisher had blown it, just two stages away from a fifth tarmac championship, handing the title to the Toyota Celica of Ian Greer.

Uncharacteristically, the mild-mannered Fisher leapt on his bonnet and kicked in the windscreen in frustration.

MacHale himself didn't have much of a year. He was in and out of the Corolla, which was not allowed to run in that year's RAC Rally because it was switched to right-hand drive. His 1999 campaign was epitomised by a massive crash on the Circuit in his Celica into which he switched in frustration with the Corolla. MacHale and Murphy's car ended upside down in a ditch after a dramatic high-speed crash which ploughed the car through a crowd of spectators on one of the stages in Northern Ireland. Miraculously, MacHale managed to avoid hitting anyone.

Fisher ended the season at the Rally of Great Britain in a Subaru Impreza world rally car, where he finished twenty-first, winning the top privateer award, but he pretty much dropped out of the scene in 2000, concentrating his efforts on his Fisher Engineering business in his home town of Enniskillen. He did compete in the 2000 Monaghan Stages Rally, where he finished second and also had a demonstration run at the Millennium Motorsport Festival at Stormont in Belfast, where he drove the Peugeot Group B 205.

However, tragedy stuck MacHale's great friend and rival in January 2001, as Fisher lost his life as result of injuries sustained after crashing his own helicopter on the outskirts of Enniskillen, which killed not only himself but also his son Mark, a promising young rally driver, and his daughter Emma. The family was returning from birthday celebrations of his wife Gladys in Ashford Castle in County Mayo when the helicopter went down just a few miles from their home. Mark and Emma died at the scene, but Bertie and Gladys were pulled from the wreckage alive. He never recovered and died thirty-two hours later after his life-support machine was switched off. Fisher's other son Roy survived the accident, along with Gladys, who sustained massive injuries but who somehow survived. The accident made national and international headlines. MacHale was devastated.

'I'd have known Bertie for years. I met him first in the late 1970s, and he'd be near enough to the same age as myself. Gladys would be at the events with him as would my wife Bernadette, and they struck up a relationship. I think it was really more a family thing that we got to know one another over the years. And then the rivalry was there, obviously, but he was a great competitor, that's for sure, and I really enjoyed competing against him. I think everyone that did would feel the same way.'

By its very nature, rallying is a tough and dangerous sport, and Fisher wasn't the only one of MacHale's rivals to suffer an untimely death. Frank Meagher, winner of the 1995 Tarmac Series, was killed while running in an old Sierra car close to his home in Cloneen, County Tipperary in March 2002.

The tragedies continued when, after the 2001 season was cancelled due to foot and mouth disease, two marshals were killed at the 2002 Donegal International Rally. Gerard McKenna from Crossmaglen in County Armagh and George Clarke from Moville in County Donegal died after a car left the road during the event at Cloghan, six miles from Ballybofey.

'Unfortunately, Frank had that accident and had a young family. It was very sad. In Donegal, the accident with the two marshals, I think, that was just a freak because it was where they were standing that the car happened to go off. We're always striving to keep the sport safer and take all sorts of precautions. In comparison to any other sports on fatalities or serious injuries – I think we're way down.'

With Fisher and Meagher now gone, MacHale appeared to be losing interest in the sport. He, like everybody else, sat out the 2001 season as rallying took a lead by cancelling its championships to protect farms which were under threat from foot and mouth. There was one major enclosed event in 2001 as MacHale's tarmac company helped to construct the Punchestown Rally Masters course for Ronan Morgan, which, at least, gave Irish competitors a chance to rev up their idle cars. Nesbitt won the 2001 event held at the Punchestown Racecourse in County Kildare, while he and MacHale tied for honours in the 2002 event.

Austin competed in only a couple of rallies in 2002, where Nesbit was crowned champion, before emerging as a force once again in

2003 in a Subaru Impreza, the must-have rally car of the early part of the new century. The hunger was back, and he contested not only the Irish championship but the British series as well. He and Murphy finished third in Ireland behind title winner Derek McGarrity but still couldn't win a tarmac round. It was MacHale's consistent points finishing that earned him his third place. The Subaru was second in the UK series behind the Corolla of Jonny Milner, just failing to emulate Coleman's feat of winning both the Irish and British Rally Championships. Amazingly, MacHale, though runner-up, didn't win a single event that season.

'We should have won the British, but we just weren't quick enough. A lot of the Irish competitors won't go over to the British rounds because they use the same stages year in year out, and, obviously, the local competitors know exactly where they're going. You could say the same thing about Irish rallies, but we tend to change the stages, reverse them and run them differently each year. It takes a year or two to get in the British Championship rounds, to know where the stages are and to know what they're like.

'Actually, I had no great ambition to win the British Championship. I think the Irish series is far, far superior, and it's a lot more competitive. Our main sponsor Sanyo are a British/Irish-based company, and that is why we did the British Championship, but I had no great ambition to win it. If we had done, all the better, but I didn't stay in the sport just to try and win the British.

'I think rallying is very, very popular in this country. All you have to do is go to any of the championship prize-givings or to any of the events and take comparisons to European or British Championship rounds, there's practically nobody there at the finish of their events. But if you go to Donegal, Killarney or any of these places, and there's thousands and thousands of people there.'

MacHale knows that he is involved in a growing sport. Many, if not all, of the rallies in Ireland were oversubscribed, and Ireland has such a reputation for the sport that Ronan Morgan and his co-promoter Sean Connor persuaded the FIA to run the penultimate round of the WRC in the north-west of the country in 2007. What upsets

MacHale no end is the lack of coverage his sport gets from the national media.

'For the amount of people that are involved in the sport and for the amount of followers, television and press coverage is not there. I think it's maybe ignorance more than anything, or else they're not getting the information. There are certain newspapers that are definitely doing a good job reporting on the events, but I think an awful lot more needs to be done, because it's got to be such a popular sport now. Obviously, a lot of the rounds are on during the summer when Gaelic Games take precedence, and the GAA have the most popular sports in the country, but we definitely need to get more publicity.'

In 2004, there was yet another change for MacHale with the first introduction into Ireland of the Ford Focus world rally car, which saw its first outing in Galway as Austin looked to add to his tally of seventeen Irish Tarmac Rally wins and break a sequence of no wins since the 1998 Circuit of Ireland. By now though, MacHale, although consistent, couldn't keep pace with the front-runners. Andrew Nesbitt had won two titles, Derek McGarrity one, and there was a new threat in former national champion Eugene Donnelly, who was competing in an old Toyota Corolla but who was blisteringly quick.

Despite his all-singing, all-dancing new machine, MacHale, again, didn't win an event in 2004, as Donnelly and McGarrity shared the Irish championship, with MacHale in third.

That season ended menacingly with sabotage performed on Donnelly's car. On the very last stage of the last round in Cork, McGarrity, who was first on the road, was only nine seconds in arrears as he flew through the stage in a desperate bid, not only for victory in Cork, but also for the title itself. After McGarrity went through the mid-point of the final run in his Subaru, a sinister plot emerged as Donnelly came across boulders and planks of wood which had been thrown onto to the stage, forcing the Corolla to crash, ending Donnelly's involvement and blocking the stage. The actions of a few had handed the series to McGarrity. He turned it down and, instead, decided to share the honour with Donnelly. It's never been properly explained as to why Donnelly was nobbled on that infamous day in Cork back in October 2004.

MacHale, once again, made an assault on the British series in 2005, where, again, he was runner-up, this time to David Higgins. He missed some of the early rounds, which, perhaps, cost him the UK crown, and there were some out on the stages who obviously didn't want an Irishman winning their series. In one of the latter rounds, a plastic bag containing oil and flour was hurled at the window of the Focus with MacHale and Murphy travelling at high speed.

Donnelly won the 2005 and 2006 Irish championship in his Corolla, as MacHale only did sporadic rounds in the Focus, concentrating instead on the progress of his two sons. Aaron won the 2003 Group N National championship, and Gareth won the 2005 Forestry title and then stunned the rallying world by taking sixth place in Rally Mexico in an M-Sport prepared 04 Ford Focus, becoming the first Irish driver since Coleman in the 1980s to take points on a world championship round.

Gareth was also a consistent finisher on other world rounds that year, including Monte Carlo, Japan and Germany, where his Ford Focus finished in a very creditable tenth place, just two places shy of picking up even more championship points.

With the onus now switching to his sons, Austin MacHale announced his retirement from full-time rallying at the end of the 2006 season, still chasing his eighteenth win in the Irish Tarmac Series. Age was perhaps his greatest enemy. Now over fifty and with Donnelly seemingly uncatchable, MacHale decided that being full-time in the sport in Ireland was no longer an option. He still did the odd event like Galway and even competed with Gareth in the 2006 Rally GB and the 2007 Rally Mexico.

'We need to get some good Irish competitors into the World Championship and reward the efforts of those who win the Irish Tarmac Series. I think they should be sponsored for two or three rounds of the World Championship and maybe pick the events that they'd be more familiar with – maybe one gravel and two tarmac events as a prize for winning the Irish title. Motorsport Ireland should do it, put something additional onto competition licences – even though they're dear enough – but think of some way of putting it together and getting the finance for some of our top drivers to do something like that. After all, Scotland had two drivers at the top of the World Championship in Colin McRae and Richard Burns, under Jimmy McRae's influence, and they proved they were well capable of competing with the best. I think we have drivers here who are just as good.'

And co-drivers? MacHale had quite a few down the years: Brian Murphy, Ronan McNamee, Christy Farrell, Dermot O'Gorman were amongst the many that sat beside the five-time Irish Tarmac Rally Champion.

'I think I've been lucky: all my co-drivers have been very good. Brian [Murphy] was very dedicated, and I get on very well with him as I've known him for a long time. He's very good on notes and with the commitments needed to the current WRC cars. Dermot O'Gorman was obviously good. He did a couple of years, and I think Dermot won his first international with me in Donegal. Ronan McNamee was very professional, but he moved on to bigger things. [McNamee was co-driver to Pentti Airikkala when the Finn won the 1989 Rally of Great Britain in a Mitsubishi Galant.]

'I think, at the end of the day, the man who had the hardest job was Christy Farrell, who was in at the start of all this. At that time, all the stages were blind, and Christy was excellent on maps, which was a huge advantage to me because he'd be able to call the roads as good as if you were on pace notes, and I really got to trust him.

'Of the other drivers, well, probably the hardest to beat I would think was Bertie. Billy Coleman was always very competitive, as he probably had that much more experience than everybody else at the time, and when pace notes came into the country first, he was very competitive straight away. It took us a while to get close to him. Frank Meagher was good, and when I started in the sport back in the 1970s, Richie Heeley was excellent and very competitive, but the toughest of them all was Bertie Fisher.'

And so, by the end of the 2006 season, Austin MacHale bade farewell to full-time rallying to concentrate on others: namely, his two sons and their efforts on the domestic and world scene.

'Yeah, it's great really. Gareth is the youngest, and they say at times that maybe he gets spoiled. But he did the Peugeot 206 championship in Britain and won the Forestry Championship in 2005 before we got the deal together with M-Sport and Sanyo to do the WRC in 2006. Aaron went a different route. I don't want two brothers competing against one another, and Aaron is very competitive. I think they're safe, and they have enough of sense that if they're getting beaten or they have problems they would back off until the time was right.

'A three-day rally or even a two-day international takes a lot more out of me than it used to maybe ten or fifteen years ago. But Rallycross is very good, and Ireland's Dermot Carnegie has won the British and the Irish Championships I don't know how many times now. He's a great ambassador for Irish motor sport, and it would be a very hard act to follow, but it was something that we wouldn't mind doing and maybe getting involved in.'

When MacHale looks back at his career, there seemed to be many more highs than lows.

'I think the year that we won our first international, which was Cork 20, and won the championship in 1983 is something that will always be in my mind. I suppose you'd have regrets over things like leading Donegal by three or four minutes and putting the car through the hedge or taking a wall out of it. But, overall, I have no complaints. To me, it has been a great sport. People often say to me, "Why didn't you get involved in the world championship back in the 1980s?" But you know, I had a young family at the time, and I'd no ambition really to go down that road. I was happy enough building up the business and looking after the family.

'I did many rallies abroad, but my first passion is the Irish Tarmac Rally Championship. It's nice to do foreign events. We did a rally, a European round, in East Germany, which was on gravel, and we finished second in it. I really enjoyed that. We did rallies in

Poland, Belgium, and I've done most of the European rounds, but you know, I still think that the Irish events are very competitive, and we have probably the best rallies in Europe.'

12

Eddie Irvine

Edmund 'Eddie' Irvine was to become *the* playboy of world motor sport in the mould of the 1976 Formula 1 World Champion James Hunt. But, unlike Hunt, who died of a heart attack in his mid-forties, broke and alone, Irvine has used his personality, skill and business acumen not only become a grand-prix winner but also to amass a personal fortune, and, love him or loathe him, he remains an Irish motor-racing icon. Alongside Derek Daly and John Watson, Irvine is only one of three Irish drivers to race full-time in the world's top formula, a series in which he so very nearly became World Champion in 1999.

The mention of his name in motor-racing circles brings out different emotions. There are those on his side, recognising that Irvine was a quick and talented driver. There are others who are not so quick to praise, his brashness and quickness of comment perhaps turning many off his personality.

There is no doubt, however, that Irvine could drive – and drive to win. His early honours included being British Formula Ford Champion and Festival Winner and a runner-up in the 1993 Japanese Formula Nippon Championship. He was initially reluctant when he got the call from Eddie Jordan to race in Formula 1 in 1993 at the penultimate race of the season in Japan, his father helping persuade his son, against his own inclination, that the time was right to enter the world's top racing series.

And what a start to his Formula 1 career. Irvine became one of only a handful of rookie drivers to score points in his very first drive in Formula 1. For good measure, he got a smack on the mouth from Ayrton Senna in Japan when Irvine had the audacity to up-lap himself, his Jordan re-passing the Brazilian's Williams in the latter stages of the race, which led to Senna storming into the Jordan motor home and planting one on Irvine.

Andrew Mueller of the *Guardian*, writing in 1995, gave his readers an insight into the Irishman who became known as 'Irv the Swerve'.

'You knew someone like Eddie Irvine at school. He copied your homework and got better marks than you, won everything on sports day, beat you up, ran off with your girlfriend, dumped her a week later, and you still never quite managed to dislike him.'

Throughout his career, Irvine was never one to shy away from controversy – or from memorable quotes for that matter. As Senna stormed out of the Jordan motor home after their infamous dust-up in Japan, Irvine shouted at the Brazilian, 'Insurance claim there!'

He seemed to have a devil-may-care attitude and once said, 'Fear is an irrational business. The things that really scare the shit out of me are earwigs, which used to infest our home in Ireland. I'd rather do 180mph around Monza than even see an earwig, let alone have one crawling around on me. I don't like snakes, either, but they are about the only two things that scare me, except for weddings, of course, and commitment, but that's another story.'

Eddie Irvine was born in Newtownards on 10 November 1965 to parents Edmund and Kathleen. The family didn't stay long in the town after his birth, moving instead to the little village of Conlig near the seaside town of Bangor, where he was joined not long after by a sister Sonia, who eventually became Eddie's fitness coach during his Formula 1 days and who later opened an exclusive night club in Monte Carlo.

Irvine says that he and Sonia had a happy childhood. For many, growing up in the North in the 1970s was a time of real trouble and strife, but Irvine claims the bitter hostilities that pervaded the province of Ulster at the time weren't a problem for him.

'It was just totally normal,' says Irvine, 'I was living in the country between Bangor and Newtownards, and it wasn't an issue. The most exciting thing that happened to us was when parts of Bangor were blown up by an incendiary bomb and all the fire-damaged stuff was dumped near my house. All the kids went rummaging for what they could find.

'I loved where we lived. We were in the middle of the countryside where there were foxes and badgers; and it was right beside Lord Dufferin's estate. I went poaching for the brown trout in his lake; there was a golf course right beside the house and a reservoir. There was everything you would need to have a great upbringing.'

After an unremarkable schooling, Irvine first sat behind the wheel of a racing car in 1983 at the age of seventeen. His father was a keen amateur racer and drove historic racing cars from time to time, and young Irvine started racing in his dad's cars, skipping the now-near-obligatory starting point of karting and moving straight into single-seater racing in Formula Ford 1600, powered by the world-famous Kent engine.

'I used to go to racing in Kirkistown with my father. We spotted this Crosslé, which cost around £1,200, and we had a Capri which we had painted and polished ourselves. We swapped it for this Crosslé, and we went motor-racing for a laugh. It really cost nothing to run. We just took it down to the circuits on a trailer. You'd have one engine build once a year, and we were using three-year-old tyres, so it didn't cost anything. The entry fee was the most expensive thing, along with the petrol.'

Irvine almost quit motor sport at the end of the 1986 season but for a timely intervention.

'Well, I was very lucky, because I had made the sort of agreement with myself that at the end of 1986 I was going to give it up because I was buying and selling cars, and I was doing very well at that, paying for my racing out in an old Van Diemen of my car-dealing. At the beginning, it went very well, and, all of a sudden, I went off the pace.

'At the end of the year, Ralph Firman asked me to come and test-drive the works Van Diemen, and because of that, I won everything in 1987, the two Formula Ford Championships in the UK as well as the Festival at Brands Hatch. Having said that, I nearly lost the Esso Championship because I was concentrating so much on the RAC, which was the big one. The Formula Ford Festival though was fairly straightforward. I led every lap, through every heat and won the final.'

From Irvine's point of view, it may well have been straightforward, but the Formula Ford Festival is probably one of the most difficult race weekends to win: 200 cars and drivers battling over two days racing at Brands Hatch, the former home of the British Grand Prix. Many drivers arrive at the prestigious festival thinking they have every chance only to get knocked out in one of the qualifying heats. Irvine, though, remembers sailing though the event.

'I won my heat, quarter-final and semi-final, and I won the final. I'd done thirty-something races that year and had been on pole position twenty-nine times. I'd basically won every race I'd finished, and the Formula Festival was the big one. Not to have won, that would have really hurt me big-time, probably not career-wise, but it would have hurt me personally because I loved the Formula Ford Festival. It was bigger than Formula 1 for me then, and to win it was . . . it was just mega. I could only lose it really, and it was just a massive relief to win it.'

Irvine is quick to praise Ralph Firman, who had a huge influence on a lot of Irish drivers around at that time, including Michael Roe, Derek Daly and David Kennedy as well as Irvine himself.

'If it wasn't for Ralph, I wouldn't have been in Formula 1, there's no doubt about it. I would have retired in 1986. I really had made my mind up, but Ralph was brilliant. At the start of the 1987 season, I was really, really quick. I was on pole for almost every race, but I was a marked man, and I just got involved in accidents – always, something happened.

'Ralph said, "Look, just don't worry about it. You're the quickest. Just go out there and you are going to win the race," and boom,

boom, boom, it was one win after another. He's a very cool charac-
ter, much laid back, and a real star. He loves motor-racing and,
although he is English, he did have a real love for Irish drivers. His
wife Angie was Irish, so I guess there was that – and Tommy Byrne.
He was in love with Tommy Byrne, and, you know, he probably saw
a little bit of Byrne in me or whatever, probably a more controlled
version.'

Irvine also acknowledges just how big an influence winning the
British championships and the Festival itself was to have on his future development as a driver.

'Well, that was the year [1987] that Marlboro picked me up and
started to sponsor me. They had started this staircase of talent, and
at that time, I was winning everything. Actually, looking back, I
wasn't picked initially because they thought I was a bit old. But I
went into a Formula 3 car instead of Formula Ford 2000.'

Formula 3 remains the breeding ground of future Formula 1 racers, and Irvine finished fifth in the 1988 Lucas Formula 3 series,
behind championship winner Jyrki Järvilehto of Finland, who became better known as J.J. Letho when he was in Formula 1. After the
championship was decided, most of the drivers involved in the British series, including Irvine, headed to Macau, a small territory on
the southern coast of China which was ruled by Portugal until 1999
– the oldest European colony in China which dates back to the sixteenth century and whose streets are turned into a motor-racing
circuit to host the biggest end-of-season Formula 3 races.

The track suited Irvine's Alfa Romeo, and, after putting it on pole
position, he won his heat and, in the process, set a new lap record. In
the second heat, he didn't make the best of starts; Rickard Rydell
and Irvine came together, putting both out of the race and ending
the Irishman's weekend. Irvine is convinced, to this day, that he
should and would have won in Macau had he not made that bad
start to Heat 2.

'I would have won it easily, but the Marlboro guys said, "Look,
qualify well and you'll be stepping up to Formula 3000," because
they believed that my engine wasn't that good, and I'd been getting

beaten only by the more experienced drivers like Martin Donnelly and Geoff Brabham, and all these guys who'd been in Formula 3 for quite a few years.'

At that stage, Irvine was making the natural progression in world motor sport. It doesn't happen so much these days – with the amount of money around, younger drivers can buy themselves into Formula 1 – but Irvine was doing the more familiar route from Formula Ford 1600s in Formula 3, and in 1988 into Formula 3000, a series which at one point was a support race at Formula 1 weekends before it was replaced by the new GP2 class, and the final stepping stone for many drivers on their way into the world's top motor-racing championship.

'Yeah, well, that's the way it should be, you know. I think it's a shame that it's now a bit fragmented. Senna, for me, had kind of the perfect career. He went Formula Ford 1600, Champion; Formula Ford 2000, he won the championship; Formula 3, Champion and then into Formula 1. The Formula 1 step was a bit too big really in those days, but it was, for me, the beautiful career. Formula Ford, Formula 3, GP2 (which replaced Formula 3000) is probably the way it should be, and they should get rid of all this other bullshit.

'Now, you've got Renault doing their little thing; you've got Nissan doing their little thing; and they should be told, "No, you can't do it. If you want to do it, you sponsor a driver." But, it's the FIA that's at fault; it's not the best-run organisation in the world.'

Irvine's initial foray into Formula 3000, however, didn't go to plan. He had a rotten season for Pacific Racing in 1989, partnering Lehto. Then, in 1990, he came into contact with Eddie Jordan, who was running his *own* Formula 3000 team, EJR.

Jordan had already won the 1989 Formula 3000 championship with Jean Alesi, and, by the time that Irvine came on board, the team was preparing for its move into Formula 1. Irvine won a Formula 3000 round in Hockenheim in Germany and finished a creditable third in the drivers' standings that year, but he has mixed feelings about the 1990 season.

'Well, it was good in one way and a disaster in another because they'd won the championship the previous year with Alesi, but they were going Formula 1 the following year, so E.J. basically raped the Formula 3000 budget and put it into his Formula 1 team, and it showed. I won one race, but we were nowhere.'

Irvine did have a Formula 1 test session while he was with EJR for the now-defunct Onyx team at the Paul Ricard circuit in the south of France. By his own admission, the team didn't want him there.

'I was forced on them by Marlboro, but they didn't give me any time, and they didn't give me new tyres. Looking back, I shouldn't have done it, but . . . any chance, you know. I was naive at that stage. I just wanted to get into Formula 1, but I didn't realise the politics involved with the Onyx team.'

Irvine was now at a crossroads in his career. He was finished with Formula 3000, and he knew it. He stepped back into Formula 3 to race in Macau again, but there was no option in Formula 1, so he decided to look east and race in Japan in their Formula 3000 Championship, which would eventually become Formula Nippon, a series latterly won by two other Irish drivers: Ralph Firman Jnr. in 2002 and Richard Lyons in 2004.

Irvine spent three years in Japan, where he also drove sports cars for Toyota, finishing fourth for the team at the Le Mans twenty-four hours in 1993 and second in 1994. The decision to go to Japan was a pivotal point in his career.

'A Japanese team approached me and said, "Do you want to come here?" and I said, "Why not?" They offered me $80,000 and prize money; there was no option to go to Formula 1, and I needed to get paid. There was no point in doing European 3000 again, so I went to Japan, and I thought that's it, the end of story, you're going to stay in Japan and make a lot of money.'

Irvine finished seventh in 1991, eighth in 1992, and he should have won the 1993 championship. However, he finished level with Kazuyoshi Hoshino after being disqualified from an earlier round. As the Japanese driver had more race wins, Hoshino was awarded the driver's title.

Despite that, Irvine was happy in Japan, but at the end of the 1993 championship, Eddie Jordan came a-knocking again, this time offering a chance to take him to Formula 1 with the Sasol Jordan-Hart Formula 1 team. Irvine, though, wasn't in any particular hurry to leave the Far East and enter into the world's top racing series.

'I had such a blast in Tokyo, I loved it. It's just such a fun city. I ended up being the highest-paid driver in Japan very quickly, and I had a great team whom I loved working with.

'For the following year [1994], I had something in the order of $1.3 million worth of contracts in my bag. I'd prize money and all that stuff to go on top of it and little side deals. I was keeping an eye on F1 of course, and Damon Hill was with Williams, and not all the guys that we raced against rated Hill. I remember Marco Apicella saying that if Damon Hill won a race in Formula 1, he would retire. [Apicella still races sports cars.] Damon was a bit of a joke in a way, and I had no respect for Formula 1 really at that stage because I realised that it was too much about the car, too much about politics. In Japan, we had qualifying tyres, our teams looked after us like gods, and we were making good money, and, you know, E.J. was offering me 120 grand or something like that, and I had $1.3 million already guaranteed in Japan.'

So, if he was being offered a lot less to go to Formula 1, why did he move? Irvine attributed a lot of his decision on the influence exerted by his father.

'I was in Barbados with my father, and I could see how much he wanted me to go to Formula 1. When you stand outside motor sport and look in, you're very passionate, and it's an amazing sport and all, but when you get inside, you start realising the politics, and you start realising that some drivers you have no respect for at all, were racing in Formula 1 and doing well in Formula 1. It was a bad decision on my part, put it like that.'

If the world of motor sport didn't know much about Irvine before he landed in Formula 1, they certainly sat up and took notice after his opening race, the 1993 Japanese Grand Prix in Suzuka where he partnered Brazilian Rubens Barrichello, who went on to finish fifth that day.

Irvine knew the Suzuka circuit very well, having raced there many times in Japanese Formula 3000. His rookie race went well, and he was looking to pick up a maiden Formula 1 championship point, when, late in the race, he did the unthinkable. He was initially passed by Ayrton Senna, which put Irvine's Jordan a lap down. However, the Irishman wasn't one for reputations, and when he came upon Senna again, he un-lapped himself, surprising the great Brazilian before shunting off Derek Warwick and finishing sixth, picking up a point for Jordan. Senna, who went on to win the race for McLaren, was so incensed by Irvine's action that he raced to the Jordan motor home, remonstrating with the team, before planting a punch on the Jordan driver, who, off balance, fell off a table in surprise.

Typically, Irvine brushes off the incident that catapulted him to world fame, not only in motor sport but also in the international media who picked up the story.

'When I think about that grand prix, I don't think about the Senna punch. I was eighth on the grid. I drove around the outside of three cars at the second corner, including Michael Schumacher, and I'm in fifth position. I could see Senna, I could see Prost, and I'm right up their gearbox. I'm only two cars behind these two guys, and I was laughing. I was thinking, What a bunch of wankers, letting me do that. I'm in a Jordan that hasn't scored any points all season, and I'm in fifth position in my first grand prix.

'It started to rain, and I radioed, telling them, "I'm coming in," and they said, "No, keep going," and I went round another lap, and that cost me an extra one or two points because the team, I felt, made the wrong choice, and I could have done better. Sixth was a good result because I scored a point in my first Formula 1 race. Prost and Alesi were the only two guys who had done it before, so it was good from that point of view, but I was really pissed off that I hadn't scored an extra two because I should have done.'

Irvine was also very surprised when Senna approached him after the race.

'Yeah, totally, because he was picking on the wrong guy. It was Damon Hill who caused the whole thing. Damon was ahead of Senna; he wouldn't let him pass; and I'm thinking, "I'm racing Hill. I can't sit here all day." So, I overtook Senna, and Damon should have moved out of the way and let him through. But Hill was with Williams, and Prost [Hill's team-mate] was leading the race, but I guess in those days they weren't so strict on blue flags [waved at slower drivers to warn that the leaders are approaching from behind].'

With a point in the bag from the Japanese race in 1993 and worldwide headlines as a result of the Senna incident, Irvine became a very marketable driver, and he signed a full-time contract with Jordan Grand Prix in 1994, but controversy was never far away. In the Brazilian Grand Prix that year, Martin Brundle, Jos Verstappen and Irvine, all fighting for seventh place, came upon Eric Bernard's Ligier, which was about to go a lap down. Brundle's McLaren slowed after overtaking, with a mechanical problem, and Bernard had to lift off (taking his foot off the throttle). Irvine turned straight into Verstappen's Benetton, which was launched into a series of somersaults. There was a mass pile-up, but, thankfully, no one was injured. Irvine was blamed for causing the accident (he still denies that he was to blame). He was given a one-race ban and a $10,000 fine. The Jordan team appealed, to no avail, and the FIA actually increased the suspension to three races.

'What a start to my grand-prix career. I got punched by Senna in my first race, crashed in my second, destroyed four cars in my third and got banned from my fourth. People are going to think I'm some kind of nutter,' said Irvine in an interview after the race in Interlagos.

He stayed with Jordan until the end of the 1995 Formula 1 season picking up six points in the 1994 campaign and ten championship points the following year. His best result was third at the Canadian Grand Prix in Montreal in 1995 behind team-mate Barrichello, who was runner-up to the Ferrari of Jean Alesi (his one and only grand-prix victory). At the podium presentation, an Irish tricolour was raised above Irvine's head. Because of his Protestant background, Irvine, and his Northern Irish-based parents, in particular, received some very nasty messages in the post.

'I didn't care what flag was up there, I really didn't. Flags mean nothing to me, but there was a bit of problem, I know my parents got hate mail, but the people who are at this level, they're so low, there is no point in even bothering with them.'

After a difficult start to life in Formula 1, Jordan Grand Prix was starting to find its feet, Barrichello and Irvine became its stable and settled drivers for the 1994 and 1995 seasons, and the team was going places.

Eddie Jordan was the perfect owner, it seemed, for Irvine, and he retains a grudging respect for his fellow Irishman, although it was perhaps a case of like with like, two men with their own way of doing things – Jordan, battling, trying every trick in the book to keep his team alive, Irvine likewise. Driving well, picking up crucial championship points but always looking after number one.

'At that stage, E.J. was on the up, really focused. He was wheeling and dealing, you know. He was hungry as hell, really hungry. The team was seen as a team going places. E.J. had the golden touch, and Gary Andersen was there, a designer who could do things for a third of the price. It was a young team that seemed to be going in the right direction. After a year, I realised it wasn't. The other teams were just so far ahead, and that next step was enormous, and I realised I had to get out.

'E.J. uses people as I use people. When you're in the game of Formula 1, you can be loyal to a certain extent, but you have to look after Number One, because if you don't, you'll get screwed. E.J. tried to screw me, and I tried to screw him, and that's the way it was. I think he got $4 million from Ferrari, but he wanted more, and I thought he was being greedy, and he didn't get it.'

Before the 1996 season began, the Formula 1 grid was shocked to learn that Michael Schumacher's partner in an all-new Ferrari line-up was to be Eddie Irvine. The news of Irvine's signing with the Italian team came out of the blue. Irvine was a competent driver, but not in Schumacher's class. Surprisingly, it was a relationship that worked. Irvine at times dutifully played second fiddle to the German, who arrived at Ferrari on the back of two world championships with Benetton and who was to win five more titles with the Italian team. Before Schumacher's arrival, Ferrari hadn't won a driver's crown since South African Jody Scheckter had landed the title back in 1979.

At the end of the 1995 season, when he finished twelfth in the driver's standings, Irvine expressed the desire to leave Jordan. He was expected to go to Arrows, but when it was announced that he was going to Ferrari, the motor-racing world was taken aback to say the least.

'It was totally my initiative. I spoke with my friends at Marlboro, and they said go and speak to Jean Todt [Team Principal at Ferrari] and see what happens. At this stage, I was pretty much the top qualifier of the non-big teams. I was qualifying in sevenths and eighths; it was pretty much the big teams that were in front of me, so I was going really well, but he [Todt] didn't seem that interested.

'Tom Walkinshaw [who was now running Arrows after leaving Ligier at the end of the 1995 campaign] came to me and said, "Right, how much is it to get you out of your contract?" and I told him, "Look, it's 5 million. I'm meant to get a million back-hander off E.J., but I don't want it, just get me out of there." So he said, "OK, come down to my house and we'll sign the contract," and I said, "Well, I'll come down and meet you but I'm not signing anything." So I went down and met him, he put the contract down on the table and was offering me ten times what Jordon was offering, huge numbers considering where I was coming from at Jordan because E.J. wasn't the best payer. I saw that Walkinshaw was more serious than E.J., and I felt it was the way for me to go if I couldn't get to Ferrari.

'I went back to Jean Todt, and I said, "Look, on Monday I'm signing a contract with Arrows, and I'm just giving you warning that the opportunity will go." That was, like, a Thursday, and on the Monday I signed for Ferrari. I bought Walkinshaw the best case of red wine that he's ever had. Ferrari would never have signed me if Tom hadn't stepped in.'

Irvine left Jordan, leaving behind Rubens Barrichello to race one more year with the Irish team before he too left to sign with the newly formed Stewart Grand Prix team in 1997. Both their Formula 1 careers seemed to have become interlinked, since Irvine took his first steps into Formula 1 in 1993. They were partners at Jordan until Irvine's move to Ferrari in 1996, and the Brazilian replaced the Irishman as Schumacher's number two at the 'Prancing Horse' in 2000.

Irvine's comparison between Rubens Barrichello and Michael Schumacher, two former team-mates, is forthright.

'I think Barrichello's a very talented driver. He was very good at set-up and had a very good feel for the car, but he was just a total baby. I had no time for him at all, none whatsoever. Oh, he was a very good driver – I'm very good at dissecting professional from emotional – very good driver, very technical, great at setting up the car, and that's probably why Ferrari used him a lot, because Michael is not. But he [Barrichello] is a baby. He was just a pain in the arse to drive with because logic did not apply on decisions within the team, a very Latin thing. I had the same problems with Pedro de la Rosa at Jaguar – you know, just a baby.'

That was in contrast to Irvine partnering Michael Schumacher at Ferrari:

'Total logic, perfect, no issue. Michael was great and has done an amazing job, but I'm a much bigger Senna fan. In fact, I'm not a Schumacher fan at all. I think he's an amazing driver, but that's it. There's no other actual attractive quality. Senna had passion; he was crazy; he was fast; he looked good; he could talk so eloquently. Michael technically was better; Senna was more passionate. But Michael has no qualities apart from being able to drive a racing car very fast. Very logical, but that's very German.'

While Irvine played the role of the team's second driver Schumacher pushed hard to give Ferrari its first World Drivers Championship in 1979. The German was third in the 1996 season, with Irvine tenth, and was seemingly on his way to the 1997 title when he led to that Spanish Grand Prix at Jerez, which would have given Schumacher the crown. However, his Ferrari slowed over the last few laps, allowing Jacques Villeneuve's Williams to get past and on to take third place, enough for the Canadian to take the title.

As he had in 1995 when he wiped out Damon Hill in the final race in Australia, Schumacher showed his win-at-all-costs persona that day in Jerez as he turned into Villeneuve, his front right wheel connecting with the sidepod of the Williams. The Ferrari number one was punished by the FIA for causing an avoidable accident and was disqualified from the championship. It would be another four years before Schumacher finally took a drivers' championship for Ferrari.

Irvine was seventh in 1997, helped by his best result to that point, a second in Argentina and a fourth in 1998, with second-placed finishes following in France, Italy and Japan. However, his biggest and most successful season in Formula 1 was in 1999 when he was elevated to the team's number-one driver when Schumacher ploughed into a tyre wall at the British Grand Prix at Silverstone. It was a year in which he very nearly became World Champion, losing out in the final race, ironically at the Japanese Grand Prix, to the McLaren of Mika Häkkinen.

Irvine had started the season well, winning the Australian Grand Prix, his first victory, and, while Schumacher hadn't actually won a title for Ferrari, he was getting close, and 1999 looked like being the season when Schumacher would win a driver's title for Ferrari for the first time in twenty years. But when he ploughed across the sand trap at the high-speed Stowe Corner early in the British race and into the Silverstone tyre wall, he had broken his leg, ending his championship chances and elevating Irvine to the role as the team's number-one driver.

There remain suggestions that the German was under pressure, especially from Irvine, who was now very much on his team-mate's heels and was perhaps no longer willing to fully play the number-two role for which he had been signed.

With Schumacher out of the title equation in 1999, there are also suggestions that Ferrari didn't want Irvine to win the title instead of

Schumacher and did little help him beat the McLaren of Mika Häkkinen to the drivers' crown.

'I was paid to do the number-two driver's job, and that is what I did. I would have preferred not to have had that situation, but it was the best one available to me at that time. If I were offered the McLaren drive, I would have gone there in a heartbeat, but I wasn't.

'Michael did an interview before the British Grand Prix, and he came out with this statement, "Eddie has only moved over for me once," and that's correct in that I'd only moved over once because they [the team] told me to move over. But there were other times where I actually just let him through because I knew there was no point in holding him up because he was faster than me, so I'd just leave the door open and let him go and get on with my race. There was no point in me racing Michael Schumacher, that's the way I'd seen it. I thought, race the drivers that I can beat, so I would just let him go.

'However, when he made those comments before Silverstone that year, I said, "Now you don't come past until they radio me." I made that very clear. I made a better start in Silverstone, and he was trying to overtake me into Stowe, and there was no way he was coming past, so I just braked. I just braked as late as I could. He tried to out-brake me, locked up and went into the barrier.'

With Schumacher out of the race, Irvine went on to finish second to David Coulthard's McLaren, and the Irish driver was then elevated to Ferrari's number one in Schumacher's absence. But was the championship in reach, and did the team give him the necessary backing?

'No, I didn't see that we could win the World Championship because the McLarens were much faster. The day that Michael crashed, Ferrari took the 1999 car out of their wind tunnel and put in the 2000 car. They started to develop for the next year because they thought – which was rightly so, it was the logical decision – that the championship was over.

'I would have done the same thing if I was the boss of Ferrari. The problem was that we actually ended up doing better than we should have done because McLaren screwed up. We got a few results that we shouldn't have, and we were still in the hunt, and not until, maybe, three or four races later did the 1999 car go back in the wind tunnel, so that's what really cost us the championship. They backed me up 100 per cent. We went testing all the time, but we had nothing to test. We'd be testing roll bars and springs. These don't make the car go faster, it's aerodynamics, so it was kind of like for show.'

Schumacher was replaced by Finland's Mika Salo while he recuperated, and Irvine backed up his early win in Australia with victories in Austria and Germany. Schumacher reappeared with two races to go, and the duo had a one-two in the penultimate round in Malaysia, with Irvine ironically passing Schumacher under team orders with the German having had to ride shotgun for the Irishman. However, both Ferrari drivers were thrown out of the race by the stewards of the meeting for illegally sized barge boards, which would have handed the title to McLaren and Häkkinen.

But the FIA subsequently overturned the stewards' decision on a Ferrari appeal, which meant the championship went to the last round at Suzuka. Irvine was four points ahead of Häkkinen going into the final round. However, if the Finn won, second place would not be enough for Irvine, as Häkkinen would have won the title by virtue of having more race wins.

Despite the McLaren's overall speed advantage on the fast Japanese track, Irvine felt the title was still within reach when the team arrived at Suzuka.

'I thought there was no problem because I'd beaten him in Malaysia. I thought, this is easily my best circuit, but as I drove out the pit lane, it was like driving on ice. I went straight back in, and I said, "There is something seriously wrong here." We checked everything in the car, but there was no grip. I was lapping two seconds a lap slower than Michael.

'There was nothing I could do. I was lapping two seconds a lap slower than a guy supposedly in the same car. I couldn't have driven any faster. I crashed in qualifying trying to get within a second and a half of him. There was just no grip.'

Schumacher took pole position, but Häkkinen won the race with the German second and Irvine a distant third, which gave the title to the Finn by a mere two points.

If Schumacher had won that day, Irvine's third place would have been enough to clinch the title, but the Ferraris were no match for the McLaren. Irvine couldn't even get close to his team-mate, and there his association with the famous outfit ended.

With four years at Ferrari behind him, Irvine was replaced by Barrichello. This meant a move to Jaguar, who had bought out the Stewart Grand Prix team. This time, Irvine was brought in as number-one driver with Britain's Johnny Herbert as his partner.

'Financially, it was OK. I was offered very similar money elsewhere, but I thought the Jaguar opportunity was much better because Ford said they were going to get stuck in and do it properly.

'But they just screwed up completely. At the beginning, I was working with Gary Anderson quite a lot, but then Gary was getting pushed out by Jackie Stewart. Jackie was just in it for himself. It was a political disaster zone; it really was. You had everyone undermining everybody else. I just wanted to go as fast as I could go, and you'd all these guys looking after their own interests. They bought the team for hundreds of millions of dollars, and they sold it for nothing three years later, having spent $500 or 600 million.

'Whenever you're in sport, you always believe it's going to get better, and I always did. I scored more points than my team-mates every year. I did my part of the deal, but they proved they knew nothing about Formula 1.'

After three years at the rather unsuccessful Jaguar team, his best results a third in Monaco in 2001 and a third in Italy in 2002, Eddie Irvine's Formula 1 career ended. His last race was the Japanese Grand Prix in October 2002, and there were suggestions of a return to Jordan for 2003, but it never happened. Ford, Jordan's engine suppliers at the time, apparently threatened to pull the $2 million subsidy they were giving Eddie Jordan if Irvine was re-signed. Thus, Irvine's career in Formula 1 and, indeed, in motor-racing itself ended with a ninth-placed finish for Jaguar in the Japanese race in 2002.

And what has Irvine been doing since retirement? Well, he is fabulously wealthy, still a playboy despite his years, and now with a growing daughter, Zoë, born in 1996 after a flirtation with her mother Maria Drummond. Irvine admits that he had little or no contact with Zoë in her early years, but a television documentary on Irvine when his daughter was younger showed, perhaps, a different side to his brash exterior as he played happily with his offspring on his yacht. She is shown responding in kind. The gentler Irvine guards his life with her, refusing to let the outside world in on their relationship.

Irvine owns Cocoon, a fashionable bar off Dublin's Grafton Street, taking sole possession after a falling out with original partner John Foley. He has business and property interests around the world, but the idea of Formula 1 now seems a little alien to him, even though there was more than a suggestion that he was interested in taking over the Midland Team, the outfit run at one stage by Alex Schneider who bought out Jordan Grand Prix.

'The idea of driving a Formula 1 car does nothing for me. They're unbelievably fast – I couldn't believe how fast they are – but I just have no interest. I've moved on. I had a great career and an amazing life. I'm very lucky that I'm not married to these businesses because I've good people managing them, and I just come in and I make my opinion known and I disappear again.'

Formula 1 has gotten pretty cold and characterless now that Irvine and Jordan have gone. Now that only the top drivers are being paid, many of the younger drivers that arrive in the sport have their daddies' money behind them for their paid drives, and they lack the charisma of the likes of Senna, Irvine or Juan Pablo Montoya, who quit Formula 1 to race with the rednecks in NASCAR saloon racing in the USA in 2006.

'I think the people in charge of Formula 1 are wrong, and I don't mean Bernie Ecclestone, I mean the suits that run the motor companies. They're trying to sell cars to the family man. They think the family man wants to see the family images. Nonsense. The family man wants to see something that he can't ever get to. It's a dream.

You go to the movies to escape. You go to see a Formula 1 car that is totally unachievable. Formula 1 should be the ultimate.

'There are also new backers coming on board in Formula 1. Millionaires like [Alex] Schneider: clueless. Perhaps he looked at Formula 1 the way Roman Abramovich looked at Chelsea. Abramovich's financial resources helped Chelsea win titles as he could buy in talent, but Formula 1 isn't like that. All the money in the world won't win races; one has to develop a car. Having a successful football team is easy. Having a successful Formula 1 car is like trying to get to the moon. It's a totally different exercise, and it's much more difficult.'

A driver of Eddie Irvine's ilk will possibly never be seen again in Formula 1. Political correctness has taken over, and his outspoken attitude angered many, but he was proved to be right on many occasions. He is still making headlines. (He had a short fling with Pamela Anderson who ended the relationship because he was too nice.)

'I'm not interested in doing anything to make money. I've made my money. I'm happy just having a great time and having businesses that I enjoy. The most important thing for me is my lifestyle, and if I can make money and have a nice lifestyle, that's what I will do. I'm not going to compromise my lifestyle to make money.'

Many ex-drivers see it as a responsibility to bring new young drivers through to Formula 1. Letho, for example, was a protégé of 1982 World Champion Keke Rosberg, while his son Nico Rosberg made it all the way to the top of his sport when he signed with Williams in 2006.

'I will do the same when I see the person that I think can be the next Michael Schumacher, the next Ayrton Senna. I'm not really interested in sponsoring someone who is slightly below that level. I opened a go-kart centre in Northern Ireland, and I watch kids driving, and none of them, I have to say, look as if they really know what they're doing. Maybe it's something I would be interested in doing in a few years' time.'

There is speculation that Irvine hasn't completely given up on getting back into Formula 1 as a team owner. The FIA are looking for more teams to take part, and Irvine says he has the necessary backers. Eddie Jordan is also said to be interested in returning to the sport.

'Racing with Jordan got me where I needed to get to. It was a stepping stone, and I definitely owe E.J. a thank you, but he got 4 million when I went to Ferrari, so he can't complain too much. I didn't learn too much there, to be honest, and it was weird I didn't learn much at Ferrari either. It was when I went to Jaguar that I learnt a lot because I had seen all the things that could go wrong. We had the worst car that was ever designed in 2002, and we turned it around into a car that finished on the podium in Monza, and that was a great learning experience.

'I remember I won the Australian Grand Prix, but I don't remember any emotion. I remember I pulled a gorgeous girl that night, but I don't remember any of it really. It was just a blur to be honest; it was amazing, my ten years in Formula 1 was a blur, it really was.

'The highlight – the most beautiful thing – was on the podium in Monza, my last podium, where the whole crowd invaded the track, and they weren't chanting "Michael," they were chanting "Eddie, Eddie." Michael was first, Rubens was second, and I was on the podium in third. That was amazing, I have to say, and actually I was so close to retiring straight after that race. I was on the TV getting interviewed, and I was just about to say it, and I thought, uh, just wait, you never know, and I probably should have done then, but no one times anything perfectly.'

Appendix

Career highlights and honours

Billy Coleman
Born 8 May 1947, Cork

Irish and British Rally Champion
Fourth on Rally Corsica (best Irish finisher on World Rally round)
Three-time Circuit of Ireland, Rally of the Lakes and Donegal
International Rally winner.
Twice winner of Cork 20 and Galway International.
Inducted Motorsport Ireland Hall of Fame, 2003.
Winner of RTÉ Sport Hall of Fame, 2006.

Billy Coleman runs the family farm near Millstreet in County Cork.

Derek Daly
Born 11 March 1953, Dublin

Formula Ford Festival winner, 1976
British Formula 3 Champion, 1977
Formula 1 World Championship, 1978–82 with Hesketh, Ensign,
Tyrrell, March, Theodore, Williams (forty-nine 49 starts in sixty-four
races)
Fifteen championship points (best result, fourth in Argentina and
Germany, 1980)

IndyCar USA, 1982–9 (best result fourth in Portland, 1984)
Inducted Motorsport Ireland Hall of Fame, 2000.

Having sold his racing school in Las Vegas in 2006, Daly is a motivational speaker and racing commentator.

Hugh Peter 'Martin' Donnelly
Born 26 March 1964, Belfast

Irish Formula Ford Champion and Irish Festival winner
Two years Formula 1 with Arrows and Lotus (thirteen starts in fifteen races)
Manager of Martin Donnelly Racing in British Formula Vauxhall
Inducted Motorsport Ireland Hall of Fame, 2006.

Martin Donnelly is a racing team manager in Snetterton in England.

Steven Robert Dunlop
Born 25 November 1960, Ballymoney, County Antrim

Five-time Isle of Man TT winner
Fifteen North West 200 victories
Macau Grand Prix 1989
125 British Supercup Championship 1991
Inducted Irish Motorcycle Hall of Fame, 2005
Awarded an honorary doctorate from the University of Ulster in Coleraine, 2006

Robert Dunlop is still racing.

The Dirty Dozen

William Joseph 'Joey' Dunlop
Born 25 February 1952, Ballymoney, County Antrim; died Estonia, 2 July 2000

Five consecutive Motorcycling Formula 1 titles from 1982 to 1986
Twenty-six Isle of Man races, including three hat-tricks in 1985, 1988 and 2000
Twenty-four Ulster Grand Prix wins
Thirteen North West 200 victories.
Awarded MBE in 1986 for services to charity
Posthumously awarded an honorary doctorate from University of Ulster in Coleraine, 2006

Patrick Barron 'Paddy' Hopkirk
Born 14 April 1933, Belfast

Winner of Monte Carlo Rally 1994 in Mini Cooper
Twice winner of Acropolis Rally
Winner Tour de France, Austrian Alpine Pirelli Classic Marathon and Coupe des Alpes
Five-time Circuit of Ireland winner
British Saloon Car Championship racer.
Elected life member of the British Racing Drivers' Club in 1967.

Paddy Hopkirk is now retired.

Edmund 'Eddie' Irvine
Born 10 November 1965, Newtownards

British Formula Ford Champion and Festival Winner 1987
Winner Japanese Formula Nippon championship
Formula 1 World Championship, 1993–2002 with Jordan, Ferrari and Jaguar (148 races, four wins, 26 podium finishes)
Runner-up Formula 1 World Championship, 1999

Eddie Irvine owns property worldwide and Cocoon Bar in Dublin.

Edmund 'Eddie' Jordan

Born 30 March 1948, Dublin

Formula Ford and Atlantic race car driver
Irish Champion and winner of Leinster Trophy
Owner Jordan Racing and Jordan Grand Prix
Winner of British Formula 3 and International Formula 3000
Championship. Winner of four Grand Prix with Jordan Grand
Prix (Belgium 1998, France and Italy 1999, Brazil 2003)
Third in Formula 1 drivers' and constructors' championship, 1999.

Jordan runs Jordan Media and is Chairman of Rally Ireland.

Austin MacHale

Born 6 January 1955, Mayo

Five-time Irish Tarmac Rally Champion (1983, 1985, 1986, 1997
and 1998)
Twice runner-up British Rally Championship
Seventeen Irish Tarmac Rally wins, including six-time Galway
International Rally winner and four Cork 20 wins
Numerous World and European Rally Championship events and
winner of national rallies, including Punchestown Rally Masters,
2001.

*Austin MacHale is semi-retired from rallying and runs the family plant
hire and tarmac business in Dublin.*

The Dirty Dozen

Jeremy McWilliams
Born 4 April 1964, Belfast.

Irish Production Champion, 1988
Irish Open Champion, 1990
Irish Champion, 250 Class, 1991
Raced 500-cc World Championship and MotoGP World
Championship
Winner of 250-cc Dutch TT race at Assen, 2001
British Superbike Championship, 2005.

Jeremy McWilliams is still racing.

Michael Roe
Born 8 August 1955, Naas County Kildare.

British Formula Ford Festival Winner 1978
CAN-AM Series Winner 1984
IndyCar US 1985 (best result seventh in Portland)
Japanese and Le Mans Sportcars Championship
Inducted Motorsport Ireland Hall of Fame, 2002

Michael Roe lives and works in Naas.

Rosemary Smith
Born 7 August 1939, Dublin

Winner of Tulip Rally, 1965
Texaco Sports Star of the Year, 1965
Numerous Ladies Cup titles in domestic and European rallies
Third overall in 1968 Circuit of Ireland Rally
Irish land-speed record holder, 1978
Class winner British Saloon Car Championship
Inducted to Motorsport Ireland Hall of Fame in 2001.

Rosemary Smith runs the 'Think Awareness' campaign for transition-year students in Ireland.

John Marshall Watson
Born 4 May 1946, Belfast

Five-time Formula 1 Grand Prix winner (one with Penske and four
with McLaren)
Third in Formula 1 World Championship 1983
152 races, 2 pole positions and five fastest laps
Winner of Fuji 1000 1984

John Watson works as a journalist and motor-sport commentator.

Motorsport Ireland Hall of Fame

2000	Derek Daly
2001	Rosemary Smith
2002	Michael Roe
2003	Billy Coleman
2004	Alec Poole
2005	Noel Smith (posthumously)
2006	Martin Donnelly

RONNIE
DELANY

STAYING THE
DISTANCE

RONNIE DELANY: STAYING THE DISTANCE

In December 1956 Ronnie Delany sprinted home to win the gold medal in the 1500m Olympic final in Melbourne, setting a new Olympic record in the process. In the depressed Ireland of the fifties, Delany's win – an outsider storming ahead to beat the favourites – caught the imagination of a nation, and made him a sporting icon.

Though most famous in Ireland for his Olympic win, Delany pursued his running career in the US, where he ran thirty-four major indoor mile races and won them all. He broke the indoor world record for the mile three times.

Fifty years on from the Melbourne Olympics, Ronnie Delany tells the story of his life and career in his own engaging style.

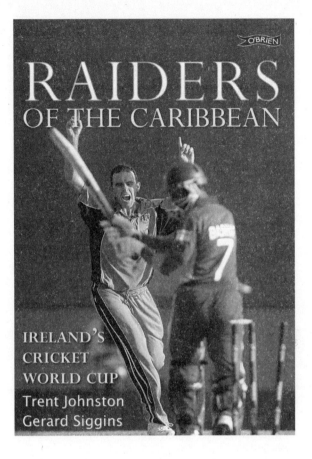

RAIDERS OF THE CARIBBEAN: IRELAND'S CRICKET WORLD CUP

When Ireland qualified for the last eight of the cricket world cup in the West Indies, they opened up many people's eyes to the mere existence of the sport here. The very English game of cricket has been played in Ireland for more than two centuries but it was only when a special group of players came together that international success was enjoyed.

Captain Trent Johnston and journalist Gerard Siggins trace the long and difficult journey Irish cricket had to make to reach the World Cup, as well as the story of Ireland's amazing victories over two of the world's best teams: Pakistan and Bangladesh.

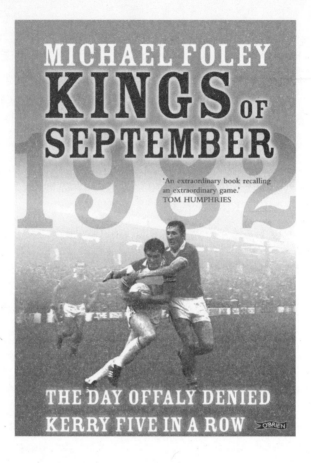

'An extraordinary book recalling an extraordinary game.'
TOM HUMPHRIES

THE DAY OFFALY DENIED
KERRY FIVE IN A ROW

KINGS OF SEPTEMBER: THE DAY OFFALY DENIED KERRY FIVE IN A ROW

On 19 September 1982, Mick O'Dwyer's Kerry ran out in Croke Park chasing immortality. Victory over Offaly in the All-Ireland football final would secure them five titles in a row, a record certain never to be matched again. And it had taken Offaly six heartbreaking years under manager Eugene McGee to drag themselves up from their lowest ebb, but now they stood on the cusp of a glorious reward. The result was a classic final that changed lives and dramatically altered the course of football history.